The European Union 1997:
Annual Review of Activities

Edited by

Geoffrey Edwards
and
Georg Wiessala

General Editors: Simon Bulmer and Andr

Copyright © Blackwell Publishers Ltd

ISBN 0-631-21190-X

First published 1998

Blackwell Publishers Ltd
108 Cowley Road, Oxford OX4 1JF, UK

Blackwell Publishers Inc.
350 Main Street,
Malden, MA 02148, USA

British Library Cataloguing in Publication Data
A catalogue record for this book is available from the British Library

Library of Congress
Cataloging in Publication Data applied for

This journal is printed on acid free paper
Printed in Great Britain by Whitstable Litho, Kent

CONTENTS

List of Abbreviations

ACP	African, Caribbean, and Pacific Countries
APEC	Asia–Pacific Economic Co-operation
ASEAN	Association of South East Asian Nations
ASEM	Asia–Europe Meeting
BSE	Bovine Spongiform Encephalopathy
CAP	Common Agricultural Policy
CBSS	Council of Baltic Sea States
CCEE	Countries of Central and Eastern Europe
CCP	Common Commercial Policy
CFI	Court of First Instance
CFP	Common Fisheries Policy
CFSP	Common Foreign and Security Policy
CIU	Catalan Nationalist Party
COM/COM DOC	Commission Document
COREPER	Committee of Permanent Representatives
DG	Directorate General
EAGGF	European Agricultural Guidance and Guarantee Fund
EBRD	European Bank for Reconstruction and Development
EBU	European Broadcasting Union
EC	European Community
ECJ	European Court of Justice
ECHO	European Community Humanitarian Office
ECSC	European Coal and Steel Community
ECOFIN	Council of Economic and Finance Ministers
ECU	European Currency Unit
EDF	European Development Fund
EEA	European Economic Area, also European Environmental Agency
EEC	European Economic Community
EFTA	European Free Trade Association
EIB	European Investment Bank
EMS	European Monetary System
EMU	Economic and Monetary Union
EP	European Parliament
ERDF	European Regional Development Fund
ERM	Exchange Rate Mechanism
ESF	European Social Fund

EU	European Union
EURATOM	European Atomic Energy Community
EUROPOL	European Police Office
FDP	Free Democratic Party (of Germany)
FYROM	Former Yugoslav Republic of Macedonia
GATT	General Agreement on Tariffs and Trade
GDP	Gross Domestic Product
GNP	Gross National Product
GSP	Generalized System of Preferences
HOSG	Heads of State or Government
IFOR	Implementation Force (of NATO)
IGC	Intergovernmental Conference
JHA	Justice and Home Affairs
KEDO	Korean Peninsula Energy Development Organisation
MAGPs	Multiannual Guidance Programmes
MEP	Member of the European Parliament
NAFTA	North Atlantic Free Trade Area
NATO	North Atlantic Treaty Organization
NGO	Non-Governmental Organization
NPT	Non-Proliferation Treaty
OCTs	Overseas Countries and Territories
OECD	Organization for Economic Co-operation and Development
OJ	Official Journal of the European Communities
OSCE	Organization on Security and Co-operation in Europe
PDS	Party of the Democratic Left (Italy)
PE DOC	Committee Report of the European Parliament
PP	Popular Party (of Spain)
PPI	Popular Party (Italy)
QMV	Qualified Majority Voting
SACU	South African Customs Union
SADC	South African Development Community
SEA	Single European Act
SEC	Internal Commission General Secretariat Document
SEM	Single European Market
SFOR	Stabilization Force (of NATO)
SIS	Schengen Information System
SMEs	Small and Medium-Sized Enterprises
SPA	Special Protection Area
SVC	Standing Veterinary Committee
TACs	Total Allowable Catches
TEN	Trans-European Network
TEU	Treaty on European Union
UN	United Nations
VAT	Value Added Tax
WEU	Western European Union
WHO	World Health Organization
WTO	World Trade Organization

Journal of Common Market Studies

Volume 36, Annual Review
September 1998

Editorial: Flexibility, Legitimacy and Identity in Post-Amsterdam Europe

GEOFFREY EDWARDS
University of Cambridge

and

GEORG WIESSALA
De Montfort University Bedford

I. Introduction

Scaffolding

Masons, when they start upon a building,
Are careful to test out the scaffolding;
Make sure that planks won't slip at busy points
Secure all ladders, tighten bolted joints.
And yet all this comes down when the job's done,
Showing off walls of sure and solid stone.
So if, my dear, there sometimes seems to be
Old bridges breaking between you and me,
Never fear. We may let scaffolds fall,
Confident that we have built our wall.

(Seamus Heaney, *Poems 1965–1975 (1980)*)[1]

If our predecessor as editor, Neill Nugent, could describe 1996 as a year of preparing, then 1997 was a year for decisions – some of which were taken, even if few of them were final. The Dutch Presidency managed to bring the Intergovernmental Conference to a conclusion on time – not least by setting an increas-

---

[1] Quoted by Deirdre Curtin in her inaugural lecture 'Post-national Democracy: The European Union in Search for a Political Philosophy', University of Utrecht, 18 April 1997.

© Blackwell Publishers Ltd 1998, 108 Cowley Road, Oxford OX4 1JF, UK and 350 Main Street, Malden, MA 02148, USA

ingly hectic pace of meetings at all levels. The resulting Treaty of Amsterdam may have failed to live up to the aspirations of many, but certainly went a good deal further than the losing British Conservative Government would have allowed. Agreement was reached, in part, by postponing some of the more fundamental issues thrown up by enlargement and also by the equally well-tried method of agreeing to the highest common rhetoric and the lowest common substance. Once agreed by the Heads of State or Government (HOSG), the Treaty was sent off to the experts to be put in 'proper' legal form. An agreement derived – again in part – from the need to re-engage the citizenry of the EU in the integration process and designed to be 'clear and comprehensible' now awaits ratification. There was a somewhat eerie silence for the rest of 1997, as Member States began to set the process in motion.[2]

Agreement on a new Treaty was not the only important decision taken. Indeed, had it not been for the final re-stitching of elements making up Economic and Monetary Union, with the Stability (and Growth) Pact joined by a European Council resolution on growth, employment and the co-ordination of economic policies, as well as the Employment Chapter in the Treaty, there might not have been a Treaty. What had been agreed at Dublin (see last year's *Annual Review*) threatened to unravel in the face of growing discontent in some of the Member States, especially in France, where President Chirac's gamble to win a more lasting majority before things got too rough came – for him – horribly unstuck. There was then a somewhat urgent need for the new French Government under Lionel Jospin to reconcile its European commitments and its domestic electoral promises if the IGC were to keep to its timetable. Insofar as this was achieved, it revealed the diplomatic and linguistic skills of EU negotiators – even if also, at times, the limits to their tempers – and possibly their prescience, if the additional focus on the economic dimension of EMU, and especially on employment, proves to be more than merely rhetoric. The subsequent special European Council on Employment – claimed as their initiative by the French and by the British (and perhaps by others) – may not have given much substance to any new specifically European efforts to deal with the problem, leaving it largely to the dynamics of the single market and to Member States themselves, but it was important in at least focusing Europe's attention on the fact that unemployment was and remains a European concern.

Some decisions were also taken within the general framework of the European Commission's ambitious project *Agenda 2000: For a Stronger and Wider Union*, published in July 1997. Many of the issues included in Parts I and III, on the policies of the Union and the new financial framework, began to be addressed only towards the end of the year when those likely to be directly affected – such

[2] Interrupted, perhaps momentarily, in the autumn by some squeaks of horror on the part of many of those teaching EU studies with the realization that they would have to take on board not only the changes agreed at Amsterdam but would also have to relearn the Treaties with all their renumbered Articles!

as regions losing Objective 1 status – began to make representations at national and European levels, or were postponed for serious consideration until after the German elections due in September 1998. But the Luxembourg European Council in December did take important decisions on further enlargement. It preserved the distinction proposed by the Commission between the six most likely to be able to cope with accession and the five others,[3] but, in the face of widespread concern over the possible divisive and destabilizing consequences of the distinction, it allowed for a degree of much-needed flexibility between the two groups ('an inbuilt and permanent *passarelle*' to quote the Luxembourg Foreign Minister: *Agence Europe*, 16 December 1997). It also set a date (30 March 1998) on which the process was to be launched. Significantly, the prospect of enlargement had not been regarded as either sufficiently immediate or urgent by the Heads of State or Government in Amsterdam to concentrate their minds and agree on a package of institutional reforms that might meet the challenge of an EU of 20 plus members. It is not therefore surprising that there was little wider debate within the Member States on the likely implications of enlargement. The Commission's and the Council's audiences were to be found rather more among the governing elites in central and eastern Europe.

II. A New Sense of Purpose?

Important as many of these decisions were in establishing a new political and economic framework for the EU, they did little to inspire or create a new sense of purpose within the Union. They did not – could not – overcome the uncertainties surrounding the move towards a single currency, whether in terms of meeting the Maastricht criteria or of winning domestic acceptance of the consequences. For Germany, with its own problems about whether it would meet all the criteria, as well as political divisions within the parties over the costs and ramifications of doing so (especially important in a pre-election year), EMU was perhaps *the* overriding concern during the year. Certainly, according to Christoph Bertram of *Die Zeit*, it was the primary influence over Germany's approach to the IGC:

> If Maastricht had been about making sure that a united Germany stays firmly committed to the European project, Amsterdam has been about making sure that France remains committed to EMU and to the Stability [and Growth] Pact to which Germany attached high symbolic importance.' (Bertram, 1997, p. 64)

The resulting modesty in Germany's ambitions for the IGC was also, and perhaps equally, engendered by a concern that German institutions (including, of course,

---

[3] The six are: the Czech Republic, Hungary, Poland, Estonia, Slovenia and Cyprus; and the five: Bulgaria, Romania, Slovakia, Latvia and Lithuania.

the Federal Constitutional Court), and the German public were already highly sensitized to issues relating to integration because of the Maastricht Treaty. Concern over renewed ratification problems meant that German decision-makers were obliged at the IGC to look over their shoulders to their domestic audience very much more than usual in an EU negotiation. Too ambitious an attempt at treaty reform at Amsterdam was regarded as likely to alienate still further those who were already moving towards greater Euroscepticism or were only very reluctant supporters of the Euro.

But such modesty in terms of objectives was not confined to Germany. Indeed, among governments, perhaps only the Italian Government continued to frame its objectives within the language of Euro-idealism – though there were still innumerable pressure groups pushing for closer integration in general or in particular. Most member governments were only too well aware of the possible costs of a domestic political agenda dominated by both the Euro and Treaty reform. Even the Commission and the European Parliament were at pains to appear 'reasonable' in their demands (Laursen, 1997). Some commentators, as a result, bemoaned the lack of leadership in Europe that this engendered (see, e.g., Ludlow, 1998).

III. The Search for Legitimacy

The Amsterdam European Council revealed clearly the wider politico-economic context from which the Treaty emerged, but what the relative lack of ambition in the IGC also revealed was an increased awareness of the problems of the general acceptability and legitimacy of the European venture. Neill Nugent referred to it last year in his editorial in terms of 'the challenge' of 'managing public attitudes and opinions' and pointed out that too little attention had been devoted to it, concluding on the need for 'caution' on the part of 'political elites as they seek to press ahead with the integration project'. As far as the IGC was concerned, it would seem that at least the need for caution was recognized. And yet, from the Reflection Group on, a key factor was seen to be 'the need to ensure that European construction becomes a venture to which citizens can relate' so that, '[i]f ... the Union's principle internal challenge is to reconcile itself with its citizens, enhancing its legitimacy in their eyes will have to be the prime objective of the coming reform' (Reflection Group, 1995).

Issues relating to the general acceptability or legitimacy of the European construct were therefore very much on the IGC's agenda – as well as, indeed increasingly, on the academic one.[4] But while there might be a general consensus

---

[4] See, e.g., den Boer *et al.* (1998), Weiler (1997), and Jachtenfuchs *et al.* (1997); though see also Obradovic (1996) and Weiler (1996); and, somewhat before those, Wallace (1993), Kaase and Newton (1995) and Laffan (1993).

on what legitimacy might entail, even if only a sense of the acceptability of the system that subsumes differences over particular policies, establishing or creating the legitimacy of the European Union was a decidedly more complex and at times controversial matter. Bringing about a sense of 'rightness' and of 'justice' in the exercise of authority by the European Union rather than the nation-state when so much of the discourse on legitimacy was in terms of building one nation at the expense of others was always going to be fraught with difficulty. Building on a common heritage to create a new supranational identity and legitimacy always faced the EU and the Member States with, to quote Helen Wallace, 'the difficulty of dealing simultaneously with the mundane and the metaphysical' (Wallace, 1993, p. 100). Maastricht, while building incrementally on the past, provided for a transition to a new polity, symbolized in its new nomenclature, and with considerably extended fields of responsibility even though they were to be rarely exercised exclusively by the EU. The implications for national sovereignty and national identity were perhaps not wholly foreseen by those who negotiated the Treaty, or at least few predicted the popular response to the Treaty. In becoming more state-like, the Union's need for a greater sense of legitimacy to justify and underpin it had become vital. On the other hand, there was no consensus among and within the Member States on quite how state-like the EU should be. Legitimating a process without agreement on the *finalité politique* in conditions of new global political and economic uncertainties has inevitably brought problems of a different order from those the Member States had themselves experienced, but it has been an order which still largely determines the debate.

IV. The Limits of the Past

In the past, with limited competences transferred to the EC and decision-making very largely carried out by consensus if not unanimity, it was, despite the radical and innovative nature of the venture, a relatively straightforward question of national parliaments and electorates holding their national representatives in the Council of Ministers to account. Even if popular support was rarely tested, there was generally considered to be a permissive consensus in favour of integration in order to ensure peace in western Europe, economic prosperity, and liberal democratic values in the conflict with communism. Moreover, the indirect legitimization through Member State governments was reinforced by growing involvement of those economic interests directly affected by Community policies, insofar as they extended their political activity to Luxembourg and then Brussels, with the expectation of policy outcomes that either protected or promoted their particular interests. And, even though it had only consultative status initially, there was a European Assembly/Parliament fighting to control not only the Commission but the Council. In addition, there was a Court of Justice to give legal validity to the legislative order.

It may never have been quite so simple, but it certainly became a good deal more complex in the 1980s and 1990s. Success, in terms of ensuring a Deutschian security community and creating a genuine single market, may have been achieved by an extension of Community competences, increased majority voting in the Council and the growing involvement of the European Parliament, including by means of co-decision. But, whether these were agreed in the interests of efficiency, effectiveness or ideological commitment, they both reflected the changed capacity of the nation-state in western Europe to manage their economies and challenged the political order. Uncertainties – sometimes deliberately encouraged by national governments – about the sources of legislation and its implementation reinforced a growing confusion, among national parliamentarians as well as publics. At the same time, the Court of Justice appeared to have established a new legal and constitutional order by claiming that it had the competence to determine what Member States had or had not agreed. Meanwhile, the burgeoning numbers of lobbyists and pressure groups in Brussels seemed – somewhat perversely perhaps – to reinforce the distance between those involved in governance and those being governed. The European enterprise appeared too often to be an elite venture, the process of legitimation top down rather than bottom up.

The complexities and opacity of Maastricht with its provisions for a European citizenship, for increased involvement in security and defence, immigration and asylum simply made the situation worse – as the Danish referendum so eloquently attested. It was signalled, too, by the continuing low interest in the European dimension of the elections to the European Parliament, arguably the strongest basis for legitimacy of the EC/EU, and a falling turn-out. In the eyes of the voters, the EP had only limited salience and, in the often zero-sum approach frequently encouraged by both the EP and national parliaments, it was no substitute for the latter (though they also had lost credibility). This, it is interesting to recall, was at a time when the EP had actually gained greater legislative authority to an extent that had roused national parliaments into attempting to put their own houses in better order – again with some support from a number of member governments.

V. Legitimacy and the Amsterdam Treaty

If all this had been taken on board by the Reflection Group, maintaining the objective of providing the basis for a greater legitimacy among the welter of competing proposals proved difficult, not least given the difficulties of simply discarding proposals – at least those from the Member States – without some compensation. The negotiators of the Amsterdam Treaty may well have sought to apply the 'principles of efficiency, democracy, transparency and solidarity in the EU', as recommended by the Reflection Group, but the end result, to quote one MEP, deserved 'a first prize for complexity, lack of clarity and transparency' (Brinkhorst, 1997, p. 49). Even the effort to gather together the various Treaty revisions into more digestible sections – freedom, security and justice; the Union and the citizen; an effective and coherent external policy; the Union's institutions; and closer co-operation and flexibility – contributed only marginally and temporarily to greater understanding. The overall framework had, of course, been determined already. The Reflection Group (REFLEX 18), for example, had pointed out that 'it would be a grave error to underestimate the Community's main contribution to the Member States and their citizens, namely the shared view of life that has ruled out war as a means of settling differences ... '. But it had then gone on to affirm a somewhat more utilitarian rationale for integration, the need to maintain a resolute path in the pursuit 'of growth, competitiveness and employment, ensuring stringency in public finances and in combating inflation as the best way to meet citizens' demands'. A clarion call for peace and prosperity based on the *acquis* was perhaps not the most obvious way of grabbing headlines. And yet, if the ratification process goes smoothly (and it may yet prove to be a big 'if' – at least if Danish polls are to be believed), governments will doubtless congratulate themselves on having set such a limited agenda at Amsterdam. That does not necessarily mean, of course, that the discernible gap between elites and the public will have been narrowed. Whether the Treaty also provides a political commitment to the construction of a Europe able to meet what could be profound challenges from the introduction of the single currency and further enlargement will doubtless be the subject of subsequent *Annual Reviews*.

Nonetheless, within the context of the IGC and the continuing debate over the introduction of the Euro, there was frequent emphasis during 1997 on the need somehow to ensure that the European public was 'reconnected' – a phrase used by Robin Cook in his presentation of the British Presidency's programme to the European Parliament in January 1998.[5] One might, perhaps, need to discount the fact that it was to be a British mission to reconnect the public, given the legacy of British Conservative Governments and the ambiguities in New Labour's statements about British and European interests. However, the new Labour Government had clearly picked up the significance not simply of 'The Union and the Citizen' aspects (especially, of course, the employment and social provisions) of Amsterdam, but also those elements involving individual security, particularly those relating to international crime, drug-trafficking, etc. to be

[5] In a sentence that spoke of 'Britain' wanting 'to reconnect the peoples of Europe with the European Union which their governments are trying to create. They need to know that the EU is relevant to their lives ... ' (European Parliament, 14 January 1998).

found in the section on 'freedom, security and justice'.[6] Richard Corbett, in his article, points to several others of the more significant changes of particular relevance to issues of legitimacy, including the reaffirmation of the importance of the principles of liberty, democracy, respect for human rights and the rule of law, non-discrimination, greater openness – or at least better access to documentation – and some further clarification of subsidiarity. The Court of Justice, somewhat surprisingly in view of the critical comments made by many member governments during the year, also saw its jurisdiction extended in several areas, though subject to certain conditions and reservations, including the need for Member States to 'opt-in' on matters under what had been Pillar III. And there is also the enhanced role of the European Parliament with, for example, some 23 additional cases of co-decision to add to the existing 15, additional rights in relation to the nomination of the Commission President and the imposition of sanctions on Member States in breach of human rights obligations, and at least some sort of consolidation of its rights to consultation on Pillar II and III issues.

Of course, the new powers given to the European Parliament were considerably less than they had hoped for, regular participation in meetings with the personal representatives, foreign ministers and HOSG notwithstanding. Moreover, a number of member governments, including the French (which had been highly critical of the European Parliament during February 1997 for 'interfering' in French internal affairs over the withdrawal of the Debré act), had pressed hard for Treaty provisions that would ensure a more well-defined role for national parliaments in the European legislative process. The result was a Protocol attached to the TEU, encouraging a greater involvement on the part of national parliaments. As Pierre Moscovici, the French Minister for European Affairs, summed it up:

> Democracy is what this is all about. A Europe which is close to its citizens implies reinforcement of the European Parliament and of national parliaments. This is why the area of co-decision has been extended, and why the parliaments of each state will increasingly be linked to the activity of the Union. They will become the privileged mouthpieces of their citizens in the European institutions. (Moscovici, 1997, p. 40)

Whether a more harmonious and purposeful relationship between the two representative levels can be established that reconnects the European elector/

---

[6] As Robin Cook put it in Dublin in a speech to the Institute for Foreign Affairs, 3 November 1997: 'We need to get Europol launched as soon as we can so that Europe's police forces can work together effectively and share intelligence … . We will sign an agreement allowing our Customs officials to work closely together. We will attack the drugs trade right at its heart, by helping the drug-producing countries of Central Asia and the Caribbean to stem the flow. This is the way to show the people that the European Union shares their concerns and is acting on them … '.

These were areas, of course, which were largely intergovernmental; there were others, as on free movement, where the British had negotiated opt-outs.

citizen remains to be seen. While the interaction envisaged is primarily via national European Affairs Committees (COSAC), a more dynamic element may be the encouragement this may give to a greater interaction among political parties, both at the European-national levels and transnationally.

One area agreed at Amsterdam of considerable potential importance for the EU's legitimacy is, as Jörg Monar suggests, that of closer co-operation.[7] Ideas about 'flexibility', 'differentiation', 'multi-speed Europe', 'variable geometry', or 'Europe *à la carte*' are not of course new (Stubb, 1996), nor its practice, whether in terms of the varying membership of defence organizations or the European Monetary System. As Neill Nugent pointed out last year in the *Annual Review*, the Schäuble-Lamers paper of September 1994 had given the idea of an inner core considerable currency. In the face of especially British negativism in the Reflection Group and much of the IGC, the idea flourished, with, for example, the then French Prime Minister Alain Juppé declaring in March 1996:

> Let's have the courage to say it. Tomorrow's Union will no doubt be made up of two distinct levels: a Union of common law, comprising the fifteen present members and those with the vocation to join it; at the heart of this Union of this first circle, a second circle, more limited, but modulable, made up of a small number of states at the centre of which will be France and Germany, nations prepared and willing to go further or faster than the others on subjects such as the currency or defence'. (*Agence Europe*, 15 March, 1996)

The issue, though, becomes not simply what 'closer co-operation' among some Member States may entail (the final Amsterdam text drops 'flexibility' completely) but what its implications may be for the legitimacy of the Union, especially in terms of Europe's identity and the public's identification with it. It may, of course, be that the provisions, *stricto sensu,* for closer co-operation will not be used – its use is, after all, strictly curtailed – though it is unlikely that the Union will forgo other established instruments of flexibility such as transitional periods for new members. Not all new instruments of policy need be used, though it might well be argued that given the genesis of the flexibility provision – to overcome the negativism of one (or two) particular state(s) – it was designed to be used. Nor does the fact that it exists necessarily influence a Member State one way or another in difficult Council discussions – certainly the British at times appeared to relish their isolation. Nonetheless, if the purpose is to maintain a momentum or create a new dynamic through closer co-operation, it inevitably creates pressures on those whose initial preferences might have been to remain outside to conform – if they can. Anxiety about exclusion, of the danger of missing the bus, may often be a last minute realization but it can, nonetheless, be a potent motivation, without necessarily making those jumping on enthusiastic

---

[7] Dealt with at greater length in den Boer (1998), de la Serre and Wallace (1997) and Edwards and Philippart (1997).

passengers. On the other hand, Maastricht and now Amsterdam allow for opt-outs for those unwilling to co-operate on a possibly permanent basis. That may, of course, remain the national preference and one that strongly reinforces a sense of national identity even if very few countries in Europe have so far been convinced of the economic benefits of standing aside. But the situation for those less unwilling than unable is even more problematic. They may be able to negotiate compensation as part of a trade-off in which they forgo the use of the veto – though a 'Schengen option' would remain for those determined to go ahead. But one of the elements signally lacking in Amsterdam is any great commitment to help those Member States willing but judged unable to co-operate. Flexibility in the sense of different speeds towards an agreed – if often vague – objective has often been a useful device in the past, as have transitional periods to incorporate new Member States. But an absence of consensus on objectives or reaffirmation of the solidarity of the Union is unlikely to make for any greater clarity, understanding or acceptance of the Union.

Amsterdam, and perhaps especially its flexibility provisions, despite the declared intentions of the Reflection Group and others, add significantly to the complexity and opaqueness of a system that has been long criticized for its lack of openness, efficiency and democratic accountability. That may be, as Andrew Moravcsik and Kalypso Nicolaïdis argue, because there was so little compelling on which Member States needed to agree. However, the move towards a single currency and, even if not inexorably, towards a wider Union without a significantly deepened sense of identity or legitimacy provides us with an interesting prospect. There are, after all, national governments as well as EU institutions pressing for change. As Lamberto Dini, the Italian Foreign Minister, put it after pondering whether Italy should try to block or suspend the IGC in Amsterdam: 'We wanted to avoid making European integration appear an ordeal, capable of bringing down governments or causing majorities to vacillate. Better to adopt the disappointed but lucid attitude of Altiero Spinelli after the Single European Act – consolidate what we have obtained and set sail again for the next objective' (Dini, 1997, p. 43). In those circumstances, it may well be that we are facing a prospect of continual constitution-building or constitution-reforming conferences. 1998 might even see the process begin as we wait for Amsterdam to be ratified.

References

Bertram, C. (1997) 'Germany'. In European Policy Centre, *Challenge Europe: Making Sense of the Amsterdam Treaty,* Brussels.

Brinkhorst, L. J. (1997) 'Pillar III'. In European Policy Centre, *Challenge Europe: Making Sense of the Amsterdam Treaty*, Brussels.

Commission of the European Communities (1997) *Agenda 2000: For a Stronger and Wider Union COM* (97)2000 (Brussels: CEC), 15 July.

de la Serre, F. and Wallace, H. (1997) 'Les coopérations renforcées: une fausse bonne idée?'. *Etudes et Recherches* (Paris: Groupement d'Etudes et de Recherches 'Notre Europe'), No. 2.

den Boer, M. *et al.* (eds) (1998) *Managing the New Treaty on European Union: Coping with Flexibility and Legitimacy* (Maastricht: EIPA), forthcoming.

Dini, L. (1997) 'The Italian Government'. In European Policy Centre, *Challenge Europe: Making Sense of the Amsterdam Treaty* (Brussels: EPC).

Edwards G. and Philippart, E. (1997) *Flexibility and the Treaty of Amsterdam: Europe's New Byzantium?* CELS Occasional Paper No. 3 (Cambridge: University of Cambridge Faculty of Law).

Jachtenfuchs, M. *et al.* (1997) 'Ideas and Integration: Conflicting Models of a Legitimate European Political Order'. Paper presented at the Fifth Biennial ECSA Conference, Seattle May–June.

Kaase, M. and Newton, K. (1995) *Beliefs in Government* (Oxford: Oxford University Press).

Laffan, B. (1993) '*The Treaty of Maastricht: Political Authority and Legitimacy*'. In Cafruny, A. and Rosenthal, G. (eds) *The State of the European Community, Vol. 2: The Maastricht Debates and Beyond* (Boulder, CO: Lynne Rienner).

Laursen, F. (1997) 'The Lessons of Maastricht'. In Edwards, G. and Pijpers, A. (eds) *The Politics of European Treaty Reform* (London: Pinter).

Ludlow, P. (1998) 'The EU on the Eve of the 21st Century: Governance, Leadership and Legitimacy'. *Report to CEPS International Advisory Council*, 5–6 February.

Obradovic, D. (1996) 'Policy Legitimacy and the European Union'. *Journal of Common Market Studies*, Vol. 34, No. 2, pp. 191–221.

Reflection Group (1995) *Report* ... (Brussels: General Secretariat of the Council).

Moscovici, P. (1997) 'The French Government'. In European Policy Centre, *Challenge Europe: Making Sense of the Amsterdam Treaty* (Brussels: EPC).

Stubb, A. (1996) 'A Categorization of Differentiated Integration'. *Journal of Common Market Studies*, Vol. 34 No. 2, June pp. 283–95.

Wallace, H. (1993) 'Deepening and Widening: Problems of Legitimacy for the EC'. In Garcia, S. (ed.) *European Identity and the Search for Legitimacy* (London: Pinter).

Weiler, J. (1996) 'European Neo-Constitutionalism: In Search of Foundations for the European Constitutional Order'. *Political Studies*, XLIV, Special issue.

Weiler, J. (1997) 'Legitimacy and Democracy of Union Governance'. In Edwards, G. and Pijpers, A. (eds) *The Politics of European Treaty Reform* (London: Pinter).

Journal of Common Market Studies

Volume 36, Annual Review
September 1998

Keynote Article: Federal Ideals and Constitutional Realities in the Treaty of Amsterdam*

ANDREW MORAVCSIK

and

KALYPSO NICOLAÏDIS

Harvard University

I. Introduction

The Intergovernmental Conference (IGC) that produced the Treaty of Amsterdam was from the start a negotiation in search of a purpose. Large-scale negotiations in EU history – from the Treaty of Rome to Maastricht – have usually centred on a major substantive agenda, normally either trade liberalization or exchange-rate stabilization, with secondary issues and institutional changes dragged in its wake. In the Amsterdam IGC, by contrast, there was no compelling reason to negotiate these particular issues at this particular time. The Member States considered no major expansions in EU competences and ignored core economic concerns almost entirely. With their primary focus clearly on managing the transition to EMU, they were extremely cautious, seeking above all not to provoke domestic debates that might upset this goal. In contrast to the Maastricht negotiations, where German unification, the Gulf War, and the impending dissolution of Yugoslavia appeared to give some urgency to foreign policy co-operation, no such crisis had such an impact on the Amsterdam discussions.

* For comments on this paper we should like to thank Youri Devuyst, Nigel Evans, Philip Gordon, Christopher Hill, Simon Hix, Kathleen McNamara, Hugo Paemen, John Peterson, Michel Petite, Jo Shaw, Helen Wallace, and participants in seminars at Harvard University, Princeton University, and the 1998 Conference of Europeanists in Baltimore, Maryland (USA).

The Amsterdam IGC arose instead out of three considerations. First, in the Maastricht Treaty the more federalist governments, notably that of Germany, had been promised rapid reconsideration of the political union issues on which no agreement could be reached. The unfinished business of Maastricht included the need to revisit Pillar II, on Common Foreign and Security Policy and, to a lesser extent, Pillar III on Justice and Home Affairs. Second, the national debates following the Danish and French referendums on the Maastricht Treaty, as well as the accession of Scandinavian countries, led to widespread calls to redress the 'democratic deficit'. Bringing Europe 'closer to its citizens' – increased powers for the European Parliament and a desire to upgrade Community competences from human rights to employment policy – became a core aim of the new Treaty. Third, in 1993 European chief executives officially endorsed negotiations on an EU enlargement to countries in central and eastern Europe. By raising the prospect of eventually doubling EU membership, they called into question existing EU decision-making procedures. It was agreed that decision-making would eventually have to become more efficient. In addition, larger governments sought a series of modest adjustments to institutional structure, notably a reweighting of votes and integration of the Schengen arrangement into the EU, in advance of enlargement. After appearing in successive European Council communiqués, these goals were summarized in the 1995 report of the intergovernmental Reflection Group chaired by Carlos Westendorp enlisted to frame the conference agenda (Ludlow, 1997a).

Given its lack of a single, clear substantive focus, it is no surprise that Amsterdam, more than any Treaty of Rome revision since 1957, became a melting pot of disparate measures lacking coherent vision of either substantive co-operation in a particular area or the future institutional structure of Europe. Given the lack of clear positive-sum gains, institutional reform tended to get bogged down in zero-sum bargaining between large and small states, or more and less federalist ones. Those elements of the agenda above that commanded consensus – such as some institutional reform to facilitate enlargement or perhaps co-operation on immigration and policing – were not very precise and, above all, not pressing, particularly by comparison to EMU. Governments could easily put them off and did so. Hence the Amsterdam Treaty neither introduces major new Community competences (symbolic proposals on employment aside) nor significantly deepens co-operation in existing substantive fields. Its provisions for institutional reform – with the exception of an expansion of parliamentary co-decision – are modest. The division of the EU into three institutional 'pillars', the second and third of which remain mired in the grey area between pure intergovernmental decision-making under unanimity and the distinctive 'Community system' of exclusive Commission initiative, qualified majority voting in the Council of Ministers, amendment by the European Parliament, and oversight by the European Court of Justice. With the acquiescence, even the advocacy, of even the most federalist governments, the Amsterdam Treaty introduced practices long considered anathema to those who support European integration, such as formal multi-track (nearly '*à la carte*') institutions in which some can move ahead without others, highly differentiated decision-making procedures, and legal versions of the Luxembourg Compromise.

Most assessments of the Treaty tend, therefore, to be highly critical. Lamberto Dini, Italian Foreign Minister, recalled: 'The long night of Amsterdam closed on a note of bitter disappointment. We would not be honest with ourselves or with the others if we did not admit this' (Dini, 1997, p. xxvii). Press commentators remained resolutely unimpressed by the results, with their assessment 'ranging from muted to sceptic' (Bertram, 1997, p. 64). To be sure, the German Government and the Commission Task Force initially attempted to present results as a success that realized the Commission's expectations in many areas; but insofar as this was correct, it reflected in large part the extent to which the Commission 'expectations' had backed away from its initial proposals for 'drastic institutional reform' (CEC, 1997; Duff, 1997a, p. xxx; Hoyer, 1997). In any case, a pessimistic – or, as one federalist commentator put it, 'realistic' – assessment soon reasserted itself (Duff ,1997, p. xxx). European Parliament reports called elements of the Treaty 'disastrous' and 'missed historical opportunities'; they 'constitute a significant reduction in democratic legitimacy'. In particular the Parliament 'deplores that the CFSP will continue to be the result of the lowest common denominator between Member States, thus largely depending on the political will of each', while 'voicing its dismay at the outcome … in the area of free movement of peoples and the third pillar'. Provisions for flexibility 'are in blatant contradiction with the Community spirit and constitute a regrettable precedent' (European Parliament, 1997, pp. 15, 23, 38, 8, 74). Subsequently the Vice-President of the Commission criticized the outcome as 'more than disappointing … disastrous' (van Miert, 1998).

Gloomy scholars and analysts echo dispirited policy-makers and journalists. Three long-time policy analysts speak of a 'comprehensive failure of institutional reform [and] of political leadership' with 'serious political consequences'. 'Heads of government', they conclude, 'have totally failed in their self-appointed task' (Crossick *et al.,* 1997, pp. 1–4). Some political scientists catalogue myriad 'output failures' (Wessels, 1997, pp. 4, 10). (Wessels' language is, it is fair to note, more loaded than his analysis. He rejects any comparisons to an 'optimal model'.) Philip Allot speaks for international lawyers horrified by the legal non-uniformity of the results: 'The Amsterdam Treaty will mean the coexistence of dozens of different legal and economic sub-systems over the next ten years, a sort of nightmare resurrection of the Holy Roman Empire...' (cited in Shaw, 1998, p. 11; also Walker 1998) A leading French federalist calls the outcome 'miserable' and 'catastrophic' (Bourlanges, 1997).

Were current failures not bad enough, the so-called 'bicycle theory' predicts that failure to restore the momentum quickly will, as one prominent former Commissioner puts it, 'place at serious risk much of what has been achieved in the last 40 years' (Sutherland, 1997, p. 31). Others predict that 'the EU cannot afford the repetition of a protracted process of intergovernmental negotiation followed by the anti-climax of negative political conclusions drawn at the end of the day' without people losing faith in integration (European Policy Centre, 1997, Conclusion; also Jørgensen and Christiansen, 1997). A seasoned scholar of EU politics asserts that 'it is urgent to recreate the global political cohesion of the Union characterized by fragmented sectorial policies, vision, and powers, and by different and even incompatible decision-making processes' (Sidjanski, forthcoming, Chapter VI, p. 11). A British federalist seeks to 'shock the citizen out of complacency about how Europe is governed' so as to assure that 'the Amsterdam IGC will have been the last of its kind' (Duff, 1997a, p. xxxviii).

In this article we seek to draw a more balanced assessment of the significance and success of the Amsterdam Treaty – issues of theory and explanation are dealt with elsewhere (Moravcsik and Nicolaïdis, forthcoming). Our central contention is that the near widespread negative assessment of the outcome is misleading, not because the results have been underestimated, but because the standard against which they are judged is unrealistic. Most criticisms of the Amsterdam Treaty implicitly or explicitly reflect a teleological understanding of European integration as moving inexorably, if at an uneven pace, toward greater substantive scope, universal participation by expanding numbers of participants, and greater uniformity in the application of institutional and legal procedures. This is the only future for Europe and if Europe does not maintain the momentum toward its, so goes the 'bicycle theory', it is doomed to slip back, endangering current achievements.

This view, we argue, is dated. Europe is entering a phase today (perhaps it has been there for some time) where this venerable federalist vision of an expanding, undifferentiated, and uniform Europe – constant increases in the substantive scope of co-operation, adherence to a undifferentiated institutional order across issues, and co-operation only if and where governments can participate uniformly – seems less compelling to Member State leaders, elites and publics. The teleological ideal – a 'United States of Europe' characterized by centralized, uniform, universal and undifferentiated institutions – is no longer an appropriate standard (if it ever was one) by which to judge further steps toward integration. Even a visionary leader like Jacques Delors now renounces such a goal: 'There will never be a United States of Europe', he stated recently, 'I refuse to identify myself with those who promote the disappearance of the nation-state ... I seek instead a federation among strong nation-states' (Delors, 1996). Governments continue to move forward towards centralized federal institutions in some areas – notably EMU – but seek pragmatic, flexible solutions in areas where the lack of negative externalities renders decentralized policy-making a workable solution.

This more measured attitude is not the result of a lack of 'political will' or 'vision' – vague, analytically unhelpful phrases generally employed to designate a general mood of rising nationalism or public scepticism toward the EU, the domestic political weakness of national leaders, the disappearance of geopolitical threats resulting from German unification and the receding Cold War, or the passing of the wartime generation. It reflects instead the lack of compelling and compatible substantive national interests in deeper, more uniform co-operation in areas like social policy, cultural and education policy, taxation, foreign policy, and even – though here there are somewhat greater incentives – environmental policy, consumer regulation, immigration, asylum, and policing. Moreover, governments now seek to balance decision-making efficiency with greater accountability and expanded membership. The problem in Europe today is not that governments have lost the ability to move forward strongly toward federalism when they acknowledge clear (generally economic) objectives – say, construct a single market, elaborate a common agricultural policy, establish a single currency, or participate in a multilateral trade negotiation. This is clear from recent movement towards EMU. It is instead the absence of clear substantive interests in doing so in new areas sufficient to justify substantial sacrifices of sovereignty. We are witnessing not a resurgence of nationalism but a diminution (or levelling off) of national interest.

Judged by the standards of the politically possible, not the federalist ideal, the Amsterdam Treaty appears instead as a creative adaptation to new, more sophisticated, more differentiated and, in many areas, more modest national demands. The ability of the Amsterdam negotiators to accommodate shifting concerns demonstrates the flexibility and responsiveness of EU institutions. This suggests that in the future European governments will spend less time seeking to expand the traditional institutions to new substantive areas and increasingly focus on determining what type of institutions and what scope of participation are appropriate to particular issues and circumstances. The resulting debates will be less substantive and more constitutional. Governments will ask – and be forced to justify – the precise level of centralization, uniformity, and scope of co-operation in particular issue areas. Such constitutional debates will not be resolved by the application of a single 'Community method', but instead by a balancing of competing philosophical and pragmatic claims for the pre-eminence of democracy, universality, uniformity, and efficiency. Future debates will reflect support for a more pragmatic, balanced evolution. Far from being 'the last of its kind', the Amsterdam Treaty is the harbinger of a new, more constitutionally self-conscious future for Europe.

II. General Institutional Reform and New Competences

Shifting the Balance between Large and Small:
A Reweighted Council and a Streamlined Commission

At Amsterdam, larger Member States called for a re-weighting of national votes in the EU's primary legislative body, the Council of Ministers. With EU enlargements since 1957, the institutional over-representation of smaller countries had grown progressively more pronounced. In an EU of 26, some calculated, a qualified majority could be achieved with the support of government representing only 48 per cent of the EU population; even some smaller states conceded that such an outcome might be viewed as illegitimate. Yet appeals to principle could not hide the essentially distributive nature of the conflict. At the Extraordinary Summit at Noordwijk, two weeks before Amsterdam, negotiations on Council reform had became an exercise in pure distributional bargaining between larger and smaller states. Calculators in hand and tables from the Commission and the Dutch Presidency by their side, negotiators assessed and reassessed the impact of competing formulae on their country's role in potential blocking alliances under different enlargement scenarios.

Two proposals for reweighting Council votes were considered: an increase in the relative weight of the five largest states (Britain, France, Germany, Italy, and Spain) and a 'dual majority' voting system in which decisions must achieve a fixed percentage of weighted votes *and* votes from states representing some percentage (also generally 60 per cent) of EU population. Smaller states supported the dual majority system, which would increase the ability of larger states to block legislation without diluting their own veto, but this was rejected by the French, because it would for the first time grant Germany more votes than France. Germany, seeking not to embarrass itself or France, sat on the fence – a symbolic setback – while other governments advanced special demands. Since smaller states lost out from a reweighting, no matter how it was structured, it was proposed to offset changes in the Council by streamlining the Commission – limiting the number of Commissioners to one per country. This proposal was presented as a means of rendering the Commission more efficient after enlargement, when the number of Commissioners would expand to 30 or more, but in fact was a *quid pro quo* to smaller states. Matters were complicated even further when the Spanish announced that if they lost a second Commissioner, they would no longer be willing to accept fewer Council votes (eight rather than ten) than the other large countries, and the Netherlands, despite its presidential role as an 'honest broker', demanded greater representation than Greece and Belgium, each with a population 50 per cent smaller. A French proposal to streamline the Commission to around a dozen members was a non-starter among the small states – who felt that their Commissioner was an indispensable conduit for information. Many in any case felt that France was either bluffing or sought thereby to reduce the Commission to a conventional secretariat.

Had the large states really wanted an agreement, surely they could have attained one during the last few weeks. Yet Chancellor Kohl, concerned about domestic ratification of EMU, proposed that the status quo be maintained for the time being and, along with President Chirac – one former head of government reports – quietly encouraged the Dutch presidency to postpone agreement. Despite last-minute wrangling, the Treaty postpones reform to a subsequent IGC with two *caveats*: first, a new comprehensive review must take place at least one year before EU membership exceeds 20; and, at Spanish insistence, there would be one Commissioner per country at the date of the first enlargement, if agreement had been reached on the re-weighting of votes in the Council.

The significance of the failure to reach agreement on institutional reform is easy to exaggerate. Internal Commission studies show that results in Council votes of the prior three years would have remained unchanged under any of the reweighting formulae – though this does not take account of the possibility that some decisions are taken 'in the shadow' of the vote. As far as Commission reform is concerned, internal reorganization and consolidation appears to be a much more significant determinant of efficiency than the number of Commissioners *per se*. After all, many national governments (not least the French), function coherently with a larger number of ministers. It is also unlikely – despite Commission efforts to generate a sense of urgency with this claim – that stalemate jeopardizes the timing of enlargement by requiring that yet another IGC would have to be held to settle institutional reform before the EU exceeds 20 members. As one top Commission negotiator remarked afterwards, the outlines of the likely agreement were so clear to the participants that at some future date it could be negotiated 'in 24 hours'; the problem being simply to select the optimal domestic political moment to do so. Finally, while governments were concerned above all to avoid the impression of symbolic failure, they remained concerned to avoid any domestic ratification controversy that might threaten the transition to EMU – a far more important and immediate priority for all member governments, not least that of Germany.

'Enhanced Co-operation': How Flexible should the EU be?

If Maastricht enshrined the notion that reluctant states cannot be forced into action, Amsterdam pursued the allegedly complementary notion: reluctant states cannot stop others from employing EU institutions to pursue actions they favour.

As one participant put it, 'In Maastricht we took care of the rights of the minority – to opt out; in Amsterdam, we took care of the rights of the majority'. In the Reflection Group, all governments accepted some form of 'flexibility' clause permitting a majority of states to move forward without necessarily including all. The motive force behind the shift in European orthodoxy reflected not the opposition of Eurosceptics, but the conversion of relatively federalist states like France and Germany, who sought a means of bypassing reluctant states like Britain or potential laggards in the east and south. This idea was introduced in the CDU/CSU paper prepared by Wolfgang Schäuble and Karl Lamers in September 1994, then taken up in an ambitious Franco-German proposal.

Broadly speaking, the Member States split into two groups – probable members of a federal core and probable candidates for exclusion – each of which sought an arrangement that afforded its members the greatest freedom of manoeuvre while restricting the strategic options of the others. Leaving aside specific provisions for foreign policy, governments considered three aspects of flexibility: the procedure for invoking it, the scope of its application, and provisions for the participation of excluded states. On invoking flexibility, Britain, supported by Greece, Denmark, Sweden and Ireland (and, to a lesser extent Spain and Portugal) insisted on veto rights over any flexible arrangement – a position France and Germany resisted. The resulting compromise, proposed by Britain and closer to its position, permitted a qualified majority to establish flexible arrangements but with a veto possible 'for important ... reasons of national policy' – echoing the terms of the much maligned Luxembourg Compromise. On scope, there was a consensus that the formal flexibility clause ought not to threaten the *acquis communautaire,* with the result it can only be employed, among other conditions, outside areas of exclusive Community competence; where existing programmes are not affected yet within current EU powers, where it does not discriminate among EU nationals, and where trade and competition remained unimpeded. Even on a narrow interpretation, these *caveats* probably preclude much meaningful co-operation outside the third pillar. On the accession of new participants, potential outsiders sought guarantees that they could opt in at any time, provided they undertook the commitments. The last minute replacement of a Council vote by a Commission assessment of the suitability of new members represented a significant victory for the potential 'outs'.

Redressing the Democratic Deficit?
Parliamentary Powers and Unemployment

Perhaps the most surprising result of the Amsterdam IGC was an increase in parliamentary co-decision. Maastricht had introduced a new EU legislative procedure – 'co-decision' – in which the Parliament and Council negotiated face-to-face over proposed parliamentary amendments in 15 categories of first pillar legislation. At Amsterdam, Member States expanded and reformed the co-decision process. They replaced references to the other major form of parliamentary involvement, the 'co-operation' procedure, in nearly all Pillar I business, excluding EMU – bringing to 38 (after five years 40) the total number of legal categories subject to co-decision. Areas like fiscal harmonization and CAP reform remained outside; only procedures for consultation applied. The co-decision process was reformed, moreover, to remove the (negative) 'third reading', which had previously given the Council a final opportunity to pass legislation by QMV in the case of a failure to reach an agreement in conciliation between the Council and Parliament, subject only to veto by an absolute majority vote of the Parliament. At the end of the legislative process, the Parliament was now on equal footing with the Council; if agreement is not reached, the legislation is dropped. The Parliament also gained a formal right to approve the new Commission President, though it remains difficult for the Parliament to exploit veto power to compel acceptance of a particular candidate. Finally, with the encouragement of the new British Government, steps were taken towards a uniform proportional representation electoral arrangement for parliamentary elections.

The central issue at stake in the expansion of parliamentary powers, it is important to remember, is not the balance between national and supranational authority but the balance of power among supranational institutions. Leaving aside the surprising decision to eliminate the third reading, the precise implications of which are disputed, the primary formal impact of expanded co-decision is to transfer influence from the Commission to the Parliament. Co-decision erodes the Commission's traditional control over the text of proposals throughout the EU legislative process. (As long as the two institutions agree substantively, there may be a joint gain in influence via increased democratic legitimacy (Noël, 1994, pp. 22–3).) Under co-decision, the Council is able to pass any compromise emerging out of the conciliation procedure with Parliament by a qualified majority, while the Commission could no longer compel a unanimous vote on changes it opposes. Whether the Commission also lost its formal right to withdraw a proposal after the conciliation procedure remains a matter of legal dispute, but exercise of such a prerogative in the face of a united Council and Parliament would surely be politically costly (Nickel, 1998).

The Commission did manage, however, to avoid more extreme curtailment of its powers. The German Government, which had advocated at Maastricht that the Parliament share the Commission's power of initiative, repeatedly proposed at Amsterdam that the Council be permitted to revise Commission proposals by qualified majority vote. This proposal, which would have severely curtailed the latter's agenda control, was acceptable neither to smaller states nor to the Commission, whose representative immediately threatened to recommend its resignation *en masse* (Nickel, 1998). For its part, the Parliament held back from demanding the power of initiative, knowing that this would trigger similar demands from the Council – perhaps to the disadvantage of supranational institutions as a whole (Petite, 1998). Co-decision aside (and notwithstanding the dispute over trade policy competence), there was greater support among national governments for maintaining traditional Commission prerogatives at Amsterdam than had been the case at Maastricht.

The increase in parliamentary power is particularly striking given the marginal role played by the Parliament in the negotiations (Petite, 1998). As in the SEA and Maastricht, parliamentary representatives were active in early meetings but played a marginal role in later deliberations (cf. Moravcsik, 1998c). The expansion of parliamentary prerogatives was supported instead primarily by the successive national presidencies and by Germany, which kept co-decision provisions in the negotiating text. Also important were shifts in national positions. Shortly before Amsterdam the new French Socialist government, with Elisabeth Guigou as Justice Minister, pressed strongly for parliamentary powers; President Chirac acquiesced and was reported to remark to his advisers that it was an issue of marginal importance. Moreover, the new British government of Tony Blair was less adamantly opposed than its predecessor. Elsewhere, given that the elimination of the third reading was not seen as a major shift – given the rarity with which it appeared to influence actual outcomes – it seemed a relatively easy concession to quell democratic sentiment.

Council Efficiency: Majority Voting in the First Pillar

The Council of Ministers remains the most powerful institution within the EU system of governance; hence reform of the Council through increased use of QMV was considered by the Commission and others as the most significant reform under consideration at Amsterdam (Devuyst, 1997, p. 14; Petite, 1998). The Commission, of course, preferred a maximalist solution, namely expansion of QMV to all areas – a proposal generally supported by the Benelux countries, Italy, and some new entrants like Austria and Finland. (For this, the Commission advanced the superficially persuasive, if analytically fallacious, argument that the probability of a veto would be many millions of times greater with 30 members than with 15. This neglects that the probability that any single government will oppose a measure is generally correlated to the probability that others will do so; Council politics are typically coalitional, not unilateral.) France, too, came to advocate QMV in these areas after an internal analysis revealed that it had much less chance of being outvoted than of seeing decisions it favoured overcome a potential veto by another Member State (Petite, 1998). Neither a Conservative nor a Labour Government in Britain was willing to contemplate extension of QMV to social policy (rules of worker representation and redundancy were proposed), but only to market liberalization.

While an attractive idea in principle, general QMV proved less promising in practice. Of around 65 Pillar I articles requiring unanimity, nearly half concerned monetary and financial issues and would therefore become obsolete with the transition to EMU. An additional dozen concerned core institutional and financial competences, such as structural funding and nominations to the Commission, on which governments were unlikely to favour QMV. (These issues are poised to become *more* controversial in coming years.) There remained 25 residual regulatory and single market issues, of which over half were areas in which governments had extreme reservations toward extending QMV – including free movement of peoples, social security, professional services, indirect taxation, culture, industrial policy, social policy and employment. (CEC, 1997; Petite, 1998). On some of these issues, opposition from Britain and numerous smaller counties might have been surmounted had it not been for German reticence.

German scepticism was not new. Germany had entered into previous IGCs with strong rhetoric on QMV but long lists of exceptions. In negotiating the SEA, Kohl had insisted on the insertion of Art. 100a4 granting derogations to governments with higher standards than the European norm – a clause strengthened in the environmental area at Amsterdam. (If backed by new scientific evidence, governments may derogate, regardless of their previous voting record.) Germany had subsequently been outvoted in the EU Council more often than any other government. In the Amsterdam IGC, this reluctance took the form of pressure against QMV from the German Länder, which held exclusive or shared jurisdiction in Germany's federal system in most of the areas under consideration. Third pillar issues were especially sensitive. Diplomats, including Germany's chief negotiator in Brussels, apparently expected Kohl to override domestic opposition at the last minute in the name of federalism. Yet the Chancellor, surely with one eye on the approaching transition to EMU, surprised all his partners in the final weeks and hours before Amsterdam by opposing compromise proposals for a broad extension of QMV. Extension of majority voting to a dozen relatively insignificant matters – such as creation of an advisory body on data protection, aid to the outmost regions of the EU, and R&D, an area governed by voluntary participation and (albeit less and less over time) *juste retour* – fooled no one. One top Commission official termed the outcome 'meagre' (Duff, 1997, pp. 155–6).

New Competences: Employment

Symbolically more salient, though substantively less significant, was the joint declaration at Amsterdam concerning unemployment in Europe. Unemployment reached 11 per cent across Europe in 1996. Despite healthy scepticism concerning the ability of governments to do anything in this domain, publics nonetheless considered action in this area as a test of EU relevance. The result was a chapter on employment – the only exception to the informal agreement among governments not to consider new substantive competences in the Amsterdam Treaty. Countries like France and Sweden spoke of this chapter as embryonic 'economic government' to counterbalance the new European Central Bank (ECB) – e.g. the long overdue spelling out of Article 103 of the Maastricht EMU provisions – a position opposed by Britain, Germany and the Netherlands, who watered down the provisions. The Germans flatly refused to consider last-minute proposals by the new French Socialist government of Lionel Jospin for the use of EU funds for job creation or research (Duff, 1997, p. 64). The new chapter does permit the European Council to issue annual employment policy guidelines, surveillance of the employment policies of Member States, and a pilot project of incentive measures to encourage intergovernmental co-operation – the latter watered down to a pilot project. An Employment Committee was created. While, as one commentator noted, these 'cosmetic' changes permit the EU to 'do nothing about unemployment it was not able to do beforehand', at most they may provide a basis for eventual efforts to encourage co-operation by 'shaming' member governments. Modest changes were also made in EC environment, consumer protection, and public health policies.

III. Foreign Policy and Home Affairs Pillars Revisited

The Maastricht Treaty had reinforced co-operation in the two major non-economic areas – foreign policy (including defence) and home affairs (immigration, asylum, and police co-operation). Of the large countries, such co-operation was of primary importance to Germany, which had a far less viable unilateral foreign policy than France or Britain and was the destination of well over 50 per cent of immigrants to the EU. In addition, immigration, justice, and policing were salient and potentially popular electoral issues for Kohl's centre-right coalition. At Maastricht, France, Britain, and others had refused to communitarize these sensitive areas. Instead, member governments agreed to the French proposal that divided the EU into three pillars.

Reform of the second and third pillars was given a sense of urgency by the failure to achieve any significant results after the entry into force of the Maastricht Treaty. This failure was much noted by commentators despite the absence of objective evidence that policies would have been different under more centralized institutions. Some mistakenly argued that the Bosnian War would have been dealt with differently had CFSP been given more institutional backbone – a view largely discredited by the historical record. A marginally stronger case can be made that co-operation in the third pillar would be deepened by more centralized administration. Yet this, too, is unclear. Bureaucracies remain insular; some governments see little advantage in co-operation. Still, encouraged by the Commission spokesmen and ongoing German concern, these areas, particularly the third pillar, came to be viewed as natural areas in which small steps toward deeper co-operation could be taken at a modest political price.

The Second Pillar: Common Foreign and Security Policy

The Maastricht Treaty had provided for a Common Foreign and Security Policy that functioned through classical intergovernmental means, thus formalizing the way 'European Political Co-operation' had functioned for two decades. At Amsterdam, the governments considered introducing greater QMV, flexibility, and better administrative support, but the gains were modest. Instead, Amsterdam confirms the essentially intergovernmental nature of EU foreign policy, but fine-tunes procedures in the name of efficiency.

Introducing greater QMV was the most significant potential reform of CFSP considered at the IGC. The Treaty introduces QMV in the General Affairs Council (where foreign ministers are represented) for 'joint actions' and 'common positions' implementing 'common strategies' previously adopted by unanimity at European summits. These terms are not well defined and may lead to disagreement. A truly determined government could seek to employ narrow and detailed initial delegation – objectives, duration, and permissible means – to restrict all *de facto* use of QMV. Still, the generalized adoption of QMV for second-tier decisions on implementation shifts the implicit default in such circumstances and had thus long been resisted by the UK, France, and Greece. However the Treaty permits a government to wield a 'political' veto by declaring its opposition to the adoption of a decision by QMV 'for important and stated reasons' of national interest. In such cases, the ministers may refer the matter to heads of state and government in the European Council, which then decides by unanimity.

An equally significant innovation lies in a unique flexibility clause introduced into CFSP. 'Constructive abstention' creates the possibility for a sub-group of Member States to conduct joint actions using EU institutions with the acquiescence but not the participation of reluctant Member States. If one-third of the Member States abstain, no action is possible. If a group representing less than one-third abstains from a decision, they are not obliged to apply it but do accept that the decision commits the EU as a whole. A subtle difference from the enhanced co-operation clause of the first pillar was that states are called upon, though not formally obliged, to refrain from any action likely to conflict with or impede EU action. If this procedure, already part of the implicit functioning of CFSP, has any impact, it will be because it permits dissenting states to register their dissent very visibly, often necessary for domestic reasons, without actually blocking joint action and retaining the option to opt in later. Non-military actions, moreover, may be funded out of joint funds, regardless of abstention, though operations to complete 'Petersberg tasks' (see below) must raise ad hoc levies. Constructive abstention provides governments with greater flexibility, though it should not be exaggerated. The policy tools that can be manipulated in this way are limited; unless abstaining countries actually implemented EU policy, for example, it would be difficult to impose effective sanctions or embargoes.

A third area of potential CFSP reform was centralized administration and leadership. Maastricht had created an independent secretariat to oversee CFSP, but there remained differing views concerning how to institutionalize collective political leadership. The Commission and the French Government took traditional positions. The Commission pursued its long-standing desire to centralize foreign policy-making authority, like authority in so many other areas, in the Commission itself; it criticized the pillar design, noting that it might hamper coordination between the EU economic and diplomatic policies. This proposal gained little support and was never discussed seriously (Petite, 1998). The French, by contrast, sought to empower a senior political figure with a high degree of independence from the Commission. This position, dubbed 'Mr/Ms CFSP' (or rather perhaps M/Mme PESC), cynics noted, was likely to be held by a Frenchman, possibly Valéry Giscard d'Estaing. President Chirac's quixotic insistence on a more political post until the very last hours of the IGC testifies to the high priority attributed by the French side to this issue – perhaps the only one where a distinctively French proposal had any chance of acceptance.

Yet this was not to be. Most governments sought to maintain an intergovernmental structure. The result was a 'lowest common denominator' compromise of sorts, one that moved only modestly from the status quo. While denying the French 'Mr/Ms CFSP', the result reinforced the Anglo-French victory at Maastricht, which had preserved Member State initiative in this area. EU representation for CFSP would continue to be handled by the rotating presidency, but the Secretary General of the Council (SG) would centrally administer CFSP and serve, alongside the national presidency, as EU envoy and representative of CFSP. The creation of a new Deputy SG would underscore these new responsibilities. Critics argue that this does little more than authorize a 'bureaucrat' to assume the post of 'special envoy' already created by the Maastricht Treaty; defenders point to the potential for greater continuity. In the end, something approaching the French vision is possible only if a substantial majority of governments cease supporting the appointment of a national civil servant as SG, as in the past, and turn to a major political figure. Even this might not be enough. The Commission is to be 'closely associated'; in other words, it can be invited to participate in discussions. This outcome marks a clear victory for the pillar design and, within it, the classically intergovernmental Council Secretariat over the Commission's more centralized, administratively uniform vision; short of a radical change in nomination practices, no serious competition to national foreign ministries is likely.

Turning lastly to defence co-operation, we observe only modest change. The French spoke of an independent EU defence identity, but advanced so few concrete proposals that others soon questioned their motives. Instead the French, whether out of commitment or calculation, joined Germany in an eleventh-hour plan, backed by the other four original EC members and Spain, for a progressive merger between the EU and WEU with an explicit timetable and flexibility provisions. Traditional pro-NATO countries such as Britain and Portugal, sceptics like Greece, and traditional neutrals like Sweden and Ireland remained sceptical; it was an issue on which numerous governments seemed willing to impose a veto.

The final outcome came closest to the sceptical position held by the neutrals and was not far – particularly when we consider firm commitments rather than rhetoric – from the completely negative views advanced by Britain. A protocol called on the EU to draw up proposals for closer co-operation with the WEU within a year, yet the language is non-committal and preserves a veto; the EU may recommend actions to the WEU. Governments may discuss a three-stage timetable for closer EU/WEU co-operation. EU defence policy may not prejudice the specific character of NATO. The only explicit step was the incorporation, following a Swedish-Finnish initiative, of the so-called 'Petersberg tasks' as part of CFSP. These tasks, which had became part of the WEU mission in 1992, include humanitarian intervention, rescue, peacekeeping and crisis management – all issues that are increasing in importance in the post-Cold War world, as the line between 'crisis management' and more traditional defence operations is increasingly blurred. The Nordic countries, along with Ireland and Austria, were the most adamant proponents of such inclusion, not only for positive reasons but also because it subtly disguised their opposition to further moves towards a more traditional European defence. For those dedicated to a European defence identity, Amsterdam was viewed as a straightforward 'failure'.

Finally, while not strictly connected with CFSP, another foreign policy issue of extreme interest to the Commission concerned the scope of 'exclusive competence' pertaining to international trade negotiations under Article 113 (Meunier and Nicolaïdis, 1997). Under the Treaty of Rome the Commission enjoyed a monopoly over external representation in World Trade Organization (formerly GATT) negotiations (though overseen by a Council committee), with governments taking final decisions by QMV. With the Uruguay Round, however, Member States (led by France) successfully argued that new issues – services trade, intellectual property, and investment – were not traditional 'trade' issues and therefore lay outside the scope of exclusive Community competence. This subjected them both to unanimous vote in the Council and to ratification by individual national parliaments. At Amsterdam, a majority of Members States led by the Commission sought to extend Community competence but the outcome reiterated the status quo. Even the Germans proved cautious. The only mitigating factor is that in the Treaty the Council can decide the status of new issues by unanimity before upcoming negotiations – another procedural hybrid that allows for some future extension of Community competence without Treaty revision.

The Third Pillar: Justice and Home Affairs

Reform of the third pillar introduced by the Maastricht Treaty, justice and home affairs, was the most intensely debated issue in the negotiations. Three broad topics were discussed together: reform of the common policy toward immigration and asylum *vis-à-vis* third-country nationals, the integration into the EU Treaty of the so-called 'Schengen *acquis*' (the provisions on visas, borders and procedures negotiated under the Schengen Agreement, which aimed to abolish checks at intra-EC borders, signed on 14 June 1985); and co-operation in matters of policing and justice. These three concerns were linked not simply because they all generally concern the movement of people across borders and because they are all handled by justice and home affairs ministries, but also because co-operation on judicial, police and immigration matters becomes more imperative as internal borders among EU Member States dissolve, a single market emerges, and enlargement to the east draws near. Even among sceptical governments, there was some concern about the need to pool resources both to manage the pressures of migration (and domestic demand for action associated with it) and to respond to the internationalization of crime, not least drug trafficking. The third pillar was seen from the start, therefore, as the substantive area where progress at Amsterdam was most likely.

Governments that favoured more intense third-pillar co-operation called for 'communitarization' – the integration of the third pillar into the normal EU economic policy-making institutions, as well as an expansion of activities already conducted by the EU. Germany, a country on the front line *vis-à-vis* eastern Europe, led by a Christian Democratic government for which 'law and order' was an attractive and popular issue, and currently responsible for taking well over half of EU asylum-seekers and immigrants, took a leadership position. Communitarization of the Schengen *acquis* was also a particularly desirable strategy because it would automatically mean folding all current agreements under Schengen into the EU – including bilateral arrangements between Germany and its eastern neighbours, obliging the latter to accept the return of any illegal immigrants to Germany who transited through their territory, regardless of their country of origin (Burrows, 1998). Even Chancellor Kohl rejected any automatic transition to QMV, however, in part because it threatened current Länder prerogatives.

In the run-up to Amsterdam, critics made much of the lack of substantial results in the third pillar since the entry into force of the Maastricht Treaty. Such critics, like those who criticize EU second pillar arrangements for failing to resolve the Yugoslav crisis, seldom explained the precise nature of preferred policies or how institutional reform would have assured that better policy would emerge. Surely the lack of policy outputs reflected substantial opposition among the Member States, as well as institutional bottlenecks. Immigration issues remained politically volatile in all countries, not least Germany, France, and Britain, because of right-wing opposition, fundamental concerns about institutional sovereignty, or geographical specificity.

More importantly, governments found themselves with widely disparate interests. Not only were some not members of the Schengen Accord, but at least two non-members of Schengen – Britain and Ireland, the former with only 23 ports of entry – were far better able to impose *de facto* control over movements across their borders than almost any continental country. As a corollary, internal policing was traditionally far less intrusive than on the continent. Hence Britain and Ireland rightly perceived less benefit and considerable cost imposed by international co-operation, a view that changed little with the election of the Labour Government. Despite the temptation to find *some* area in which to declare 'success' in the negotiations, opposition to communitarization by the UK, Ireland and Denmark meant that agreement was far from obvious until the last weeks before Amsterdam.

The introduction of a new title in the Treaty on free movement of persons, asylum and immigration and the concurrent shift of these issues from the third to the first pillar have been described as a success by many observers. Communitarization extends not only to visa, asylum and immigration policy but also to some judicial co-operation in the civil matters having cross-border implications; police co-operation and criminal matters remain in the intergovernmental third pillar. Hence the scope of the newly communitarized policies is slightly broader than even the Commission initially sought. The Commission gained the right of initiative, albeit shared by the Council for at least five years, which may help place on the agenda politically sensitive proposals that some Member States could not endorse publicly. (It will be interesting to see whether there in fact exist viable proposals that no single Member State would propose but the Commission does.)

The Treaty undeniably brings about gains in efficacy and accountability. Control by the Court, albeit excluding matters concerning the maintenance of law and order and the safeguarding of internal security, provides greater guarantees for the protection of individual rights – although the Court's rulings on the interpretation of the Title may not affect judgments of Member State courts which have become *res judicata*. The replacement of the secretive 'K4 committee' by traditional COREPER structures may increase democratic accountability in this field as well as the coherence with other domains. A transition to QMV may be possible after five years without national parliamentary ratification. Finally, EU directives or regulations need no longer be ratified by national parliaments – a striking contrast to the uneven ratification of conventions under Schengen and Maastricht arrangements. Since Maastricht entered into force only one convention (actually negotiated before the Treaty was signed) has been approved by all 15 parliaments; a number of agreements are still to be examined by national parliaments, including on the operations of EUROPOL, customs co-operation and the fight against fraud.

Still, even on the most optimistic of readings, these gains are moderate compared to those to which advocates aspired. The transition to QMV will not occur for at least five years and only then with unanimous support. For the moment, the Commission lacks the exclusive right of initiative, except on rules governing visas, for which there had already been a partial exception under Maastricht. A proposal for automatic transition to QMV, either immediately or in five years, was opposed not just by the traditional recalcitrant countries, but by Chancellor Kohl, who was responding to pressure from the Länder, as well as other substantive concerns. Even in the longer run, it is hard to envisage an alternative to unanimity – in effect imposing new 'potential citizens' onto a Member State by qualified majority – occurring soon. The delicacy of the compromise is reflected also in the extreme legal complexity and ambiguity of the resulting arrangement. Some detractors suggest that the incorporation of the Schengen *acquis* into the Treaty will add complexity. NGOs supporting immigrant rights criticize the communitarization of bilateral arrangements that permit west European Member States to deport immigrants. Finally, communitarization was possible only by granting broad opt-outs and flexibility to Britain, Ireland, and Denmark. The UK and Ireland each obtained two opt-out protocols, one regarding the new free movement of persons, the other recognizing the Common Travel Area between the UK and Ireland. Denmark obtained a similar opt-out, made even broader by the inclusion of any decisions with defence implication. The transition from Schengen to the EU will take place under an 'enhanced co-operation' procedure not involving all Member States. In this area, a precedent has been set for an extremely loose form of variable geometry, if still a bit short of a pure 'Europe *à la carte*' scheme, in which recalcitrant countries choose the precise measures on which they would like to co-operate – though such co-operation would require unanimous approval – and governments can collectively choose whether to act under the EU or Schengen. This raises interesting legal and strategic issues for the future.

IV. Success and Failure Reconsidered: Flexibility and Differentiation as Creative Adaptation

It is traditional, at least among European federalists, to evaluate major EU agreements teleologically. EU agreements are successful if governments embark on new schemes for substantive co-operation and embed those schemes by deepening a uniform legal and administrative order centralized in Brussels. Only this, in the teleological view, generates irreversible integration. This is the sort of vision that inspired the then Commission President, Jacques Delors, to proclaim in 1988 that 80 per cent of national regulations would soon be made in Brussels – a statement that, while (almost) true, betrays a rather rule-bound perspective on what is most important about integration. The teleological approach takes for granted that deeper co-operation is in the fundamental interest of Member States; failures to agree are therefore secondary factors: weak, ignorant or ill-intentioned politicians, random and incidental domestic pressures, the absence of compelling geopolitical motivations for co-operation, or a general lack of 'political will'. Evaluation is simple. Whatever deepens and widens co-operation and, in particular, whatever pools and centralizes authoritative decision-making, marks progress. In the teleological view, finally, it is essential to overcome difficulties quickly not simply in order to exploit future possibilities to move toward federal union, but because continuous forward motion – thus the 'bicycle theory' – is required to preserve existing gains.

From this perspective the Amsterdam Treaty seems bitterly disappointing. It maintains the 'pillar' logic introduced at Maastricht rather than expanding the full 'Community method' to foreign policy. Within the first pillar, the Treaty disappointed the Commission's ambition to generalize QMV, expand its own participation, and extend (or retain) Community competence to new trade negotiations (Devuyst, 1997). Explicit provisions for vetoes, akin to the Luxembourg Compromise, and extensive provisions for differentiation and flexibility are now embedded firmly in the Treaty. In striking contrast to the strategy employed in the original Treaty of Rome, in which unanimous voting procedures became QMV nearly automatically, future movement after Amsterdam continues to require explicit issue-specific unanimous votes of the Member States. While some third-pillar issues of immigration and asylum – the one set of issues in the negotiations where there are clear economic or regulatory benefits from co-operation – were moved into the first pillar, the maintenance of unanimity voting and the lack of a unique Commission right of initiative mean that evolution toward a supranational decision-making system will be at best slow.

Some flexibility provisions move close to a 'pick and choose' Europe '*à la carte*' (Shaw, 1998, p. 13). Even if the result does not, as one commentator asserts, 'push the Union in an integovernmental direction, it does reflect a striking willingness on the part of member states to eschew the "Community method" where satisfactory hybrid deals are possible' (Devuyst, 1997, p. 13). No wonder – as we saw in the introduction to this essay – that those who mark the successes and failures of integration against an ideal federal standard see Amsterdam as a catastrophic failure. At the very least, it limits the scope for future supranational solutions.

Yet this teleological mode of evaluating progress toward European integration – and the pessimistic assessment that follows from it – increasingly appear dated. Though newspaper columnists never tire of reciting how the Europeans seek to form a cohesive whole the size of the US and supranational officials and members of federalist groups continue to promote centralization for its own sake, national politicians, interest groups, and individual citizens increasingly doubt that the vision of a centralized, uniform, undifferentiated Europe, let alone a 'United States of Europe,' is either desirable or feasible. Among EU member governments at Amsterdam, only Belgium and Italy consistently adopted anything resembling the traditional position; neither Germany nor the Netherlands was nearly as unambiguous, not to speak of France, Britain, and others. Even the Santer Commission, with the public approval even of Delors, shied away from proposing a radical overhaul of the pillar structure (Delors, 1996). There is an expanding consensus that the EU properly provides a structure to complement, co-ordinate, even in limited ways supplant the policies of nation-states, correcting for their manifest weaknesses; yet the EU has not, will not, and should not replace the nation-state (Milward, 1993; Moravcsik, 1998c; Weiler, 1996).

Traditional federalists attribute such caution to contingent factors: the purported shift in public opinion away from support for European integration, for which there is little evidence; the decline of geopolitical pressure for co-operation after the Cold War, German unification, and the passing of a generation with personal experience of World War II; or the domestic weakness and general lack of 'political will' among national politicians – all of which results in a deficit of 'leadership', not least from the 'Franco-German motor' (Devuyst, 1997). This both misinterprets the dominant motivations underlying European integration in the past and misunderstands the current mood. Governments have traditionally pooled or delegated sovereignty in order to lock in implementation and compliance with agreements that offer clear (generally economic) gains. Consensus on institutional form has been greatest where there is underlying consensus on substantive goals, even when key participants – we need think only of Charles de Gaulle, Helmut Schmidt, or Margaret Thatcher – were openly critical of supranational officials, institutions, and ideology (Moravcsik, 1998c; Milward, 1993). And today, if we are to believe that the modesty of the Amsterdam Treaty stemmed from atavistic nationalism or an extraordinary sensitivity to sacrifices of sovereignty, how do we explain simultaneous progress toward EMU?

The failure to move forward more strongly stems, more fundamentally, from the lack of any compelling substantive reason to deepen co-operation. What governments and publics seem to desire today – as they always have – is a European structure that solves practical problems while undermining state sovereignty to the minimum extent possible. While the need for the EU structure trade liberalization was obvious, it is far less clear whether the gains from deeper economic regulation fully offset the sacrifice of control over free movement of peoples, social security, professional services, indirect taxation, culture, industrial policy, social policy, employment, or fiscal policy – or, more precisely, governments have far more diverse preferences concerning these forms of co-operation. In comparison with previous treaty reforms, nearly all of which were driven by an overriding substantive, generally economic goal – the elimination of tariffs and quotas, the construction of the common agricultural policy, exchange-rate co-ordination, the completion of the single market ('Europe 1992'), and monetary union – the Amsterdam Treaty was preceded by a near total lack of concrete substantive proposals for policies that could be pursued under new institutional provisions. In the future, modest forward movement is likely in justice and home affairs, due to relatively clear substantive gains for a majority of states from co-ordinated visa and policing policies; elsewhere the prospects are less promising.

In historical perspective the Amsterdam debate was striking in its vagueness. The SEA and Maastricht were preceded by detailed substantive agendas in the form, respectively, of the 'White Paper' with its almost 300 proposals formed into a plan for 'Europe 1992' and the vision, whether technically sound or not, of a single currency and 'Economic and Monetary Union.' By contrast, the preparation for Amsterdam was strikingly devoid of discussion about precise scenarios and concrete purposes for which second and third pillar institutions were to be reformed, let alone the concrete benefits of co-ordinating residual economic regulation, culture, education, taxation, or social policy. In short, there has been much debate about who belongs in the 'core' of Europe and much less about what the core is. One reason is that European governments simply do not agree on overriding objectives.

Peter Ludlow is therefore half right when he observes, 'The age of the pioneers is over. That of the system managers is already with us – or ought to be. [Amsterdam] was bound to be different from its predecessors – for the very good reason that the latter had done most of the system building that was needed'. It could only be successful if it managed 'to show that its modesty was its glory rather than its shame' (Ludlow, 1997a, pp. 4, 13). Ludlow is correct that the EU is moving beyond an era in which the primary focus has been on the expansion of common policies. Far from being the last of its kind, the Amsterdam Treaty is the harbinger of the future. Yet we should not assume, therefore, that there remains nothing fundamental to be debated at future IGCs. We have not reached the 'end of history' in Europe in which one can only, as did Alexandre Kojève in his time, retire to Brussels and cultivate the CAP.

Europe stands instead before a series of ongoing constitutional debates. The focus in the future – disguised up to now by the increases in the scope of EU policy-making in core economic areas where a common legal order and universal participation were and remain unquestioned – will be on the construction of a legitimate constitutional order for policy-making responsive to the desires of national governments and their citizens. The question facing the EU today is no longer how to expand the ideal of centralized institutions and uniform participation to new areas, but whether and when to do so. As in most constitutional polities, fundamental issues of this kind are unlikely to be resolved by the application of a single definitive principle, let alone by commitment to a centralizing teleology. Constitutional bargains tend instead to emerge from the balances between different underlying principles (Shaw, 1998; Coglianese and Nicolaïdis, 1998). Not since the days of Charles de Gaulle have such questions been debated as explicitly as they are today.

Within the EU, tensions are emerging between fundamental principles of democratization, uniformity, universality and efficiency (Brinkhorst, 1997). Further democratization of the EU legislative process, for example, clearly requires either reduction in the prerogatives of the Council of Ministers or reduction in those of the Commission. The former is unlikely and, accordingly, the Commission found itself in a defensive position at Maastricht and Amsterdam, as the more radical proposals for strengthening the Parliament, particularly those advanced by Germany, came at the expense of the traditional Commission monopoly on the right of initiative. How long will it be before the French desire to strengthen the Council and the German desire to strengthen the Parliament come together in an open alliance against the Commission? Yet might this not undermine the record of success of the Commission-centred system more insulated from special interests, more technocratic in its decision-making, and, therefore, more effective at promoting the common European interest?

Similarly, there is increasingly open tension between a universal and uniform legal order, on the one hand, and effective decision-making, on the other. At Amsterdam the result was a greater willingness of governments to dilute the uniformity and universality of EU commitments (outside core EU issues, such as market liberalization) in the interest of achieving substantive co-operation of interest to some governments. Despite efforts to simplify the legislative process, divergent institutional procedures are employed and different sets of members are involved across issues. Clearly, if some flanking policies become key to the success of monetary co-operation, laggard states cannot impose a veto; if some Member States disagree with a foreign policy action, they need not be involved; and if countries hold to different traditions of internal and external control of personal movement, they cannot be compelled to join a border-free Europe. In such circumstances, 'evolutionary pragmatism' increasingly dominates legal simplicity – even more so than has been the case since the signing of the Treaty of Rome in 1957. Procedures ranging from no EU involvement at all to full communitarization are instituted, with each designed to create a distinctive balance between national prerogatives and community competence. Policy innovation in the years to come will be ever more focused within the grey area between the classical extremes of intergovernmental and supranational institutions.

This was not a novel innovation at Amsterdam, as federalists who attribute the result to recent geopolitical or ideological shifts would have it. It was instead the extension of a deep, accelerating trend over decades within Europe toward greater differentiation across countries and issues. Article 233 of the Treaty of Rome governing the Benelux countries, the EMS and EMU, the Schengen agreement, ESPRIT, Article 100a4 of the SEA, British and Danish opt-outs on issues like social policy, budgetary bargains, and European Political Co-operation all involved *de facto* acknowledgements that not all governments would be treated the same. Credible threats to exclude recalcitrant Member States were critical to both the SEA and Maastricht agreements. Prospective enlargement to 21 or more increasingly diverse Member States only intensifies the problems. It seems clear that the CAP will not be applied to new members in the same way it is applied to existing members – with long transition periods serving to differentiate between the two groups to an even greater extent than in the Iberian enlargement of the 1980s.

The difference between Amsterdam and previous negotiations lies in the legitimacy and openness of such proposals. In 1988, Margaret Thatcher's call for a 'multi-track' Europe in her notorious Bruges speech was dismissed as the height of Euroscepticism (Moravcsik, 1998c). Even after Maastricht, flexible arrangements were still spoken of by most Europeans as unfortunate exceptions, with a uniform *acquis communautaire* the clear ideal. In the decade that followed, the debate over Europe has been turned on its head. Today it is the more federalist countries that demand differentiation and flexibility – now termed 'differentiated solidarity', 'avant-garde', 'federal core', or 'enhanced co-operation'. In response and over the objections of traditional federalists, the Amsterdam Treaty elevated 'flexibility into one of the constitutional principles of the

EU' (Ehlermann, 1997, p. 60; de La Serre and Wallace, 1997). The debate has shifted to the relative burdens to be accepted by 'ins' and 'outs' – whether Europe should provide choices '*à la carte*' or be centred on 'hard core'. Will flexibility undermine the threats of exclusion that have forced recalcitrant states to accept European solutions in the past – witness threats aimed at the French in the early years of the EU and the British more recently – or will it offer new opportunities for governments to make such threats? The answer depends on the outcome of the emerging constitutional debate (Pisani-Ferry, 1998).

The European project has evolved into the most successful example of voluntary international co-operation in history. For its first four decades, this was achieved through the progressive extension of the scope of co-operation among Member States. With EMU and intergovernmental co-operation in the second and third pillars, this phase is nearing completion. Amsterdam represents the beginning of a new phase of flexible, pragmatic constitution-building in order to accommodate the diversity of a continent-wide polity.

This is not to say that the EU is dissolving. The opposite is true. The 'bicycle theory', whereby integration will recede if it does not progress, is a fetching metaphor but one without substance (Ash, 1998). The EU is proving quite capable of moving forward where it is perceived as necessary, as in EMU, and it is proving capable of protecting the *acquis communautaire*. The one point of agreement at Amsterdam, from the most Eurosceptical government to the most federalist, was the sanctity of provisions guaranteeing free trade in goods and services.

Even less plausible is the spectre of World War III – fear that makes unlikely rhetorical bedfellows of Helmut Kohl and Martin Feldstein (Feldstein, 1997). Those who assert that the failure to continue progressing towards a federal Europe (or the collapse of certain schemes currently directed to that end) will spark a geopolitical conflagration are forced to invoke historical analysis and political science over two generations old. The primary cause of peace in postwar Europe has not been European integration, but the law-like propensity of developed democracies to avoid war with one another. The major geopolitical bargains underlying post-war Europe – the US commitment, the repatriation of the Saar, the remilitarization of Germany, the formation of NATO, and the like – were precursors, not products of the Treaty of Rome in 1957 (Moravcsik, 1996, 1998c). What has held Europe together and propelled it forward has been a series of mutually beneficial bargains, largely economic in nature, to promote the interests of European producers and consumers. Those who continue to believe that the EU is fragile – too fragile to withstand constitutional debate – because it has been powered forward by fears of reliving World War II, doses of federalist idealism, constraints imposed by federal institutions, and the intermittent 'political will' of national leaders, rather than a stable pattern of co-operation tailored to the convergent economic interests of national governments and their citizens, are today's true Eurosceptics.

References

Ash, T.G. (1998) 'Europe's Endangered Liberal Order'. *Foreign Affairs*, Vol. 77, No. 2, March–April, pp. 51–66.

Bertram, C. (1997) 'Germany'. In European Policy Centre, pp. 64–5.

Bourlanges, J.-L. (1997) 'The Amsterdam Paradox'. In European Policy Centre, Brussels p. 70.

Brinkhorst, L. J. (1997) 'Efficiency and Democracy'. In European Policy Centre, p. 57.

Burrows, N. (1998) Presentation at the Conference of Europeanists, Baltimore, MD.

Coglianese, C. and Nicolaïdis, K. (1998) 'Securing Subsidiarity: Mechanisms for Allocating Authority in Tiered Regimes'. In Woolcock, S. (ed.), *Subsidiarity in the Governance of the Global Economy* (Cambridge: Cambridge University Press).

Commission of the European Commmunities (1997) 'Assessing the Achievements of the Commission's Objectives for the IGC (1996 IGC Task Force), Brussels MP/bw D(97).

Crossick, S, Kohnstamm, M. and Pinder, J. (1997) 'The Treaty of Amsterdam'. In European Policy Centre, pp. 1–4.

de la Serre, F. and Wallace, H. (1997) 'Les coopérations renforcées: une fausse bonne idée?' *Série études et recherches*, No. 2 (Paris: Groupement d'études et recherches, Notre Europe).

Delors, J. (1996) Speech at Harvard University.

Devuyst, Y. (1997) 'The Treaty of Amsterdam: An Introductory Analysis' . *ECSA Review*, Vol. 10, No. 3, Fall.

Dini, L. (1997) 'The European Union after Amsterdam'. In Duff 1997b, pp. xxvii-xxix.

Duff, A. (1997a) 'Supranational Institutions for Post-national Europe' in Duff 1997b, xxx-xxxviii.

Duff, A. (ed.) (1997b) *The Treaty of Amsterdam: Text and Commentary* (London: Federal Trust)

Ehlermann, C. (1997) 'Flexibility'. In European Policy Centre , pp. 59–60.

European Parliament, Committee on Institutional Affairs (1997) 'Report on the Treaty of Amsterdam – Annex' (Brussels: European Parliament).

European Policy Centre (1997) *Making Sense of the Amsterdam Treaty: Challenge Europe,* Brussels.

Feldstein, M. S. (1997) 'EMU and International Conflict'. *Foreign Affairs*, Vol. 76, No. 6, November, pp. 60–74.

Hoyer, W. (1997) 'The German Government'. In European Policy Centre, p. 41.

Jørgensen, K. E. and Christiansen, T. 'The Amsterdam Process: A Structurationist Perspective on EU Treaty Reform'. In Edwards, G. and Philippart, E. (eds) *Theorising European Integration* (forthcoming).

Ludlow, P. (1997a) 'The Intergovernmental Conference: An Evaluation' (Brussels: Centre for European Policy Studies), unpublished mimeo.

Ludlow, P. (1997b) 'Institutional Balance'. In European Policy Centre, p. 52.

Meunier, S. and Nicolaïdis, K. (1997) 'National Sovereignty vs. International Efficiency: The Delegation of Trade Authority in the European Union'. Paper presented at the Center for European Studies, Harvard University, December.

Milward, A. S. (1993) *The European Rescue of the Nation-State* (London: Routledge).

Moravcsik, A. (1996) 'Federalism and Peace: A Structural Liberal Perspective'. *Zeitschrift für internationale Beziehungen*, Vol. 2, No. 2, Spring.

Moravcsik, A. (1998a) 'European Integration in the 1990s: Meeting the Challenges of Deepening, Diversity, and Democracy'. In Moravcsik (1998b).

Moravcsik, A. (ed.)(1998b) *European Integration in the 1990s: Meeting the Challenges of Deepening, Diversity, and Democracy* (New York and Washington: Council on Foreign Relations and Brookings Institution).

Moravcsik, A. (1998c) *The Choice for Europe: Social Purpose and State Power from Messina to Maastricht* (Ithaca: Cornell University Press).

Moravcsik, A. and Nicolaïdis, K. (forthcoming) 'Negotiating the Treaty of Amsterdam: Interests, Influence, Institutions', *Journal of Common Market Studies*.

Nickel, D. (1998) 'European Institutions after the Amsterdam Treaty'. Paper presented at the Seminar on the EU, NAFTA, and the WTO, Harvard University.

Petite, M. (1998) 'The Commission and the Amsterdam Treaty'. Paper presented at the Seminar on the EU, NAFTA, and the WTO, Harvard University, April.

Pisani-Ferry, J. (1998) *Variable Geometry in Europe* (Brussels: Centre for European Policy Studies).

Shaw, J. (1998) 'Constitutional Settlements and the Citizen after the Treaty of Amsterdam'. In Neunreither, K-H. and Wiener, A., *Beyond Amsterdam: Institutional Dynamics and Prospects for Democracy in the EU* (Oxford: Oxford University Press).

Sidjanski, D. (forthcoming) *The Federalist Future of Europe* (Ann Arbor: University of Michigan Press).

Sutherland, P. (1997) 'Has the IGC Succeeded?'. In European Policy Centre, pp. 29–31.

Van Miert, K. (1998) 'EU Institutions after the Amsterdam Treaty'. Paper presented at Harvard University, April.

Walker, N. (1998) 'Sovereignty and Differentiated Integration in the European Union'. Paper prepared for Workshop in Legal Theory and the European Union, Edinburgh, February.

Weiler, J.H.H. (1996) 'Legitimacy and Democracy of Union Governance: The 1996 Intergovernmental Agenda and Beyond'. Oslo: Arena Working Paper, November.

Wessels, W. (1997) 'The Amsterdam Treaty in View of the Fusion Theory'. Paper presented at BISA Annual Conference, Leeds, December.

Journal of Common Market Studies

Volume 36, Annual Review
September 1998

Governance and Institutions

RICHARD CORBETT

Member of the European Parliament for Merseyside West

I. Introduction

The key institutional event in 1997 was the conclusion of the Intergovernmental Conference (IGC) and the signing of the Treaty of Amsterdam. Other developments took place within the context of the existing Treaties, not least the preparations for the single currency and the beginning of preparations for enlargement. Routine institutional life also continued.

II. The Treaty of Amsterdam

One and a half years of Intergovernmental Conference preceded by half a year of work by the Reflection Group culminated in agreement on a Treaty which many found to be disappointing in failing adequately to address a number of problems facing the Union, not least in view of its forthcoming enlargement. Nonetheless, the Treaty, if ratified, will bring in about 20 significant changes to the institutional structures and the governance of the European Union. Of particular significance are the following.

  1. The UK opt-out of the Social Agreement will come to an end, thereby enabling it to be integrated into the body of the Treaty and ending a two-tier system in this field.

2. A new chapter containing new procedures on employment policy was agreed, highlighting thereby the need for Union policies to shift in emphasis and for national employment policies to be co-ordinated.

3. The importance of democracy and respect for human rights as a condition of membership of the Union was further highlighted in the Treaty and a procedure laid down for the first time for the suspension of any Member State that ceases to respect such fundamental criteria.

4. The Union is empowered for the first time to adopt anti-discrimination legislation to outlaw discrimination on the grounds of race, gender, religion, sexual orientation, disability or age. However, the procedure for adopting such legislation involves the unanimous agreement of the Council.

5. The use of qualified majority voting (QMV) was extended marginally within Pillar I and more extensively in Pillar II (CFSP), though in the latter case it is combined with a procedure allowing individual states to veto a decision, i.e. a limited formal introduction of the Luxembourg Compromise..

6. The co-decision procedure, whereby Council and Parliament jointly adopt EU legislation through a procedure involving up to three readings in each body, was extended to 23 new articles. As a result, most EU legislation outside the fields of agriculture, and justice and home affairs, will now be subject to co-decision in what is virtually a bi-cameral system.

7. The co-decision procedure has itself been changed, taking up the three key changes advocated in the IGC by Parliament itself, namely:

(a) The abolition of the negative version of the third reading in which, in the event of the conciliation committee failing to agree, Council could confirm its own text which would become law unless Parliament rejected it by an absolute majority within six weeks. The elimination of this option underlines that it is only by compromise and agreement with Parliament that Council can adopt legislation.

(b) Elimination of the phase, 'intention to reject' in which Parliament had first to announce its intention to reject and then to confirm it in a second vote following a meeting with Council. Simple rejection in a single vote will now be possible.

(c) Introduction of the possibility of adopting a text in a single reading when both institutions agree.

8. Parliament is given the right formally to approve or reject the European Council's nominee for President of the Commission. Under Maastricht, this vote was legally consultative, albeit politically binding in the view of the Parliament and, on the one occasion it was used, in the view of the nominee for President and of the President of the European Council (see *Annual Review 1994*).

9. The position of the President of the Commission within the college is upgraded in that he/she will henceforth be able to agree on the composition of the

rest of the Commission with the Member State governments. The President's role in the allocation of portfolios to Commissioners and eventually in reshuffling those portfolios is acknowledged and reinforced.

10. The provisions of the second pillar regarding a common foreign and security policy (CFSP) have been revised. In addition to QMV for implementing a joint action or adopting a common position (unless a government vetoes the decision for 'important and stated reasons of national policy'), a new mechanism of 'positive abstention' is created, whereby a Member State may abstain and not be obliged to apply the decision in question, whilst accepting that the decision is binding for the Union as such. A new Policy Planning and Early Warning Unit is set up, headed by a high representative who will be the Secretary-General of the Council. The high representative is intended to provide for continuity in the external representation of the Union, alongside the rotating Presidency of the Council and the responsible member of the Commission (the 'new troika'). The Policy Unit will consist of officials drawn from the Council Secretariat, the Member States, the Commission and from the WEU, whose relationship with the Union was otherwise unchanged. The Treaty, for the first time, mentions specific security issues as falling within the remit of the Union, namely the 'Petersberg Tasks' of peace-keeping, humanitarian aid and crisis management, including peace-making. The Union is empowered to enter into agreements with third countries in the CFSP field and a procedure is laid down to this effect. (The Presidency is to negotiate, assisted by the Commission, and approved by Council unanimity.)

11. The Council is empowered to extend the application of Art. 113 (external trade) of the EC Treaty to cover international agreements concerning services and intellectual property, but only on the basis of unanimity.

12. A number of matters are transferred from the third pillar (justice and home affairs) to the field of community law in the first pillar. These include matters relating to immigration, asylum, the granting of visas, refugee policy and judicial co-operation in civil matters. Such matters will continue to be governed by the need for unanimity in the Council, except as regards visas. However, the Treaty provides for a Council decision after five years which would transfer all or some of these matters to the domain of qualified majority voting and co-decision with the European Parliament. This decision would not require national ratification. In the immediate future, the effect is to bring the matters within the field of competence of community law, including a role for the Court of Justice, but with references from national courts limited to those from courts of final instance and precluding rulings on measures concerning the maintenance of law and order or national security.

13. The Schengen agreement is absorbed by the European Union and will henceforth be dealt with within the Union framework. However, the two Union

states which were not party to the Schengen agreement – the UK and Ireland – will not be bound by measures adopted in this field, though the Treaty does give them the possibility of opting into any such measures. The UK and Ireland are granted the right to maintain border controls at their frontiers.

14. Only police and judicial co-operation in criminal matters will now remain in the third pillar. In this pillar, a new instrument, namely 'framework decisions' – similar to a directive in the Community pillar – will be available. Conventions will now enter into force among the Member States which have ratified once half of them have done so. Member States may opt into ECJ jurisdiction for the third pillar. The European Parliament will now be formally consulted on all framework decisions, or conventions in the third pillar.

15. Provisions are laid down on openness and transparency in decision-taking, largely at the behest of the Nordic countries and the European Parliament. Implementing measures will be necessary, but the implication of the provisions is that there will be a right of access for citizens to internal Community documents. It will also, for the first time in the Treaty, be specified that the results of votes on legislation in the Council must be made public, as must any statements in the minutes or explanations of vote.

16. The investigatory powers of the Court of Auditors are strengthened.

17. A start was made on codifying and simplifying the European Treaties, deleting redundant articles and repetition and consolidating texts. Such a process brings greater clarity to the myriad of EU Treaty texts, but is also seen by many as strengthening the characteristic of the EU Treaties of being a constitution.

18. A protocol is added to the Treaty laying down the conditions and the criteria for applying the principles of subsidiarity and proportionality. It is largely a codification of the declaration adopted at the Edinburgh summit on these matters.

19. A new concept of closer co-operation is introduced whereby the Union framework may be used to develop policy areas even when not all Member States wish to do so. A decision to allow such closer co-operation may be taken by a qualified majority on a proposal from the Commission, but if a single state objects then the matter is referred to the European Council.

The outcome of the IGC thus contained a number of items of benefit to the European Parliament. This must be attributed partly to the enhanced participation of the Parliament in the IGC. As reported in last year's *Annual Review*, a compromise was reached at Turin regarding Parliament's participation such that it was able to name two representatives who were able to have monthly meetings with the IGC working group (largely of European affairs ministers or permanent representatives), receive all the documents, table their own documents and amendments and take part in informal gatherings and dinners. Furthermore, the monthly meetings of foreign ministers in the IGC framework opened with an exchange of view with the President of the European Parliament and the two representatives. For this purpose, Parliament nominated Elisabeth Guigou (a French Socialist, later to be Minister of Justice in the Jospin Government) and Elmar Brok (a German Christian Democrat) who reported back regularly to Parliament's Committee on Institutional Affairs and to the various political groups.

The area where the new Treaty failed to make adequate provision was that of the institutional changes necessary to cater for the further enlargement of the EU. The European Council itself recognized this fact and added a protocol to the Treaty on the institutional aspects of enlargement. This provided for a two-phased approach: before even a single new Member State joins the European Union, agreement must be reached on a reweighting of the votes in the Council and on the size of the Commission. Before six states join, a wider institutional reform is necessary.

In practice these two aspects are likely to be telescoped together. This is because the initial set of enlargement negotiations will indeed be with six countries, and also because there appears to be growing support for significant overhaul of the institutions before any enlargement takes place. Belgium, France and Italy appended a declaration to this effect to the Treaty of Amsterdam and a similar view was expressed by the Parliament when it approved the Amsterdam Treaty and by the European Commission.

Parliament in particular felt that the two issues specifically mentioned by the European Council – weighting of votes in the Council and size of the Commission – whilst important, were not as significant as the need to replace unanimity, where it is still required under the Treaties, with some form of majority voting. Unanimity of 20 plus states would lead to paralysis in the policy areas concerned.

As regards the two issues highlighted by the European Council, the fear of the largest states was that a succession of small states entering the Union, which had already begun with the 1995 enlargement, would dilute the voting strength of the largest states (which would continue to represent a majority of the population of the Union) to about one-third of the weighted votes. Although the Amsterdam European Council was rumoured to have been very close to an agreement in which the five largest states give up their traditional rights to a second Commissioner in exchange for extra votes in the Council, this did not in the end materialize.

The Treaty was signed in Amsterdam on 2 October 1997. It is expected that ratification, which in Denmark and Ireland will involve a referendum, will require the whole of 1998.

III. Economic and Monetary Union

The main legal instruments still necessary for the preparation of the changeover to the single currency were agreed on 16–17 June in Amsterdam at the European Council; namely the legal framework for the use of the euro, the new Exchange Rate Mechanism to link the euro and non-participating EU currencies and the Stability and Growth Pact. The latter strengthens the surveillance of budgetary positions and the co-ordination of economic policies of the Member States and specifies more fully how the relevant provisions of Art. 104c of the EC Treaty (Excessive Deficit) will apply.

The Stability Pact provisions are intended to ensure that Member States continue to apply the budgetary disciplines required for monetary union after the start of the single currency. In particular it provided that the 3 per cent reference value for public sector deficits should be applied in such a way as to allow Member States to exceed 3 per cent only in the event of an economic recession leading to the fall of GDP. If the fall is by more than 2 per cent, states will automatically be allowed to go beyond 3 per cent. If the fall is between 0.5 and 2 per cent of GDP, the Council must evaluate the situation, needing a qualified majority to find a deficit to be excessive. These provisions leave room for political debate and assessment within the Council without everything being predetermined by automatic triggers. However, the margin for such political assessment is limited.

In December, the European Council meeting in Luxembourg reached agreement on economic policy co-ordination within EMU. The Council, meeting at the level of economic and finance ministers, would be the central decision-making body for such co-ordination, but ministers of the single country currencies would be able to meet separately to hold informal discussions on issues related to the single currency.

IV. Other Developments

Citizenship

The transposition of the directive allowing citizens the right to vote and stand as a candidate in municipal elections in their Member State of residence, even when they are not nationals, was transposed into national law by all the Member States except Belgium which was taken to the European Court by the Commission on this.

1997 was European Year Against Racism and Xenophobia, with projects and activities organized across the Union. A permanent European Monitoring Centre on racism and xenophobia was established in Vienna and the Treaty amended to allow the adoption of anti-discrimination legislation on a Union-wide basis.

Co-decision Procedure

In 1997, 28 'Acts of the European Parliament and the Council' were adopted under the co-decision procedure (30 in 1996) with a slight increase in the number of times that Parliament and Council had to have recourse to the Conciliation committee in order to reach a compromise (which, however, still remained fewer than half of all cases). No legislative proposals were rejected outright by Parliament in 1997. An issue which frequently divided Parliament and Council was that of 'comitology'.

Commission Implementing Powers and Comitology

The procedures for conferring implementing powers on the Commission and subjecting them to the scrutiny of committees of national civil servants able, in some cases, to refer a matter to Council, continued to cause controversy. In 1997 implementing powers were conferred on the Commission using the Advisory Committee procedure in fewer than 20 cases, the Management Committee procedure in about 60 and the Regulatory Procedure in over 40, including four using variant (b) which allows a Commission implementing measure to be blocked indefinitely even when Council cannot agree on an alternative.

The IGC failed to reform this 'comitology' system, but issued a declaration calling on the Commission to put forward a proposal by the end of 1998 for a new system to replace the 1987 framework decision and implicitly the *modus vivendi* agreed with Parliament. The Commission agreed to put forward a proposal to this effect by June 1998.

Budget

The procedure for adopting the 1998 budget resulted in the adoption by Parliament of a total of 91,013m ECU in appropriations for commitments (up 2.10 per cent on the previous year) and 83,529m ECU in appropriations for payments (up 1.41 per cent).

These figures represent a modest rise and include a small fall in agricultural spending, despite the BSE crisis. They leave substantial margins available below the ceilings of authorized expenditure laid down in the financial perspectives, of 3,731m ECU as regards commitments and 7,052m ECU as regards payments. Indeed, the total payments adopted for 1998 represent 1.14 per cent of the Union's GNP, as compared to the 1.26 per cent ceiling.

This margin of unused resources, together with the (optimistic) projections for economic growth, enabled the Commission to conclude in its *Agenda 2000* document on the finances and policies of the enlarged Union, that it would not be necessary to raise the ceiling on the Union's resources before the year 2006, despite enlargement.

Monitoring the Application of Community Law

The Commission continued to monitor the application of Community law by the Member States. It started 1,422 infringement proceedings (up from 1,142 in 1996) and issued 331 reasoned opinions (435 in 1996). One hundred and twenty-one cases were referred to the Court of Justice (up from 92), the breakdown per country being as follows: Italy 20, Germany 19, Belgium 18, France 15, Portugal 14, Greece 10, Luxembourg 8, Spain 7, Ireland 6, Netherlands 3, UK 1 and Denmark 0, Austria 0, Finland 0, Sweden 0 (provisional figures).

V. The Institutions and Other Bodies

The Commission

In the course of 1997 the Commission held 48 meetings. It presented for adoption by the Council, or by Parliament and the Council together, 52 directives, 238 regulations, 245 decisions and 14 recommendations. This total of 549 proposals was slightly higher than the 524 presented in 1996, but below the number of 600 presented in 1995. It also presented 283 memorandums, communications and reports (down from 294 in 1996). The Commission's establishment plan for 1997 comprised 16,014 permanent posts (up from 15,574 in 1996) and 810 temporary posts (down from 875), supplemented by 3,558 permanent and 154 temporary post in its research bodies (back to just above the 1995 level after a decline in 1996 to 1453 and 161 respectively), 525 permanent posts in the publications office (unchanged), 52 at the European Centre for the Development of Vocational Training (down from 81) and 29 at the European Foundation for the Improvement of Living and Working Conditions (down from 82).

The Council

The Netherlands held the Presidency of the Council for the first half of the year and Luxembourg for the second half. The Council held 83 meetings in 1997 (down from 87 in 1996) in the following formations:

	1997	(1996)
General Affairs	15	(13)
Agriculture	11	(13)
Economic and Finance (Ecofin)	10	(8)
Labour and Social Affairs	5	(4)
Environment	4	(4)
Transport	4	(4)
Telecommunications	3	(5)
Fisheries	3	(5)

Energy	3	(3)
Internal Market	3	(3)
Justice and Home Affairs	3	(3)
Industry	2	(4)
Development	2	(3)
Research	2	(3)
Education	2	(2)
Budget	2	(2)
Consumers	2	(2)
Culture/Audiovisual	2	(2)
Health	2	(2)
Tourism	1	(1)
Youth	1	(0)
Ecofin and Labour Social Affairs Jointly	1	(0)
Civil Protection	0	(1)
Total 1997 Council sessions	83	(87)

The Council adopted 34 directives (down from 58 in 1996), 209 regulations (down from 247) and 164 decisions (down from 179). Of these, 20 directives, 1 regulation and 7 decisions were adopted jointly with the Parliament under the co-decision procedure. In 48 cases, Council acted by qualified majority. Council's establishment plan comprised 2,417 permanent (up from 2,404) and 18 (unchanged) temporary posts.

The European Council

The European Council again met four times in 1997. The first of these was an informal meeting in Nordwijk on 23 May devoted to IGC matters. The others were in Amsterdam on 16–17 June and two meetings in Luxembourg on 24 November and 12–13 December. The November meeting was the first European Council meeting devoted specifically to the issue of employment. The two main European political parties continued to organize meetings of their respective Prime Ministers and party leaders prior to each regular meeting of the European Council.

The European Parliament

The distribution of seats among the political groups was as follows by the end of the year (the figures for 1996 are in brackets):

Party of European Socialists	215	(215)
European People's Party	181	(182)

Union for Europe	55	(57)
European Liberal, Democratic and Reformist Left	41	(43)
Confederal Group of the European United Left/		
Nordic Green Left	33	(33)
Green Party	28	(28)
European Radical Alliance	19	(19)
Group of Independents for a Europe of Nations	18	(18)
{Non-affiliated	31	(31)}

Just at the end of the year, two Labour members of the Party of the European Socialists informed the President that they were joining the Green Party. This automatically led to the termination of their membership of the Socialist Group (and indeed of the Labour Party) but only took effect as regards the above figures as of 1 January 1998, by which time one of them had decided to join the European United Left instead.

During 1997, the European Parliament adopted 154 opinions under the consultation procedure (154 in 1996); 19 first readings (31) and 15 second readings (34) under the co-operation procedure; 34 first readings (34), 27 second readings (37) and 21 third readings (9) under the co-decision procedure; and 15 assents (8). It also adopted 329 own-initiative reports, other opinions and recommendations. It adopted 24 (27) budgetary decisions or resolutions.

Members of the Parliament addressed 3,838 written questions to the Commission (3,772 in 1995) and 393 to the Council (359); 40 oral questions with debate to the Commission (160) and 45 to the Council (101); and at question time, 689 questions were put to the Commission (738) and 335 to the Council (315).

At the end of 1997 there were 3,491 permanent (3,443) and 602 temporary (602) posts on Parliament's establishment plan.

Court of Auditors

The Court of Auditors adopted its Annual Report and its Statement of Reassurance on the reliability of the accounts on 16 October. It gave a positive assurance on the reliability of the accounts and on the legality and regularity of revenue and commitments. However, for payments the Court was unable to give a global positive assurance because of an unduly large number of errors detected, most of which originated in the Member States.

The Court also produced 7 special reports, 15 specific reports and 6 opinions. Its establishment plan comprised 413 permanent (503 in 1996) and 92 temporary (73) posts.

Economic and Social Committee

The committee held 9 plenary sessions at which it adopted 179 opinions and 3 information reports (173 and 2 respectively in 1996). In 63 cases, the request for its opinion was compulsory and 89 cases it was optional. The committee also issued 27 own-initiative opinions, including 5 additional opinions. Its establishment plan comprised 135 permanent posts and 519 in the organization structure which it shares with the Committee of Regions.

Committee of the Regions

In this last year before its reappointment, the Committee adopted 66 opinions (43 in 1996) and 5 resolutions (3). The Committee organized a summit of Regions and Cities in Amsterdam in May, a month before the conclusion of the IGC. Besides its regular meetings with Commissioners, the Committee was addressed in January by the President of Portugal, Jorge Sampaio, and in November by Valéry Giscard d'Estaing, former President of France and Chairman of the Council of European Municipalities.

European Monetary Institute

The EMI continued to prepare for the single currency and the establishment of the European Central Bank. It focused in particular on banking supervision, accounting, statistics and communications systems. It launched the test phase of the TARGET (Trans-European Automated Real-Time Gross Settlement Express Transfer) system for cross-border payments in euros. It agreed with the Council on the date for the introduction of euro notes and coins (1 January 2002) and presented the final design for the bank notes.

Wim Duisenberg took over from Alexandre Lamfalussy as President of the EMI.

European Investment Bank

In 1997 the EIB granted loans totalling 26,203m ECU (23,200m in 1996) including 3,2455m ECU which went to non-Member States (2,254m in 1996).

Journal of Common Market Studies   Volume 36, Annual Review
                                                              September 1998

Internal Policy Developments

JOHN REDMOND

University of Birmingham

I. Introduction

In the field of internal policy, 1997 is perhaps best characterized as a 'forward looking' year. Much of the focus was on preparation for the future, particularly for economic and monetary union and for a genuine single market; and, of course, *Agenda 2000* set out the development of the budget, the structural funds and agricultural policy for the next few years. The other striking feature of the year was the increasing emphasis being given to employment policy, not just at the special 'Jobs Summit' in Luxembourg in November but, more generally, through linkages with many other policy areas.

II. Economic and Related Policies

Internal Market Developments

The main development in 1997 was the Commission's *Action Plan for the Single Market*, presented and endorsed by the European Council in Amsterdam in June. This effectively provides a summary of the shortcomings of the Single European Market (SEM) which it seeks to remedy by linking the SEM's completion to the introduction of the single currency on 1 January 1999 and by setting four strategic targets:

1. Making the SEM rules more effective through simplification, better implementation and enforcement, and efforts to tackle deficiencies in the legal framework.
2. Dealing with specific distortions caused by the tax system (especially VAT) and state aids.
3. Removing sectoral obstacles, particularly in the service sector (telecommunications, energy, pension funds, the allocation of slots at airports, etc.) and improving the business environment (the European Company Statute).
4. Delivering the direct benefits of the SEM for citizens more effectively, through more information, increased labour mobility, an enhanced social dimension, and wider knowledge of and access to the rights stemming from the SEM.

An annex listing a timetable for the implementation of the required actions was attached to the plan.

Progress of Member States in implementing the plan is measured by an SEM 'scorecard', first presented by the Commission in November, which provides a measure of progress based on the rate of transposition of SEM directives and the number of infringement proceedings. However, the deadline for the implementation of the first elements of the *Action Plan* (1 October) was met by only some of the Member States, despite Commission pressure, even though nearly 30 per cent of the SEM common rules were still not being enforced by all of them. Indeed, the Commission continued its relentless pursuit of infringements throughout 1997 and, in November, proposed new measures to speed up its procedures.

Difficulties also arose as the EU approached its target date of 1 January 1998 for the liberalization of the telecommunications sector. At the beginning of 1997, the accompanying regulatory framework was still incomplete and it was not until December that all the necessary directives were agreed. However, the real problem was caused by the growing realization that half the Member States would not be ready by the target date. Partial derogations of up to three years were given to some countries (Ireland, Portugal, Luxembourg, Spain and Greece), but the Commission also felt it necessary to initiate infringement proceedings against those Member States which had failed to transpose essential legislation (Belgium, Greece, Luxembourg, Germany, Portugal, Italy and Denmark).

The EU's other endeavours to facilitate the completion of the SEM in 1997 were subsequently embedded within the *Action Plan* (as will be the case in 1998). These included the efforts to move forward on the European Company Statute (ECS) which were boosted by Vicomte Davignon's Report. This tried to break the 25-year impasse caused by the deadlock on the question of worker participation by proposing that there should be freedom of negotiation (and agreement on a company-by-company basis) underpinned by 'reference provisions' for situations where negotiations failed, rather than a uniform system. However, despite this successful relaunch of the debate and the Commission's optimism, opposition from Germany, Spain, Italy and the UK in December made agreement impossible in 1997.

In March, the Veil Group presented its report on the free movement of people. It stressed that the deficiencies stemmed not from the lack of, but from the poor application of legislation, and made 80 recommendations to fill the gaps. In October, the Parliament adopted the Tappin Report on public procurement. The Report noted that public procurement accounted for 11 per cent of the EU's annual GDP (720m ECU), that the SEM rules were not being honoured, and advocated strengthening the enforcement powers of the Commission. In November, the second (and final) phase of the Commission's campaign to inform people of their rights within the SEM – the *'Citizens First'* initiative – was launched.

Finally, Italy (October) and Austria (December) became the eighth and ninth full members of the Schengen area. More fundamentally, it was agreed at the June summit that the Schengen Accord would cease to be a 'parallel' agreement and that the Amsterdam Treaty would incorporate it into the framework of the European Union.

Economic and Monetary Union

Preparations for the third stage of Economic and Monetary Union (EMU) continued at an increasing pace and with growing attention to detail. The year began with the EU's Statistical Office – Eurostat – seeking to define various rules concerning accountancy practices, to prevent Member States concealing parts of their deficits in order to meet the Maastricht criteria. The designs for euro coins and notes were finalized. The June summit approved the main elements of the 'new' exchange rate mechanism (ERM2) which will have fluctuation margins of ± 15 per cent. By December, ten Member States had published their national transition plans which specify the role the euro will play in their economies in the transition phase (1999–2002). The Commission also produced a preliminary analysis of the external aspects of EMU, particularly the possible role of the euro in the international monetary system. More specifically, there are the questions of the exchange rate policy of the euro and the external representation of the states in the euro area (in, for example, the IMF).

In April, the Commission adopted its Broad Guidelines for Economic Policy which sought to continue the economic recovery and help create more jobs. The Commission also added two countries (Finland and the Netherlands) to its list of Member States without excessive budgetary deficits (Denmark, Ireland and Luxembourg) and noted that Spain, Greece and Portugal had attained their budget objectives for 1996, thereby fulfilling the condition required for their continued access to the Cohesion Fund. The Commission's autumn forecasts were similarly optimistic and suggested that 14 Member States should qualify for participation in Stage III by the time when decisions had to be made in March 1998. Nevertheless, question marks were periodically raised against the Italians who perhaps fuelled the doubts by floating the idea of postponing Stage III of EMU for a year. Moreover, in October, the UK made clear its decision to exercise its right to 'opt out' of participation in Stage III.

The EMI produced a series of reports in 1997: on the single monetary policy (January), potential monetary strategies for the European System of Central Banks (ESCB) (February) and, with the Commission, on the impact of the introduction of the euro on capital markets (July). There were two reports in September – on the probable monetary policy instruments of the European Central Bank (ECB) and on the 'Target' system which will manage cross-border payments in euros from 1999 – and also the EMI's annual report in April which expressed satisfaction with the preparations for Stage III but concern about unemployment. Finally, the EMI had a change of President when, on 1 July, Alexandre Lamfalussy was succeeded by Wim Duisenberg (the former Governor of the Dutch Central Bank).

A debate was triggered by a proposal for a 'Stability Council', comprising 'Euro-participants' (only) as a political counterweight to the future ECB. This soon met with strong opposition and it was (eventually) merely agreed that informal meetings of the Member States participating in Stage III were permissible, with the attendance of the Commission and the ECB when appropriate.

Finally, work continued on co-ordinating national taxation systems culminating, in October, in a Commission communication to the Council. This identified the need to tackle harmful tax competition between Member States (in their efforts to attract investment, for example) and the comparatively heavy tax burden on labour (which discourages job creation). One of its proposals was taken up – a (non-binding) code of conduct for business taxation, designed to limit harmful competition in the field of company taxation – and is effective from the beginning of 1998. The Commission has been asked to work towards the preparation of other appropriate draft directives in 1998.

Growth, Competitiveness and Employment

There were particularly significant developments in this area in 1997. First, it was agreed to include a chapter on employment in the Amsterdam Treaty, thereby formally incorporating employment policy within the competence of the EU. Second, there was a special summit on employment in Luxembourg in November, which ensured the centrality of this policy area in EU affairs for much of the second half of the year. More specifically, 'guidelines' for employment policy were agreed which were designed to co-ordinate and strengthen national policies; this in effect implemented elements of the new title on employment in the Treaty of Amsterdam in advance of ratification. There were also two specific initiatives:

- an EIB Action Plan to invest in small and medium-sized enterprises (SMEs), new technology and trans-European networks (TENs) with total expenditure of up to 10bn ECU;
- a new budget heading – the European employment initiative – of 450m ECU over three years, targeted at helping SMEs.

However, the outcome of the summit was criticized for its failure to specify a target for the number of jobs to be created and the lack of sanctions for those not obeying the guidelines.

There was also a series of other measures taken during the year. In April the Commission published a document on 'benchmarking', a technique for identifying gaps in competitiveness by comparing practices in Europe with those elsewhere. The Commission put forward principles and guidelines for the use of 'benchmarking' and, more concretely, initiated some pilot projects and created a high level group on 'benchmarking'. In May the Commission established a second Advisory Group on Competitiveness which will identify problems and make practical proposals over the next two years. In June, following French pressure, the European Council issued its Resolution on Employment and Growth, which sought to provide new impetus to efforts to promote employment and job creation.

The trans-European networks programme continued to make slow progress. The 'Kinnock Group' reported in May: it sought to indicate measures to facilitate the funding of TENs by public/private partnerships and proposed more innovative means of EU financing. However, the year ended with the Commission bemoaning the continued lack of a sound and credible financial structure.

Structural Funds and Regional Policy

Significant changes in the operation of the structural funds (SFs) to promote greater simplicity and efficiency were proposed in the *Agenda 2000* document issued in July. For the 2000–06 period the SFs' share of the EU budget would be maintained at 33 per cent of the total (and held at 0.46 per cent of the EU's GDP), but economic growth would mean that SF expenditure would rise to 275bn ECU, compared to 200bn ECU in 1993–99. (This should allow allocations to new members joining in 2000–06 to be covered, providing total SF receipts did not exceed the current levels of 4 per cent of a Member State's GDP). The number of objectives would be reduced from the current seven to three:

(1) Regions lagging behind in development, defined as those with a GDP per capita of less than 75 per cent of the EU average; current Objective 1 regions with higher GDP levels would receive reduced allocations as they were phased out during a transition period; this objective (like the current Objective 1) would account for about two-thirds of SF expenditure.

(2) Economic and social reconversion: this objective would address problems relating to certain types of regional activities, such as areas undergoing industrial transformation, rural areas in decline and areas dependent on fisheries.

(3) A new strategy on human resources to help Member States adapt and modernize their systems of education, training and employment.

In addition, Community initiatives would focus on only three themes: interregional co-operation, rural development and human resources. Finally, the Cohesion Fund would continue to help countries with a GNP per capita of less than 90 per cent of the EU average (thereby potentially excluding Ireland) at its current level of expenditure or less.

More mundanely, the Commission launched pilot projects exploring new and innovative ways of creating jobs (August), set minimum standards to regulate SF spending and ensure value for money (October), assessed the impact of the 89 territorial pacts for employment being funded by the SFs (November), and produced guidelines to reduce and concentrate national regional aids (December). Also in December, the Commission indicated that 11 regions, including Northern Ireland and the Highlands and Islands of Scotland might lose their Objective 1 status after 1999 (although South Yorkshire might gain it).

Finally, Italy continued to come under fire in 1997 for delays in using its SF allocations, in spite of its assertions that it would soon 'catch up'. Ultimately, the Commission lost patience and cancelled a 6.5m ECU grant awarded in 1992 to promote SMEs in Italy.

Industrial and Competition Policies

A number of sectors received attention in 1997. In April, the Commission proposed several measures to address problems in the information and communication technologies sector. In shipbuilding the expiry of the seventh directive on 31 December led to a debate throughout the year (especially concerning the provision of aids to the industry). In December, it was agreed to extend the directive by one year but Commission proposals for a new, stricter (lower state aids) regime from 1 January 1999 were still being discussed. In September and December respectively, the Commission drew attention to the need for restructuring in the aerospace industry and for a strategy for defence-related industries.

In addition, efforts continued to help small and medium-sized enterprises (SMEs). Specifically, the Commission issued guidelines to facilitate improved SME access to capital markets (May), set up a task force ('BEST') to make recommendations to simplify the administrative and regulatory framework for SMEs (September), and approved the Joint European Venture (JEV) programme, with a budget of 5m ECU for 1997, to promote the development of joint transnational companies between SMEs from different Member States (November). Finally, in June, the Commission published a Green Paper on the patent system in Europe.

In January, the Commission launched a Green Paper on future policy on vertical agreements which restrict competition (exclusive distribution and purchasing agreements, franchising, etc.) and proposed modifications to the provisions for agreements of minor importance; specifically, it sought to reduce the number of cases examined in order to allow it to focus only on the more significant cases. After a period of consultation, the Commission adopted appropriate changes to the regulations in October.

In 1997 the Commission was notified of 172 planned mergers which were mostly cleared at the first stage (within one month); the 11 that proceeded to the second stage (a further four months) were also authorized, in most cases subject to various conditions and/or modifications. In April the Council agreed to modify the EU's merger regulation to make it applicable to cases involving the competition authorities of three or more Member States at lower thresholds than normal – a 'world threshold' (accumulated turnover throughout the world) of 2.5bn ECU (compared to a 'norm' of 5bn ECU) and an 'EU threshold' of 100m ECU (250m ECU). This extension is expected to bring approximately ten more cases per year within the scope of the regulation. However, the Commission's efforts to reduce the thresholds for all mergers remain blocked in the Council.

Other Developments

Efforts to conclude a bilateral agreement on road *transport* with Switzerland continued throughout the year. Negotiations for a 'Euro tax disk' (or *'Eurovignette'*) for heavy goods vehicles, the cost of which would be related to the pollution caused, also dragged on. The two issues became linked but the year ended with agreement on neither. The problems of Alpine transit were magnified by the continuation of infringement proceedings by the Commission against Austria for increasing tolls on the Brenner motorway.

In April, the Commission proposed a new *Strategy for Road Safety (1997–2001)* and also an EU framework for charges to airlines for airport services. In addition, the Commission continued its attempts to extend its negotiating mandate to enable it to negotiate an 'open skies' agreement between the EU and the US, but the Council refused to make further concessions as Member States preferred to make their own bilateral agreements with the Americans. In December, the Commission responded by renewing infringement proceedings against the nine Member States that had negotiated such agreements on the grounds that they were in breach of single market regulations.

In April, the Commission published an overview of EU *energy* policy which identified three principal issues for the future: coping with increased dependency on outside supplies; ensuring more competitive energy prices; and making energy policy more compatible with environmental protection. To face these strategic challenges, the Commission proposed (in November) a 'framework programme' for the energy sector to group all current and future measures, with a budget of 200m ECU over five years (1998–2002), designed to improve co-ordination, efficiency and transparency.

In December, a second multi-annual programme – *Altener II* – to promote renewable energy sources was agreed to run for two years (1998–99) with an annual budget of 11m ECU; the programme to foster international co-operation in the energy field (*Synergy*) was extended for a further year with a budget of 5m ECU; finally, some limited progress was made towards the creation of a common market for gas and efforts to achieve this end will continue in 1998.

In the field of *research and development* the year was dominated by Commission proposals for the *Fifth Framework Programme* (1999–2003) which were initially presented in April and sought to concentrate funds on a more limited number of (six) priority areas – three 'thematic' ones: life resources and the ecosystem, the information society, and sustainable and competitive growth, and three 'horizontal' programmes: international co-operation, innovation and participation by SMEs, and growth of human potential. The *Fifth Programme* is intended to be more flexibly managed and better co-ordinated, and should promote growth, employment and competitiveness wherever possible. In July, the Commission proposed a budget of 16.3bn (compared to 13.1bn ECU for the *Fourth Programme*).

Meanwhile, the dispute between the Council (100m ECU) and the Parliament (200m ECU) over additional funding for the *Fourth Framework Programme* dragged on until eventually, in September, a compromise figure of 115m ECU was finally agreed.

Turning to *education*, the *Jean Monnet Project* supported a further 210 actions in 1997, including 57 new chairs. The *Kaleidoscope* programme provided 6.8m ECU to support 128 *cultural* projects in 1997 and, after some difficulty, agreement was reached on the *Ariane* programme (books and translation) in May (7m ECU over two years) and the *Raphael* programme (cultural and artistic heritage) in July (30m ECU over four years). Finally, in November, the Commission published its guidelines for future policy (2000–06) with six priority areas: mobility of learners and teachers, use of technology, increased European co-operation, language skills, innovation and European reference sources.

In June, the Commission established a scientific steering committee to report on and co-ordinate work on consumer *health* and food safety and, in December, the Council reached a common position on a measure to ban tobacco advertising (which now passes to the Parliament for a second reading).

The Council discussed a revised version of the *Philoxenia* programme, designed to improve the quality and competitiveness of European *tourism* (1998–2002) in November, but it remained blocked by Germany and Britain. Financial irregularities within the section of the Commission responsible for tourism continued to concern the Parliament.

III. EU Finances

The focus in the early part of the year was on fraud, with a parliamentary committee of enquiry examining fraud in the area of transit, in particular, and making recommendations in March. (The Committee estimated a loss in revenue of 3.5bn ECU per year.) The Commission responded with an *Action Plan* to modernize the transit system and make fraud easier to detect. Also in March, the Commission adopted the *Fiscalis* programme (1998–2002), to combat VAT and excise duty fraud. A Commission report in May estimated that known fraud in 1996 amounted to 1.3bn ECU in 1996 and lamented the EU's lack of powers to recover lost funds and punish the guilty parties.

As part of *Agenda 2000,* the Commission published its proposals for the next financial perspective (2000–06) in July. It recommends that the 1999 ceiling on the size of the budget (1.27 per cent of EU GNP) be maintained through to 2006 and that the additional expenditure needed to finance the EU's coming enlargement will be generated by economic growth; thus the size of the budget will increase – by 20bn ECU at 1997 prices – as GNP grows, but the ceiling will not. Agricultural spending will continue to be constrained to rise each year by no more than 74 per cent of GNP growth, the structural funds (SFs) will be held at 0.46 per cent of GNP (even after enlargement) and other expenditure will grow, on average, in line with GNP. However, choppy waters lie ahead: whilst the Member States welcomed the tone of the proposals, the Parliament has questioned the continuation of the 1.27 per cent ceiling and Germany and the Netherlands have raised the matter of excessive net contributions.

In January, the Commission made it clear that for 1998 it would propose an 'austerity budget', increasing by no more than 3 per cent over the 1997 budget; indeed, as the EU was already committed to increased SF expenditure of 8 per cent, this implied rises of no more than 1 per cent for other items. In fact, the Commission eventually produced an even stricter preliminary draft budget with an increase of commitment appropriations of only 2.4 per cent (2.9 per cent for payments) – 91.3bn ECU (commitments) and 84.7bn ECU (payments), well

JOHN REDMOND

Table 1: European Community Budget, 1997 and 1998, Appropriations for Commitments

	1997 Budget (m ECU)	1998 Budget (m ECU)	1998 Budget (% of total)	% Change 1998 over 1997
1. COMMON AGRICULTURAL POLICY				
Markets (price support)	38,956.0	38,154.0	41.9	−2.1
Accompanying measures	1,845.0	2,283.0	2.5	+23.7
TOTAL 1	40,805.0	40,437.0	44.4	−0.9
2. STRUCTURAL OPERATIONS				
EAGGF guidance	4,026.1	4,183.1	4.6	+3.9
FIFG (Fisheries guidance)	490.7	464.2	0.5	−5.4
ERDF	12,989.7	14,000.4	15.4	+7.8
ESF	7,639.1	8,628.1	9.5	+13.0
Community initiatives	3,273.4	2,856.1	3.1	−12.8
Transnational/innovation/anti-fraud measures	301.1	350.2	0.4	+16.3
Cohesion fund	2,749.0	2,871.0	3.2	+4.4
EEA financial mechanism	108.0	108.0	0.1	0
Negative reserve	−100.0	−	−	−
TOTAL 2	31,477.0	33,461.0	36.8	+6.3
3. INTERNAL POLICIES				
Research	3,500.0	3,491.0	3.8	−0.3
Other agricultural operations	163.4	145.9	0.2	−10.7
Other regional operations	22.0	17.0	−	−22.7
Transport	21.6	19.1	−	−11.8
Fisheries and the sea	50.0	48.1	0.1	−3.7
Education, vocational training, youth	377.9	411.1	0.5	+8.8
Culture and audio-visual media	119.9	99.2	0.1	−17.3
Information and communication	107.8	102.5	0.1	−4.9
Other social operations	172.9	165.4	0.2	−4.3
Energy	38.1	33.0	−	−13.4
Euratom nuclear safeguards	15.8	16.0	−	+1.4
Environment	31.8	140.5	0.2	+6.6
Consumer protection	19.6	20.9	−	+6.6
Aid for reconstruction	3.9	3.0	−	−23.2
Internal market	219.0	157.3	0.2	−28.2
Industry and labour market	130.1	275.1	0.3	+111.5
Statistical information	28.2	29.8	−	+5.6
Trans-European networks	465.5	559.9	0.6	+20.3
Co-operation in justice/home affairs	13.1	15.8	−	+20.7
Measures to combat fraud	19.9	5.4	−	−72.9
Negative reserve	−26.0	−	−	−
TOTAL 3	5,594.4	5,755.7	6.3	+2.9
4. EXTERNAL ACTION				
Food and humanitarian aid	904.5	914.5	1.0	+1.1
Co-operation – Asia	401.2	396.2	0.4	−1.3
Co-operation – Latin America	255.7	274.5	0.3	+7.4
Co-operation – southern Africa	145.0	137.5	0.2	−5.2
Co-operation – Mediterranean countries	994.7	1,142.0	1.3	+14.8
Co-operation – central/eastern Europe	1,206.5	1,124.8	1.2	−6.8
Co-operation – former Soviet Union	540.5	530.4	0.6	−1.9
Co-operation – former Yugoslavia	254.1	259.0	0.3	+1.9
EBRD	−	33.8	−	−
Other co-operation measures	407.7	407.1	0.4	−0.1
Human rights and democracy	78.9	97.4	0.1	+23.4
International fisheries agreements	280.0	295.7	0.3	+5.6
Other external aspects	108.7	88.1	0.1	−19.0
Common foreign and security policy	30.0	30.0	−	−
TOTAL 4	5,607.3	5,730.8	6.3	+2.2

Table 1: *(Contd)*

	1997 Budget (m ECU)	1998 Budget (m ECU)	1998 Budget (% of total)	% Change 1998 over 1997
5. ADMINISTRATION				
Commission	2,797.7	2,843.1	3.1	+1.6
Other institutions	1,485.5	1,510.3	1.7	+1.7
TOTAL 5	4,283.3	4,353.4	4.8	+1.6
6. RESERVES				–
Monetary reserve	500.0	500.0	0.5	+2.7
Guarantee reserve	329.0	338.0	0.4	+2.7
Emergency aid reserve	329.0	338.0	0.4	+1.6
TOTAL 6	1,158.0	1,176.0	1.3	
7. COMPENSATION				
Compensation	212.0	99.0	0.1	–53.3
TOTAL 7	212.0	99.0	0.1	–53.3
TOTAL APPROPRIATIONS FOR COMMITMENT	89,137.0	91,013.0	100.0	+2.1
of which:				
Compulsory	42,761.6	42,424.3	46.6	–0.8
Non-compulsory	46,375.3	48,588.7	53.4	+4.8
TOTAL APPROPRIATIONS FOR PAYMENTS	82,365.5	83,529.2	100.0	+1.4
of which:				
Compulsory	42,905.1	42,488.5	50.9	–1.0
Non-compulsory	39,460.4	41,040.7	49.1	+4.0

Source: CEC (1998) *General Report on the Activities of the European Union in 1997* (Luxembourg: CEC), Table 19, pp. 385–6.

Table 2: Budget Revenue (% of Total)

	1997 (Outturns)	1998 (Estimates)
VAT	43.2	40.9
Customs duties	16.9	14.8
GNP-based own resources	34.1	43.0
Agricultural levies	1.3	0.8
Sugar and isoglucose levies	1.4	1.4
Budget balance from previous years	5.4	–
Other	–2.3	–0.9
Actually assigned own resources (%GDP)	1.165	1.127
Maximum assigned own resources (%GDP)	1.240	1.260

Source: CEC (1998) *General Report on the Activities of the European Union in 1997* (Luxembourg: CEC), Table 18, p. 384.

within the budget ceiling. The Council went even further and pursued a 'zero growth' option (actually a 0.7 per cent increase) partly by cutting back on SF spending. The Parliament objected but a compromise was reached and the budget was approved on time: 91.01bn ECU (commitments) and 83.53bn ECU (payments), with increases over 1997 of 2.1 and 1.4 per cent respectively.

The volume of loans granted by the European Investment Bank (EIB) amounted to 26.2bn ECU in 1997 (up 13 per cent on 1996), of which 23bn ECU was advanced within the EU and the rest externally (mainly to countries in central and eastern Europe and the Mediterranean region). The loans within the EU were provided for regional development (14.4bn ECU), trans-European networks (5.8bn ECU), industry, services and SMEs (5.4bn ECU), environmental projects (7.29bn ECU), and energy projects (2.6bn ECU). (The total exceeds 26.2bn ECU because some projects fall into two categories.) The shares of the five largest EU Member States continued to account for over two-thirds of all internal loans, with the share of Germany (15 per cent), France and Spain (12 per cent each) similar to last year and Italy (15 per cent) lower and the UK (16 per cent) higher.

Finally, the EU's first 'own resource' – the European Coal and Steel Community (ECSC) levy, paid by EU coal and steel producers – was abolished for 1998, a year ahead of schedule, as the ECSC budget is dismantled as the expiry of the ECSC treaty (2002) approaches An unexpected surplus in the ECSC budget in 1997 made the 1998 levy unnecessary.

IV. Agriculture and Fisheries

Agriculture

The first half of the year was dominated by 1997–98 price package negotiations and the second by the debate on CAP reform. Turning to the former, in the face of budget austerity at both national and EU level, the Commission essentially proposed a price freeze, with only a few minor (downward) price changes. However, and more controversially, the package also included plans to reduce aids to arable crops (originally put forward last year); this would have raised the 1.4bn ECU needed to finance emergency measures for the beef industry. Predictably, this non-price element was opposed in the Council where the usual individual Member State 'shopping lists' were also in evidence. Agreement was eventually reached in late June but only at the expense of softening the sanctions on excess production of arable crops to the point of not adequately addressing the budget deficit forecast in 1998 because of the BSE crisis.

The reform debate began in earnest after the publication of *Agenda 2000* in July which sought to extend the 1992 CAP reforms by continuing the shift away from price support to direct payments. The Commission therefore proposed significant price cuts for cereals (22 per cent from the year 2000), beef (30 per cent between 2000 and 2002) and dairy products (10 per cent by 2006) with some offsetting compensation payments of various kinds in all three sectors. These proposals met with predictable opposition from farmers' groups and a very mixed reaction and numerous reservations from Member States. Fourteen of the latter – Spain refused to subscribe due to its fears about the future financing of the CAP – were able to endorse a rather general report for the December summit which was duly noted. However, the real debate will continue in 1998.

The BSE crisis (and the embargo on imports of British beef) continued throughout 1997. In the face of criticism from the Parliament and threats of censure, the Commission announced modifications to its management procedures for veterinary and health matters, implemented action programmes to promote (quality) beef and introduced a new identification system for cows and their meat. However, the situation was not helped when it became apparent that quantities of British beef were still being exported (fraudulently and illegally) through Belgium. Meanwhile British efforts to get the embargo lifted through a new British programme for certifying herds and through legal action in the ECJ continued.

Following the end of the drought in Spain, a wine surplus reappeared. The Commission introduced some limited measures to help restore market balance and eventually announced new proposals for longer-term reform which are currently under consideration. Efforts to reform the olive oil regime (plagued by surpluses and fraud) continued. The Commission favoured a radical revision of the policy but was opposed by the main producer states (Portugal, Spain, Italy and Greece) and no significant progress was made. Milk quotas also continued to cause problems and, in March, the Commission temporarily suspended CAP payments to Italy, Spain and Greece because of their failure to pay fines for exceeding their 1995–96 milk quotas. However, despite these tribulations, the Commission is not seeking radical reform of the dairy sector but wishes to extend the quota system until 2006.

In September, the Council began to discuss the Commission's proposals for rural development contained in the *Agenda 2000* document. Basically, the objective is to extend policy to include not only the adaptation of agricultural structures but also the development of alternative activities to agricultural production (in rural areas) and the reinforcement of agri-environmental measures. The debate will continue.

Fisheries

The first half of the year was dominated by the need to agree the fourth *Multi-Annual Guidance Programme (MAGP IV)* which determines restructuring measures for the 1997–2001 period; the sense of urgency was increased by the Commission's decision temporarily to suspend reconstruction and modernization aids. Eventually, agreement was reached in April with some difficulty – France and the UK voted against – for less radical restructuring than originally proposed by the Commission but bigger than that being discussed in the compromise package at the end of 1996: fishing effort is to be reduced by 30 per cent for stocks threatened with extinction and 20 per cent for overexploited stocks.

Also in April the Council replaced transitory provisions by permanent arrangements for the management of fisheries in the Baltic Sea. The new measures included conditions for access to waters and resources and a fishing permit system; their introduction marked the full integration of Finland and Sweden into the Common Fisheries Policy (CFP).

Meanwhile, the new British Government maintained the pressure to seek a solution to the 'problem' of 'quota hopping' (purchase of licences and hence access to the quota of one Member State by fishermen from another). In particular, the British demanded closer economic links between the 'quota hoppers' and their 'home' ports.

In December, the Commission put forward total allowable catches (TACs) for 1998 which continued the restrictive policy of 1997. Following particularly lengthy negotiations, it was agreed by qualified majority – Ireland voted against – to implement TACs for 1998 that were mostly lower than those for 1997, although less so than proposed by the Commission. At the same time fisheries management agreements with a range of countries neighbouring the EU were also approved.

V. Social Policy

In January, the *European Year Against Racism* began and went on to fund 177 projects (with grants totalling 3.2m ECU) addressing four priority areas: public awareness, 'day-to-day-racism', racism in employment and the implementation of legislation. In March, the Commission adopted its first annual report on equal opportunities for women and men, and promised more initiatives in this area. A Green Paper on new work organization was adopted by the Commission in April, which was intended to launch a debate on how new forms of work organization can be used to create jobs and improve the work environment. In December, the Council adopted a directive implementing the framework agreement on part-time work concluded by the social partners in June which aims at preventing any discrimination between full- and part-time workers, improving the quality of part-time work and contributing to increased flexibility of work organization.

In May, the new British Government signalled that the UK would now abandon its 'opt-out' and sign up to the Social Chapter which it duly did. The immediate implication of this was that Britain accepted the two directives already adopted (on European Works Councils and parental leave), although the UK has up to two years to transpose these into national law. It remains to be seen if this heralds a more co-operative British approach to the EU's social policy than in the past.

The French company, Renault, encountered strong criticism when it decided to close down its Vilvoorde plant in Belgium. This triggered a fierce reaction from trade unions and the accusation that Renault had not respected EU directives relating to collective lay-offs and European Works Councils. The intended shift of production to Spain also raised questions about the acceptability of relocation within the EU primarily for the purpose of receiving regional aid. In order to prevent future 'Renaults', a code of conduct concerning company closures and relocations by European multinationals was proposed.

In a survey, the Commission showed that, at the beginning of 1997 no Member State had transposed all of the EU's social legislation (with the exception of Finland); Spain and Italy were the worst transgressors, having transposed only 72 and 78 per cent of legislation, respectively. The EU therefore set about pursuing the offenders through its infringement procedures and, by December, 14 Member States were 'in the dock' for failing to transpose a wide range of directives relating to young people, European Works Councils, working time, sex equality and exposure to biological agents.

VI. Environmental Policy

The EU was involved in two major international conferences on the environment in 1997. The first of these was the second 'Earth Summit', held in New York, which produced no firm commitments and was widely condemned as a failure. The second – held in Kyoto in December – concerned reducing the emission of greenhouse gases and climatic change. The EU's overall stance – a 15 per cent decrease in greenhouse gases by 2010 compared to their 1990 level – was agreed relatively easily but agreement for targets for individual Member States (within the overall reduction) proved more difficult and only added up to 10 per cent (with the remaining 5 per cent left to be assigned if the full 15 per cent were agreed in Kyoto). An interim objective of a 7.5 per cent reduction by 2005 was also agreed. However, the EU's proposed target for 2010 was considerable more ambitious than those of the US (stabilization at 1990 levels) and Japan (a reduction of 5 per cent). Not surprisingly, therefore, the actual agreement eventually reached was to pursue a target of a 5.2 per cent reduction by the 2008-2012 period. However, the EU accepted a somewhat higher target – 8 per cent

– and, as this applied to six gases rather than the three on which the EU's proposed 15 per cent cut was based, the Commission claimed that it approximated to 13 per cent if calculated on the EU's initial base.

Internally, the Union continued to pursue various environmental aspects of water management. In February the Commission adopted a framework directive that set out guidelines for future EU water policy with a view to ensuring the continuation of an adequate water supply, in terms of both quantity and quality. It addressed the management of the river system, the designation of protected areas, the definition of qualitative and quantitative objectives and the cost of water (the price of water should reflect the cost and the 'polluter pays' principle should apply). In December, the Council updated the 1980 directive on the quality of water for human consumption to simplify it and adapt it to reflect technical progress. The Commission's annual report on the quality of bathing water was published in May; whilst satisfaction was expressed with regard to coastal waters, there was considerable concern about the quality of inland waters.

Various efforts were made to link environmental policy to the economic mainstream. In particular, the relationship between the environment and SMEs was debated in the Council in April and the Commission was asked to reflect on possible future action. More fundamentally, on the eve of the November Employment Summit, the Commission published a paper on environmental and employment policies which sought to demonstrate their complementarity and specifically the potential of the former to facilitate the latter by creating jobs.

The *LIFE* programme – the EU's financial instrument for the environment – co-funded 188 new projects in 1997 with a total contribution of 90.2m ECU. More negatively, the year was marked by a steady flow of infringement procedures initiated by the Commission against Member States for their failure to transpose EU environmental measures into national legislation. Areas in which transgressions occurred included protection of water, waste management, access to information, noise, air pollution, and the protection of nature and animals.

Finally, in the face of the proposed CO_2 tax being permanently blocked in the Council, the Commission sought to incorporate the tax, along with the current excise regime for mineral oils, within a broader, overall system for the energy sector which would maximize coherence and allow the objectives of the CO_2 tax (such as reduced pollution) to be achieved by a different route. However, this too was controversial and made no significant progress.

References

Agence Europe (1997) *Daily Bulletin*, No. 6973, 14 May.
Agence Europe (1997) *Europe Documents*, No. 2023, 6 February.

Agence Europe (1997) *Europe Documents*, No. 2026, 5 March.
Agence Europe (1997) *Europe Documents*, No. 2030, 9 April.
Agence Europe (1997) *Europe Documents*, No. 2031, 30 April.
Agence Europe (1997) *Europe Documents*, No. 2033, 7 May.
Agence Europe (1997) *Europe Documents*, No. 2034, 8 May.
Agence Europe (1997) *Europe Documents*, No. 2039/40, 12 June.
Agence Europe (1997) *Europe Documents*, No. 2043, 21 June.
Agence Europe (1997) *Europe Documents*, No. 2052/53, 3 October.
Agence Europe (1997) *Europe Documents*, No. 2054, 9 October.
Agence Europe (1997) *Europe Documents*, No. 2055, 17 October.
Agence Europe (1997) *Europe Documents*, No. 2057, 14 November.
Agence Europe (1997) *Europe Documents*, No. 2062, 10 December.
Agence Europe (1997) *Europe Documents*, No. 2063, 11 December.

Journal of Common Market Studies

Volume 36, Annual Review
September 1998

External Policy Developments

DAVID ALLEN and MICHAEL SMITH
Loughborough University

I. General Themes

Introduction

The EU spent much of 1997 preoccupied with two major issues, both of which had external policy implications. In June, the 1996 Intergovernmental Conference (IGC) was finally concluded with agreement on the content of the Treaty of Amsterdam. In December the European Council endorsed the Commission's suggestion, as outlined in its *Agenda 2000* document published in July, that enlargement negotiations should begin in 1998 with Poland, Hungary, the Czech Republic, Estonia, Slovenia and Cyprus in the first instance. The Treaty of Amsterdam contained some minor changes to the Common Foreign and Security Policy (CFSP) provisions of the TEU, but failed to give the European Union a legal identity or to extend the competence of the EC in the field of external trade in services and intellectual property. The debate about future enlargement caused considerable internal division amongst the Member States and impacted significantly on the EU's relations with all the applicant states and, in particular, with Turkey.

The number of foreign missions accredited to the European Communities rose from 164 in 1996 to 165 in 1997 with the addition of Turkmenistan. The Commission and the Council also agreed that in the near future diplomatic relations would be opened with Tajikistan and the Marshall Islands. The Commission downgraded nine of its delegations into offices (Comoros, Djibouti, Equatorial Guinea, Gambia, Liberia, Netherlands Antilles, Solomon Islands, Somalia and Swaziland) and closed its office in Grenada. It opened a new office in Guatemala and appointed a special envoy to Croatia and non-resident heads of delegation to Armenia, Belarus and Moldova. At the end of 1997, the Commission was represented in 122 countries and five international organizations.

Foreign and Security Policy

1997 was a mixed year for the CFSP. The Member States were visibly divided on the question of intervention on Albania, on relations with Turkey, on policy towards China and united in their decision not to respond, beyond the issuing of statements, to continuing problems in Nigeria, to the deteriorating situation in Algeria or to events in Zaire. The Fifteen were, however, able to take collective action against Iran, to continue their efforts in the Middle East and former Yugoslavia and to maintain their bilateral and multilateral political dialogues with a variety of associated states.

The EU reached formal agreement on a number of CFSP instruments during the year. Altogether there were 13 new or amended joint actions and 13 new or amended common positions. Four joint actions related to Bosnia (providing extra resources to Carlos Westendorp, Carl Bildt's replacement as High Representative of the EU, supporting the electoral process and supporting the OSCE in Republika Srpska); two related to the peace process in the Middle East (establishing a programme to support the Palestinian Authority in its fight against terrorism and appointing Nils Eriksson as a special adviser, as well as extending the mandate of Miguel Moratinos, the EU's special envoy); two related to Africa (appointing Pedro Carlos da Silva Bacelar de Vasconcelos as special adviser and head of the EU electoral unit in the Democratic Republic of the Congo – formally Zaire – and extending the existing joint action); one extending the joint action on the export of land mines to their production; one on transparency in nuclear related export controls and three extending the joint action on the export control of dual use goods. Of the 13 common positions, two were on Bosnia (aimed at those who committed violence in Mostar and those whose actions threatened the Dayton peace process), one on Albania, seven on Africa (relating to conflict prevention in general and to the situations in Nigeria, Angola, and Sierra Leone), two on Burma and one on the Korean Peninsular Energy Development Organization. In addition, there were as usual a host of Presidency and EU statements relating to developing situations in most parts of the world. These statements are often rather vacuous but are faithfully recorded monthly in the *Bulletin of the European Union* and summarized in the 1997 *General Report on the Activities of the European Union* (points 726–37).

The outbreak of violence in Albania, probably the most acute crisis faced by the EU since the war in former Yugoslavia, produced a mixed reaction. After the EU had sent a couple of fact-finding delegations, Britain and Germany made it clear that they would not participate in any military action. It was left to the Italians to organize and lead a military intervention force of some 6,000 troops supplied by Italy, France, Spain, Greece, Austria and Denmark from within the EU, and Turkey and Romania from outside. Following the adoption of a CFSP common position, the Commission allocated 1.5 million ECU for support for the electoral process and organized an international donors' conference in Brussels. Alongside the Council of Europe and the OSCE, the Western European Union (WEU) added to the alphabet soup of concerned organizations by offering technical assistance to Albania's police.

When a German court found, in the *Mykonos* case, that the Iranian authorities were implicated in terrorism on German soil, the EU Member States responded rapidly by recalling their ambassadors, calling off the 'critical dialogue' with Iran and refusing to allow their ambassadors to return to Teheran until the Iranian Government allowed the German ambassador to return. Attempts to demonstrate a similar solidarity against China were dashed when France (just after China had agreed to purchase Airbus aircraft and just before President Chirac visited Beijing), with the tacit support of Germany, Spain and Italy, refused to support a Dutch-sponsored EU resolution condemning China at the UN Human Rights Commission

The Treaty of Amsterdam provides for a number of minor changes in the CFSP decision-making process. The principle of unanimity is preserved with some variations. The new consolidated Treaty on European Union introduces (Art. 23) the principle of 'constructive abstention', whereby a Member State can qualify its abstention from a vote so that the Union can take action which it (the Member State) is not obliged to participate in. The Treaty also introduces the idea of a 'common strategy' (Art. 13.2) to be decided upon unanimously by the European Council on the basis of a recommendation by the Council. Once a common strategy has been agreed, then the Council can implement it 'in particular by adopting joint actions and common positions' (Art. 13. 3) and these decisions, along with those implementing any joint action or common position, can be taken by a qualified majority (Art. 23.2). However, it should also be noted that the new Treaty also allows any Member State to oppose the adoption of any CFSP decision by a qualified majority on the grounds of 'important and stated reasons of national policy' (Art. 23.2). This is, in effect, the Luxembourg Compromise, which is given formal legal status for the first time. On balance, then, the new voting arrangements would seem to reinforce the intergovernmental nature of the CFSP.

The major institutional innovation is the creation of the post of High Representative and the establishment of a policy planning and early warning unit under his or her responsibility. The High Representative, in the first instance, is to be the Secretary-General of the Council charged with the task of assisting the Presidency in particular, and the Council in general, in the management, representation and implementation of the CFSP. There has been considerable speculation that a new foreign policy 'troika' is likely to emerge consisting of the High Representative, the Council President and the Vice-President of the Commission responsible for external relations (the Commission intends to reorganize itself to bring external relations under the overall responsibility of just one Commissioner instead of the four who presently share that task). In any case, the old troika, linking the previous, present and next Council Presidency, is to be replaced (Art. 18.4) by provisions for the Presidency to be assisted 'if need be' just by the next Member State to hold the Presidency.

The new planning cell will draw its staff from the Council Secretariat, the Member States, the Commission and the WEU. Its effectiveness will depend critically on the willingness of the Member States to grant it access to privileged information. The present Secretary-General of the Council, Jurgen Trumpf, has also called for new funds and staff to be allocated to the unit and for the Member States to decide as soon as possible how it will operate. For their part, the Member States are already divided on the size of the unit, about how closely it should be integrated into the existing Council structures and about how it will relate to the Political Committee. Political directors, based in the national capitals, may feel that the new unit represents yet another move towards the 'Brusselization' of the CFSP process.

The 1996 IGC failed to make any real progress on the question of the integration of the WEU into the EU. An inconsequential change of wording refers to the 'progressive' framing of a common defence policy, but the only substantive novelty is the inclusion, in Art. 17.2, of the so-called 'Petersberg' tasks – humanitarian and rescue missions, peace-keeping and the use of combat forces in crisis management and peace-making. The substantive record of the CFSP, discussed above, would seem to suggest that the EU is unlikely in the near future to 'avail itself of the WEU to elaborate and implement decisions and actions of the Union which have defence implications' (Art. 17.3).

External Trade and the Common Commercial Policy

The EU's external trade position at the beginning of 1997 was strong, with provisional figures showing a fourth successive annual surplus for 1996 (46.3bn ECU compared to 24.2bn ECU in 1995). EU exports to the rest of the world in

1996 had amounted to 620bn ECU, a rise of 9 per cent on 1995, and imports from the rest of the world had totalled 573.7bn ECU, a rise of 5.3 per cent. This did not mean, of course, that there were no areas of concern; in particular, deficits with China and Japan were to cause tensions as the year wore on (see below), and the impact of the financial turbulence in Asia during the second half of the year was impossible to calculate.

A first issue, which had emerged during 1996 as the preparation for the IGC went ahead, was that of the Common Commercial Policy (CCP) itself, and in particular of the Community's competence to conduct trade policy in the areas of trade in services and intellectual property. The ECJ in its opinion of November 1994 had indicated that exclusive Community competence existed only over trade in goods, and that in services and intellectual property competence was shared between Community and Member States. The Commission's submission to the IGC made a firm bid for the extension of exclusive competence to the two disputed areas, but it became apparent that this was likely to be opposed by Britain and France in particular. Despite the Commission's view that the existing situation made negotiations difficult both to initiate and to conclude by limiting bargaining flexibility, and despite the inclusion of a wide-ranging provision in the Dublin Draft Treaty, it was clear by the time of the Amsterdam European Council that little could be expected. The final result was the addition of a paragraph to Art. 113 (now Art. 133 in the consolidated European Community Treaty), which provides for the determination of competence in the disputed areas by unanimity in the Council. It is not clear whether this is seen as a once-for-all decision, or more plausibly as a provision to be used on a case-by-case basis, but it will not be long before it comes to the test, given the trade negotiation agenda for the next few years.

Apart from this 'constitutional' issue, there were other significant areas of dispute in the CCP during 1997. The most fraught was that of anti-dumping legislation, which is a much-used Community instrument (23 notices of initiation of proceedings were issued in 1997,14 of them new cases). Leon Brittan early in 1997 pursued proposals to widen the criteria used to determine 'Community interest' in anti-dumping cases (and thus to take into account the interests of processors and consumers as well as those of producers); this attracted the predictable opposition of France and other 'southern' members, whilst being supported by 'northern' countries. Tensions were focused by a wide-ranging conflict, essentially between the 'free-traders' and the 'protectionists' in the Council, which centred on the trade in unbleached cotton textiles, and affecting imports worth around 600m ECU a year from India, Pakistan, Indonesia, China, Egypt and Turkey. The Commission had imposed provisional anti-dumping duties to the tune of 36 per cent during 1996, and in early 1997 these came up for review. By March, it was clear that up to nine Member States opposed the imposition of definitive duties, and also that the duties themselves threatened thousands of jobs in the textile finishing industry and retail sectors. Despite the defeat of proposals for definitive duties, the issue would not go away; by the end of the year, new investigations had been started, despite firm opposition by the 'free traders' and a variety of vociferous lobbies, and this was taken to indicate the residual strength of French producers in particular. Another 'model' of anti-dumping procedures was provided by tensions with Japan and Korea about perceived dumping of dynamic random-access memory chips (DRAMS); an initial finding of dumping by the Commission was followed by industry-to-industry negotiations which produced a 'gentlemen's agreement' late in the year, in the case of Korea, and potentially a similar agreement with Japan.

Elsewhere in commercial policy, there was a continuation of reforms and codification, particularly of customs co-operation procedures under the 'Customs 2000' programme. A range of new customs co-operation agreements was concluded, with South Korea, the United States, Canada, Norway and Switzerland. Another area of activity was that of export credit procedures, with continuing efforts to establish Community-wide principles for official export credits. Finally, there were continuing negotiations with a number of countries to resolve issues of import and export quotas, for example with Vietnam on textiles. One interesting variation on this theme was the closing of a loophole which had allowed Member States' overseas territories to be used as a channel for imports of commodities such as rice from countries that would otherwise have been subject to quota restrictions (see 'Development Co-operation Policy' below).

Quite apart from 'internal' policy development, 1997 was a highly significant year for the EU's development of external strategy, particularly in the context of the World Trade Organization (WTO). During the year, three large-scale sectoral agreements were reached – on basic telecommunications trade, on information technology trade and on trade in financial services. In each of these areas, the EU had played a central role in establishing and sustaining the negotiations; in each of them, the major barriers to agreement had seemed on many occasions to arise from the position of the United States. In the financial services negotiations, for example, it seemed at times that a single US insurance company's interests in Malaysia were the barrier to agreement. Interestingly also, in the light of earlier discussion, the telecommunications and financial services agreements were in areas where the Community could not claim exclusive competence. Altogether, the EU's year in the WTO can be seen as one of substantial progress. In November, a WTO report on the operation of the single market praised it as the basis for liberalization, and as generating the potential for EU leadership in global negotiations. One qualification to this praise was continued debate both within the EU and in the WTO about the costs and benefits of preferential trade agreements; at EU level, the French especially wanted a halt brought to the growth of such arrangements pending the clarification of WTO rules, and although this did not delay existing negotiations with partners such as Mexico, it cast a shadow of uncertainty on the initiation of new negotiations.

As in previous years, a notable feature of the EU's external commercial policies was the impact of issues that at first glance appeared to be predominantly domestic. The most striking of these in 1997 was competition policy – an area in which the growth of transnational alliances and communications has made the internal/external distinction almost meaningless at times. The EU had to wrestle with some very knotty problems in this area, particularly in relation to the United States, and increasingly it appeared that Karel van Miert and Neil Kinnock, the Commissioners for Competition Policy and Transport respectively, were an integral part of the external policy process alongside Leon Brittan, Hans van den Broek and Manuel Marin. Not only this, but when environmental issues were raised – for example at the Kyoto conference on greenhouse gas emissions – or when labour standards were at issue, yet other Commissioners entered into the policy arena. Couple this with the increasingly turbulent context provided by the financial crises in Asia and the possible volatility associated with the coming of EMU, and the recipe for interesting times in EU external commercial policies is firmly established

Development Co-operation Policy

In October, after extensive discussions within and between the EU, the African, Caribbean and Pacific (ACP) states and the many interested non-governmental organizations (NGOs) about the future of the Lomé arrangements after 2000, the Commission presented its guidelines for the negotiation of a new agreement. Talks are due to begin in the autumn of 1998. The ambitious new objective will be to aim for reciprocal free trade by 2020 with a gradual phasing-out of trade preferences and development aid schemes so as to bring Lomé in line with World Trade Organization (WTO) rules. In future, priority will be given to promoting investment in the ACP states, encouraging private sector initiatives and using EU resources to focus on poverty alleviation. The ACP states will be relieved that the EU is prepared to consider another framework convention after 2000, but dismayed by the EU's radical proposals for its content. Under pressure from the WTO, the new arrangements will almost certainly seek to differentiate between the 71 ACP states based on their level of economic development.

There are 39 ACP states which fall into the category of land-locked and least-developed countries (LLDC) who will probably continue to receive aid and trade concessions. The remaining 32 ACP countries now fall into the middle-income category which needs to be made compatible with WTO rules. These countries will probably have to be given access to the EU's generalized system of preferences (GSP), similar to that enjoyed by the developing countries of Asia and Latin America. If the Lomé Convention is to be preserved beyond 2000, then the question of future membership will also have to be resolved. The present ACP countries are naturally anxious to preserve their special status but a new regime might open up the question of membership for the poorer nations of South Asia as well as problem countries such as Cuba.

In addition to radically overhauling the Lomé trade and aid arrangements, the Commission is also keen to inject greater political conditionality and momentum into the relationship and into its overall development policies. In 1997, the Commission also considered proposals to offer trade concessions under the GSP to those developing countries prepared to guarantee to respect international standards on social rights and the environment. This would represent a significant movement away from a sanctions policy towards an incentives policy, with the EU offering significant tariff reductions for both industrial and agricultural products. Developing countries would have to adopt International Labour Organization standards on child labour, freedom of association and collective bargaining, and countries with tropical rain forests would have to implement standards set by the International Tropical Timber Association. Some Member States would also like to see the incentives proposals extended to include respect for broader human rights.

The present Lomé arrangements were twice undermined in 1997, firstly when the EU was forced to accept a WTO ruling against its banana import regime, even though it had previously thought that its arrangements for ACP bananas had a WTO waiver and, secondly, when the Commission was forced to impose quotas on rice imports from the Caribbean. The rice problem arose because rice producers in Guyana and Suriname were taking advantage of the rule which allowed products from ACP countries, which undergo significant transformation (in this case, milling) in a dependent territory (in this case, Netherlands Antilles), to enter the EU quota and duty free. In 1997 Netherlands Antilles rose to become the world's third largest exporter of processed rice after the US and Thailand, but the Commission has now imposed a strict limit on the amount per quarter that can be imported through an overseas territory.

The Commission came under further attack from the Court of Auditors for its management of development aid to Africa, the southern Mediterranean and the countries of eastern and central Europe. The Court was particularly critical of the Commission's tendering procedures, of the time taken to execute policies, of the lack of policy transparency and of poor co-ordination both within the Commission (which has five Directorates-General responsible for aid programmes) and between the Commission and the Member States. In addition to modifying its procedures, the Commission is also considering the more radical solution of transferring all the administrative and technical aspects of its aid programmes to an outside agency which would be independent but answerable to the Commission, the Parliament and the Member States. The Commission is rapidly becoming overwhelmed by the sheer volume of aid funds that it must administer, up from 2.3bn ECU in 1990 to 7.2bn ECU in 1997. With a separate agency responsible for policy implementation, the Commission could then concentrate on policy formulation where its competence is acknowledged.

The EU remains the world's largest donor of humanitarian aid disbursing a total of 438m ECU through the European Community Humanitarian Office (ECHO). In 1997 the bulk of the aid went to the Great Lakes region of Africa (172m ECU) and Bosnia (132m ECU). Smaller sums of money were dispersed to assist victims of mainly man-made disasters in most parts of the developing world.

II. Regional Themes

EFTA, the EEA and Northern Europe

The European Economic Area (EEA), much reduced since the accession to the EU of Austria, Finland and Sweden in 1995, continued to operate on its established agenda during 1997. The EEA Council met in June and November, the Joint Parliamentary Committee in June and October, and work continued on the incorporation of single market legislation into the EEA framework. In addition, there was consultation in respect of the impending round of accession negotiations concerning central and eastern Europe, Cyprus and Turkey. Among EEA members, the most salient for the EU has always been Norway and, during 1997 as before, most of the contentious issues in EU–Norwegian relations concerned fish. In March, a meeting at Bergen attempted to find ways of conserving North Sea fish stocks, and, quite apart from the difficulties of reaching agreement on the substance, it also saw a conflict between the Commission and some Member States. Emma Bonino, the Commissioner, refused to accept an inter-state agreement, since the Community had exclusive competence in the area; this predictably outraged the Norwegians, and eventually the results of the conference had to be presented as a 'political' declaration which, in the Commissioner's view, had no binding legal force. The Norwegians also caused tensions in the Commission indirectly when Leon Brittan came to an agreement to avert the threat of anti-dumping proceedings in relation to farmed salmon. Brittan's solution was to operate on the basis of price undertakings, but Bonino and Padraig Flynn (the Social Affairs Commissioner) resisted, calling for the imposition of 14 per cent duties. Eventually, the Commission narrowly backed Brittan, but immediately EU salmon producers expressed their fears of job losses.

For the purposes of practical policy, EFTA equals Switzerland in the EU's universe; and Switzerland during 1997 came effectively to equal transport, transit and trucks. Since Switzerland's refusal even to enter the EEA as the result of a 1992 referendum, there have been continuous negotiations on bilateral issues. By early 1997, these had made substantial progress on troubling issues such as public procurement, and had even managed to establish principles for agreement on the free movement of persons, but transport and transit issues remained unresolved. Essentially, the Swiss resisted an invasion of heavy trucks from the EU, proposing substantial transit charges and attempting to transfer as much as possible of the traffic to rail. Any agreement would be subject to approval not only by the Swiss people in a referendum, but also by each of the cantons – not a recipe for rapid progress or flexibility. It was also feared by the Swiss that, after the end of the Dutch Presidency in June 1997, there would be an increasing focus on impending accession negotiations and EMU, at the inevitable expense of their interests. The uncertain effects of EMU and further EU enlargement tempted some in Switzerland to think more seriously about a new attempt to join the EU, while others were determined to resist if not to establish even more restrictive conditions for approval of any such moves.

Central Europe

The most important feature of relations between the EU and the countries of central Europe, all of whom are applicants, was the progress made in the enlargement process. In July, the Commission published its opinions on the membership applications from Hungary, Poland, Romania, Slovakia, Latvia, Estonia, Lithuania, Bulgaria, the Czech Republic and Slovenia at the same time as *Agenda 2000*. This consisted of a general assessment of the applications for accession, an assessment of the impact of enlargement on EU policies and the Commission's recommendations on the strategy to adopt to prepare the applicants for membership. The Commission concluded that, whilst none of the applicants was yet ready for membership, negotiations could begin with five of them – Hungary, Poland, the Czech Republic, Estonia and Slovenia.

There then followed a period of argument between the Member States over whether to accept the Commission's suggested list or whether to begin negotiations with a larger or smaller group of applicants. Each applicant had its own supporters within the EU (France advocating adding Romania to the list, Sweden wanting Latvia and Lithuania to join Estonia) but in the end the European Council meeting in Luxembourg endorsed the Commission proposals and agreed to convene bilateral Intergovernmental Conferences (IGCs) with the chosen five in spring 1998. At the same time, anxious to ease the difficulties for those not initially chosen, the European Council agreed to establish a European Conference involving all the applicant states (the ten central Europeans plus

Cyprus and Turkey). It was also decided to launch an accession process for the ten central European states plus Cyprus, which would involve a pre-accession strategy consisting of an accession partnership and increased assistance for each applicant.

As we shall see below, the inclusion of Turkey in the European Conference but its exclusion from the pre-accession process (even though Turkey's membership eligibility was reconfirmed) proved extremely contentious and somewhat of a distraction from the continuing concerns of the central Europeans. In Poland there were worries about the costs of membership as the EU complained about milk quality and car imports, and in the Baltic States President Santer was given a rough ride when he visited Lithuania and Latvia in November. More ominously, by the end of the year, the EU had still conspicuously failed to tackle the critical questions that must be resolved before enlargement can become a reality. These include the reform of the EU's finances, the CAP and the cohesion and structural funds, as well as essential institutional changes.

During the year, as the arguments about overall enlargement strategy raged, the structured dialogue with the countries of central Europe and the bilateral meetings provided for under the Europe Agreements continued to take up an enormous amount of time that was not always seen as well spent by either the EU or its central European partners. Under the PHARE programme 1.1142 bn ECU were allocated in 1997, and in March the Commission proposed new guidelines for future PHARE expenditure which were adopted by the Council in June. In future PHARE's two major priorities will involve institution-building, which will receive 30 per cent of the budget, and the financing of investment in the applicant countries, which will account for 70 per cent of the budget. This expenditure will underpin the accession partnerships discussed above. The Commission's intention with these new proposals is to stop PHARE being demand-driven by officials from the central European countries and to concentrate expenditure on the EU's agreed priorities. The Commission is also keen to answer criticism of its heavy reliance on consultants by encouraging direct contacts between officials from the Commission and the Member States and officials in the central European governments. The problem with implementing this new approach, which marks a further 'coming of age' for the PHARE programme, is a shortage of personnel in the east and a reluctance by budget-conscious EU governments to release staff.

The EU has continued its policy of supporting regional co-operation in the area. Both the Commission and the EU Presidency attended the Council of Baltic Sea States in Riga and, at the end of the year, the Commission adopted a report listing the various regional co-operation initiatives currently in progress in Europe.

Russia and the Other Soviet Successor States

The partnership and co-operation agreement between the EU and Russia finally came into force in December after many delays (see previous issues of the *Annual Review*). President Yeltsin's illness, which prevented him travelling, meant that the scheduled EU–Russia summit was held in Moscow rather than Brussels. The meeting itself was dominated by Russian concerns about the prospective EU enlargement and the Russian desire to begin negotiations for a free trade area, as well as Russia's ambition to join the WTO. Russia fears a loss of EU market share once the countries of eastern and central Europe become EU members, but would prefer to negotiate free access to the expanded market rather than claim compensation from the EU for the trade diversion effect of enlargement.

Despite a new agreement providing free access to the EU for Russian steel by the end of 2001, relations between the EU and Russia were mainly characterized by a series of niggling disputes over, amongst other things, textiles, inhumane methods of fur trapping, border controls, import quotas on EU carpets, steel pipes, and Trans-Siberian overflights. On the Russian side, irritation with the EU, concerns about enlargement and an eye for domestic opinion led Boris Nemtsov, Russia's first deputy prime minister, to refuse to meet Leon Brittan, the EU's chief trade negotiator, when he visited Moscow in June. Nemtsov complained about the EU's continuing classification of Russia as a 'non-market' economy and about what he described as 'fierce' EU anti-dumping procedures.

It was no coincidence that just two days after the Commission published its *Agenda 2000* on EU enlargement and one week after the NATO enlargement summit in Madrid, the EU welcomed Viktor Chernomyrdin, the Russian Prime Minister, to Brussels on a face-saving visit. During this visit Chernomyrdin spelt out Russia's ambition to become a full member of the EU; President Santer was careful not to comment directly on this ambition, although it is clear that few people within the EU consider Russian membership to be either desirable or practicable.

In September an EU–Ukraine summit was held in Kiev shortly after the EU had agreed to provide a grant of 100m ECU to help shore up the dilapidated concrete sarcophagus encasing the remains of the Chernobyl nuclear plant which melted down in 1986. For its part, the Ukraine has agreed to close down the remaining nuclear reactors at Chernobyl by the year 2000. Relations between the EU and Belarus deteriorated following the failure of the Belarusian government to take action to rectify human rights violations. In September the EU decided not to conclude a partnership and co-operation agreement with Belarus and to freeze all assistance except humanitarian and regional aid and funds for democratization.

In 1997 the EU committed 475.2m ECU under its TACIS programme which included for the first time funds for the conversion of chemical weapons plants in Russia and for combating the drug problem. The EU also undertook a review of TACIS implementation between 1991 and 1996 which revealed that 80 per cent of the projects had proceeded according to plan, 71 per cent had achieved their objectives and 87 per cent had matched the needs of their recipients (it is interesting to speculate about the 9 per cent that proceeded according to plan but which did not achieve their objectives and the 16 per cent which matched the needs of the recipients but which did not proceed according to plan!)

The Mediterranean and the Middle East

The second Euro-Mediterranean Conference of foreign ministers was held in Malta in April, after Syria refused to condone the symbolism of inviting Israel to an Arab country. Despite the tensions between Israel and Palestine and Greece and Turkey, and despite the fact that it took three weeks for diplomats to complete the final declaration, the momentum that was started in Barcelona in 1995 was just about maintained. With one or two exceptions (Morocco cancelled a meeting of industry ministers in October citing Israeli obstruction of the Middle East peace process), all the participants continue to meet regularly in pursuit of the partnership's multiple objectives. Within the Euro-Mediterranean framework, an association agreement with Jordan was signed along with an interim agreement with the Palestinian Liberation Organization on behalf of the Palestinian Authority. Negotiations for similar agreements with Syria and Algeria began during 1997 (the latter despite the rapidly deteriorating situation there and amidst growing criticism of EU inaction), but those with Egypt and the Lebanon remained deadlocked over agriculture and import duties respectively. Under the MEDA scheme for financing economic and social reform in the Mediterranean, 981,391m ECU were committed in 1997.

The EU's support for the Middle East peace process was made more difficult by the settlements policy of the Netanyahu government and by Israeli criticism of the trade arrangements between the EU and the Palestinian Authority. Nevertheless, the EU sought to use its good offices and, in July, succeeded in brokering a meeting between the Palestinian President, Yasser Arafat, and the Israeli Foreign Minister, David Levy, in Brussels, at which they agreed to resume negotiations to unblock the peace process. Towards the end of the year, economic relations with Israel deteriorated when the EU was forced to warn Israel publicly against flouting the rules-of-origin conditions of their 1995 free trade agreement. The EU was particularly disturbed to discover Palestinian flowers and shoes being exported through the Israeli quota and also noted that Israel was exporting 50,000 tonnes of oranges a year, which was exactly double the amount it was capable of producing!

The EU expressed continuing concern about the lack of progress in the implementation of the Dayton peace accords. The third international donors' conference for the reconstruction of Bosnia was postponed several times until it was eventually held in Brussels in July. At the meeting, 48 countries and 30 international organizations pledged a total of US$1.26 billion. The EU's contribution of 250m ECU made it the leading international donor. The EU continued to refine its attempts to exert influence over the states of former Yugoslavia by applying conditionality to its trade and aid relationships. As well as postponing the donors' conference, the Commission froze aid to Republika Srpska until Radovan Karadzic, an indicted war criminal, was removed from power and, in December, withdrew the autonomous special trade measures extended to Serbia in April because of concern about the behaviour of the Serbian government in the province of Kosovo.

In the eastern Mediterranean, the EU's relations with Cyprus and Turkey were made all the more complex by the debate on EU enlargement. The decisions taken at the European Council in Luxembourg further infuriated Turkey and those who support Turkish membership within the EU. Little progress was made towards a reconciliation of the two rival communities in Cyprus and, whilst Greece continued to make relations between the EU and Turkey difficult, Turkey, for its part, constantly threatened to involve the US by seeking to make a linkage between its support for NATO enlargement and a more sympathetic consideration by the EU of its claim to membership. Despite numerous attempts to mollify Turkey within the framework of the association agreement, the EU's decision to include Turkey in the European Conference but not in the accession partnership provoked a Turkish refusal to participate in the conference. As enlargement negotiations get under way in 1998, the tensions within the EU and between the EU, Cyprus and Turkey are only likely to increase. At the end of 1997, the Maltese Foreign Minister caused some agitation in Brussels by announcing that Malta might reactivate its own membership bid, suspended since the Labour Government came to power in 1996.

Africa

In March, Spain finally lifted its veto on South Africa's partial membership of the Lomé Convention despite the fact that little progress had been made in talks designed to give EU trawlers access to South African waters. In April, the ACP–EC Council of Ministers formally adopted the protocol allowing for South Africa's 'qualified' accession to the Convention, but it was not until September that South Africa finally agreed to ratify it. In particular, South Africa was concerned about a clause which exempts South African materials included in exports from other Southern African Lomé members from EU tariffs, but only on an ad hoc basis. The EU has already refused to grant South Africa the preferential access enjoyed by other ACP countries but is, instead, attempting to negotiate a separate trade and development agreement. Talks on this made little progress in 1997 with South Africa resisting EU attempts to limit imports of 'sensitive products' such as fruit and beef which countries such as Spain, France and Germany insist should be excluded from any free trade agreement. Despite the continuing problems between South Africa and the EU, a total of 127.5m ECU under the European Programme for Reconstruction and Development was granted in 1997.

The EU was accused of turning a 'blind eye' to the continuing abuse of human rights in Nigeria. In particular it was criticized for a French decision to allow Nigeria to participate in the soccer World Cup in France in 1998. Although the EU did ban all Nigerian sportsmen and women from playing in Europe after the execution of Ken Saro-Wiwa in 1995, an exception was made for sporting events which had been arranged prior to this date. France has used this exception to justify its decision to let Nigeria play, but human rights activists have also accused France of leading a group of countries, including Italy, Spain, Portugal and Greece, who have been pressing for a general easing of restrictions against Nigeria. The European Parliament joined in this chorus of disapproval when the Dutch Presidency invited Nigeria to the ACP–EC Council of Ministers despite the fact that Nobel prize winner Wole Soyinka and other human rights protesters had just been charged with treason – a charge which could lead to further death penalties. The EU's 'soft' treatment of Nigeria is in sharp contrast with the pressure it had put on neighbouring, but much poorer, Niger to reform its governmental procedures.

Events in Zaire, which became the Democratic Republic of the Congo after a civil war, produced only a subdued EU response despite the efforts of Italian Commissioner Emma Bonino, responsible for humanitarian aid. Despite French pressure, the EU rejected the idea of military intervention to protect humanitarian aid corridors as well as a Belgian proposal for an arms embargo. Instead, the EU contented itself with a number of declarations, the dispatch of the troikas of EU foreign ministers for initial contacts with the new government in Kinshasa, humanitarian assistance and a joint action in support of democratization and the holding of free elections.

Asia

At the level of interregional relations between the EU and Asia, interest centred on EU links with the Association of Southeast Asian Nations (ASEAN) and on the preparations for the second Asia–Europe Meeting (ASEM), due to be held in London in April 1998. The EU's relations with ASEAN have been established formally since an agreement in 1980, but this had effectively expired by 1997. Attention thus focused on the possibility of a new joint action plan to replace the agreement. In February, Singapore was the venue for a series of meetings: the twelfth annual EU–ASEAN ministerial meeting, followed by the meeting of the ASEAN Regional Forum (in which the EU is a 'dialogue partner') and by an ASEM meeting for foreign ministers. In the EU–ASEAN context, the desire for new agreements was severely complicated by the political dynamics of the southeast Asian region: the long-standing EU concerns with human rights in East Timor and Burma came up against the determination of ASEAN not only to make up their own minds but also to admit Burma (and Cambodia) as members. Whilst Vietnam could be added to the EU–ASEAN 'club' without difficulty, by November there was a threat that an annual meeting of EU and ASEAN officials could be cancelled because of the presence of Burma; in the case of Cambodia, the coup in spring which had led to the ascendancy of Hun Sen also meant that EU contacts were withdrawn.

One fear generated by these tensions was that the projected second ASEM might be blighted by the Burmese issue in particular. It became clear that since the ASEM depended on consensus among existing participants to determine the programme and attendance, the issue would not come to a head, and the London meeting would go ahead as scheduled. In preparation for this, and as a result of the first ASEM held in Bangkok during 1996, a wide range of activities took place. Foreign ministers met in Singapore during February, finance ministers in Bangkok during September, and economics ministers in Tokyo during September. The Asia–Europe Foundation was opened in Singapore, and preparations were made for the establishment of an Asia–Europe environmental technology centre in Thailand. There was an ASEM business conference during July in Indonesia, and a meeting of the Asia-Europe Business Forum in Thailand during November. In this way, the aim of generating a continuing network of Asia–Europe contacts was furthered, but it was apparent that when the financial crisis of the summer and autumn hit Asian economies, the EU's role was not as prominent as that of the United States and Japan. The second ASEM would clearly meet in a very different context from that surrounding the first.

The second key focus of EU policies towards Asia was China – a continuing preoccupation of EU policy-makers, given added point during 1997 by the change in status of Hong Kong. The particular focus of concern here was two-fold: first, the continuation of existing trading and other links, and second, the support for democracy in the new 'autonomous region'. The second of these led to a Council declaration issued in June, and also to British efforts to achieve EU unity on symbolic protests against the installation of the new Legislative Council, which achieved patchy success. The commercial policy links were followed up with a visit to Brussels by the new Hong Kong Chief Executive, Tung Chee Hwa, in October, and the conclusion of a new customs co-operation agreement.

China in general was a source of interest and frustration for EU officials during 1997. The main strategic concern was with the continuing negotiations on Chinese entry into the WTO, which are conducted both at a bilateral and at a multilateral level. From the Commission's point of view, the bilateral process was centred on issues such as trade in services and market access more generally, within the general context of a desire for early Chinese membership. This made slow but significant progress during the year, leading to what was described as a 'partial understanding' when Leon Brittan visited Beijing during October, but had to be seen within the context of both United States and Japanese policies, which were often either less positive (in the case of the US) or more yielding (in the case of Japan). The whole process was also conditioned by issues of human rights, and particularly by an unseemly row which broke out in the Council during the spring. The immediate occasion for the conflict was the sponsoring of an annual resolution at the UN Commission for Human Rights in Geneva, condemning China's record. This had been undertaken previously on the basis of a Council consensus, but in 1997 France, Germany and Italy withdrew their support; some commentators drew a direct line between the action and the Beijing visit of the French President Chirac. Whatever the motivation, the action exposed deep rifts among Member States. The resolution was eventually sponsored by Denmark, attracting retaliatory actions by the Chinese. The whole episode was seen as a major setback by the Dutch Presidency, and relations between Beijing and Copenhagen were 'normalized' only during the autumn.

China also attracted the usual rash of anti-dumping actions during 1997, of which the most contentious was the imposition of provisional duties on imports of handbags. China accounts for nearly half of the EU market for handbags, totalling about 150 million during 1996, and the market is worth around 1bn ECU in total. But at the 'popular' end of the market, Chinese products predominate. As a result, when duties were imposed, handbag retailers and importers, as well as consumers, were roused. At the very end of the year, controversy broke out when the EC reaffirmed its classification of China as a 'non-market economy' for anti-dumping purposes.

Asia also provided a host of developments in other bilateral relationships with the EU. Mention has already been made of Burma, and the multilateral issues encountered within ASEAN. Bilaterally, in March, the Council carried out its threat to withdraw GSP recognition from Burma, on the specific grounds of its use of child labour, and its Common Position was reaffirmed in November. Relations with Cambodia – including a proposed co-operation agreement – were effectively frozen as a result of the coup in March, whilst those with Laos were formalized through a co-operation agreement signed in April. Negotiations with India were designed to lead to a new co-operation agreement, and such an agreement was signed with Pakistan in April. Specific concerns arose with

Pakistan over food hygiene in respect of seafood imports, and with Bangladesh in respect of the detection of fraudulent export licences for tee-shirts; the latter issue threatened severe consequences not only for Bangladeshi exporters but also for importers in the EU.

One of the more complex bilateral relationships between the EU and Asia-Pacific is that between the Union and Korea. Indeed, it could be argued that Korea's status as a member of OECD, and its possible removal from 'developing country' status under the GSP, put it in a different category from other Asian countries. Part of the EU's 'Korea problem' reflects this ambiguity. During 1997, the Commission had occasion to complain about the Korean 'frugality campaign', designed to reduce imports and thus to stabilize the economy, whilst the government in Seoul maintained it was nothing to do with them. There was also a complaint from Brussels about the Korean liquor tax, which discriminates against imports much as did the Japanese version until it was ruled illegal by the WTO on an EC complaint. At the same time, there were new agreements: a customs co-operation agreement, an agreement on the opening of telecommunications procurement markets, agreement on mechanisms to deal with the trade in DRAMS (see above). Most importantly, there was finalization of the terms on which the EU could participate in the Korean Peninsula Energy Development Organisation (KEDO). The problem was that it was unclear who should represent the EU; eventually, in January 1997, it was agreed that Euratom would be the EU representative with one vote, but that two delegates would be sent, one mandated by the Commission and the other by the Council. This unlocked 15m ECU of annual EU funding, and contributed further to the EU's broad activist strategy in Asia, but also indicated continuing issues about competence and the 'division of labour' in the Union. Alongside these areas of agreement, the EU through the Council expressed its continuing support for the four-power negotiations on the future of the 'two Koreas' due to start during 1997.

Latin America

During 1997, a number of trends gathered momentum to create new interest and dynamism in EU–Latin America relations, with the potential for further development during 1998. The first set of issues concerned broad interregional relations. Visits by President Chirac of France in March, and by Manuel Marin in September contributed to the formalization of proposals for a conference of Heads of State and Government from the EU, Latin America and the Caribbean. The initial target date for this conference was ill defined, but when it was incorporated in the conclusions of the Amsterdam European Council there was reference to it occurring by the year 2000. Assuming that this does happen, the conference could be seen as a parallel to the ASEM, and with some of the same aims in terms of asserting EU interests in an area previously dominated by the United States.

If the EU–Latin America conference does occur, it will complement an already existing set of interregional relations with several groupings. Perhaps the most far-reaching of these is the relationship with Mercosur (the southern common market), whose members are Argentina, Brazil, Paraguay and Uruguay with Chile as an associate. A framework agreement with Mercosur was signed in December 1995, with the aim of working towards a full free trade area, but progress has been slow. The annual ministerial meeting between EU and Mercosur took place in April 1997, and it was agreed that negotiations could begin in 1998 with the aim of establishing a free trade area by 1999. Difficulties remain, including Mercosur concerns about agricultural trade and the impact of the Asian financial crisis, which led in late 1997 to a 25 per cent increase in the Mercosur external tariff.

Other interregional relationships were subject only to incremental change and development during 1997. The links with the 12-member Rio Group were maintained through a ministerial meeting in April, and the same applied to the Andean Group (in fact, the meetings with Mercosur, the Rio Group and the Andean Group all took place in parallel during April). The San José Group of central American states met in its 12th Ministerial Conference with the EU in the Hague during February, with the EU represented by the troika of the Netherlands, Luxembourg and Ireland alongside Manuel Marin for the Commission. Discussion centred on the (slow) implementation of the 1996 'solemn declaration', and also on agricultural issues (inevitably tinged by the dispute over the EU banana regime). Each of these groups also met with the EU during the United Nations General Assembly meeting in September.

Bilateral developments with Latin American countries were generally also incremental rather than radical during 1997. Tensions with Brazil (over automobile tariffs) and Argentina (over footwear and textile imports to the EU) were dealt with in the WTO context. There were continued tensions between Spain and Cuba, and the Council reaffirmed its common position on the issue, whilst a new framework co-operation agreement was signed with Chile. The most significant bilateral developments were in relations with Mexico, where a new co-operation agreement was signed in December as the prelude to far-reaching negotiations on a free trade agreement. Whilst it was conceived as a strategic move in competition with the United States in particular, the mandate for this set of negotiations was complex to say the least, since it dealt at one level with a 'standard' co-operation agreement, at another with free trade negotiations, and in the latter context with trade in both goods and services. The Mexican government was keen to stress that the eventual package should be agreed as a whole or not at all, so this may be an extended story.

The United States, Japan and Other Industrial Countries

In 1995, the United States and the EU agreed the New Transatlantic Agenda and its associated Action Plan. Alongside this there had also been the development of a Transatlantic Business Dialogue (TABD), which focused on the evolution of co-operation in such areas as mutual recognition and product standards. During 1997 there were important developments at both of these levels which affected EU–US relations. Two EU–US summits were held, the first in the Hague during May, the second in Washington D.C. during December. At the first, the centrepiece of institutional development was the signing of an extensive Mutual Recognition Agreement, which had been the subject of intense negotiations during the first half of the year. This agreement covers conformity assessment practices in pharmaceutical products, information technology equipment, telecommunications, medical equipment and pleasure craft, and is estimated to save the sectors at least $200m per year once in operation. Under-Secretary of State Stuart Eizenstat suggested at the time that 'this is the first down-payment on plans to create a new transatlantic marketplace', and plans were made to follow it up with negotiations on biotechnology, electronic commerce and intellectual property. Unfortunately, by the end of the year implementation had proved to be slower than expected, and one or two of the additional areas – in particular, electronic commerce – were causing tensions.

EU–US relations are also central to the development of the broader global institutional framework, and this was demonstrated in concentrated fashion during 1997. The three major sectoral agreements under the WTO reached during the year – on IT trade, on telecommunications and on financial services – all depended heavily on the ability of the US and the EU to agree, and were all shaped by the reluctance of the United States to reach agreements not in the interests of US industries. The EU and the US also played a central role in the so-called Quad group, alongside Canada and Japan, which met in Toronto in late April and early May, and in the Group of Seven industrial countries whose summit was held in Denver during June. As the year passed, two particular developments began to shape EU–US relations in new ways. First, Americans began to recognize some of the implications of EMU for the dollar and for international monetary relations; and second, the financial turmoil in Asia led at least some Americans to place greater emphasis on relations with the EU as the most reliable and wide-ranging of their international partnerships. Whilst this was particularly true in the area of economic relations, linkages to such issues as the Middle East conflict and NATO enlargement were also made by many commentators.

It was in the area of political – or politicized – co-operation, nonetheless, that some of the sharpest EU–US disagreements were to be found. During 1996, there had been often intense conflict over the application of the so-called Helms-

Burton Act (properly called the Cuba Liberty and Solidarity Act) which threatened extra-territorial sanctions against those 'trafficking' in assets expropriated from Cuban citizens by the Castro regime. The early part of 1997 saw continuing efforts to defuse this tension, under the pressure both of US threats and of an EU challenge in the context of the WTO. As the EU moved towards an overt confrontation over what they saw as a trade restraint and the Americans as a matter of national security, negotiations during April produced a 'truce'. This interim agreement allowed the US President to continue waiving parts of the Act, whilst the EU undertook to 'discourage' certain types of investment in Cuba. Nothing was settled, however, and the end of the year saw renewed threats of confrontation in the WTO.

Meanwhile, a new 'time-bomb' had appeared in the shape of the 'D'Amato Act' (the Iran-Libya Sanctions Act), which threatened to punish EU companies investing in those countries. Since many EU petroleum companies envisaged precisely such investments, the potential for conflict was clear. In particular, the French Total company and Royal-Dutch Shell committed themselves to investments in Iran during the year, but US retaliation was not immediate, perhaps because of the actions taken by the EU members in the wake of the *Mykonos* case (see above). Indeed, by the end of the year opinion in the USA itself was shifting, albeit glacially, towards a more relaxed view and a feeling that American companies should have some of the investment action. A further irritant was added during the year by the emergence of state-level legislation in the United States, for example the Massachusetts Act which forbade purchases from firms doing business with Burma; here, although the EU might protest, even the US government had an unsure leverage on the state authorities.

The political tensions caused by extra-territoriality went alongside a number of more or less sharp trade disputes of a more conventional type. The biggest single issue was the US complaint to the WTO about the EU banana regime – a long-running saga which saw a WTO panel ruling in favour of the US during the spring, an abortive appeal by the EU, and eventual acceptance of the need to amend the regime (to the dismay of Caribbean banana producers). A cluster of disputes concerned food production and especially food hygiene: the first was caused by EU regulations about the treatment of meat products which threatened to de-recognize US practices (a sharp contrast to the spirit of mutual recognition evident elsewhere!) and which led the US to threaten both a virtual ban on imports of EU products and a reference to the WTO. The second dispute, again long-standing, concerned EU regulations aimed against artificial growth hormones for beef. Here, the US reference to the WTO produced a finding against the EU and another failed EU appeal, although the Union was granted time to produce more scientific evidence. Finally, the EU's regulations designed to prevent the spread of 'mad cow disease' (BSE) caused anger in the US when it was realized that they might prevent exports to the EU of pharmaceutical and other products containing (however indirectly) 'specified risk materials'. In other trade disputes, the US continued to resist agreement with the EU on the use of leghold traps, raising the possibility of a ban on imports of US furs from the beginning of 1998 (again, the dispute was provisionally settled at the end of the year), and the EU (some Member States with the support of the European Parliament) continued to have reservations about the import of genetically altered plants and seeds.

Perhaps the sharpest EU–US trade exchanges were reserved for areas involving competition policy. Three cases were central to the year. In the first, the Commission became concerned about the proposed merger between British Telecom and MCI, the US telecommunications company. The case rather faded away when the merger itself collapsed later in the year. More enduring were two other cases: the proposed British Airways–American Airlines alliance, and the merger of the Boeing and McDonnell-Douglas aerospace companies. The BA/AA issue raised not only issues of competition on the North Atlantic routes; it also linked with the whole question of 'open skies agreements' between EU Member States and the US (on which the Commission wished to assert its competence) and with the question of 'slot trading' at airports, on which Commission opinion was divided. As a result, it engaged the intense efforts of airlines and governments on both sides of the Atlantic, and the outcome was undetermined by the end of the year after Commission threats of fines and compulsory yielding of slots at Heathrow airport. The Boeing/McDonnell-Douglas merger was a unique case in many respects, since neither company had extensive operations in the EU, but the Commission could justifiably claim that the merger would significantly affect the European market. On this basis, and after acrimonious exchanges as the Commission threatened sanctions, the issue was eventually settled when Boeing agreed to rescind exclusive long-term supply contracts with several airlines (opinion is divided as to whether this 'concession' makes any real difference). Other competition policy issues began to appear at the end of the year, the most interesting being the prospect of EU–US tensions over regulation of the Internet and of 'electronic commerce', and the possible implications of EU efforts to restructure defence industries.

In contrast to these dramas, EU relations with Canada and Australia presented a serene aspect. The dispute with Canada about leghold traps was settled early in the year (thus changing the context for negotiations with the USA), and tensions over the Canadian film distribution system did not lead to open conflict. The EU–Canada variant of the transatlantic agenda proceeded smoothly, and there was a considerable meeting of minds over the implications of Helms-Burton, D'Amato and other US challenges. The EU–Canada summits, one at Denver alongside the G-7 summit and the other in Ottawa during December, revealed a stable relationship. EU relations with Australia were buttressed in June by a Joint Declaration which, whilst it fell short of the 'transatlantic declaration', did create a new impetus for joint action.

EU–Japan relations moved in short steps during the year, with a summit in June the centrepiece of formal contacts. There were a number of relatively limited disputes – over pigmeat imports from the EU, over Japanese port practices – whilst in the latter part of the year there was some renewed attention to the growth of Japanese automobile imports. The existing monitoring arrangements for car imports are due to end in 1999, and Japanese companies are set to increase their share of the EU market, either through manufacture in the EU or through increased imports. Imports themselves surged during 1997, partly as a result of the Asian economic crises, but the informal quotas were not breached since planned imports had been well below the ceiling. EU–Japan contacts betrayed a greater focus than before on political co-operation, and this represents a Union priority for the future; but it cannot be pretended that Japan was at the epicentre of EU concerns during 1997, even compared with other parts of Asia.

© Blackwell Publishers Ltd 1998

Legal Developments

NIGEL FOSTER

Cardiff Law School, University of Wales

I. Introduction: Business as Usual

With a change of authorship of this section, it would do no harm to restate its aims. The main focus will continue to be a review of the judicial developments of the European Court of Justice (ECJ) and the Court of First Instance (CFI). It cannot take the form of a comprehensive review of all movements of law or a close scrutiny of how specific provisions are interpreted and applied, but a selective review of cases which are regarded as adding to the body of Community law. Some of these cases will merely be continuations of past developments but by inclusion will confirm a trend or particular line of development. The structure previously developed by my predecessor, Jo Shaw, will be retained, for the sake both of continuity and ease of comparison with past reviews. However, as in the past, some change is inevitable, where, e.g., there are no cases of mention in particular sections or where there are developments in areas that have not previously appeared. Consolidation or re-casting of sub-sections may also be considered appropriate.

In line with a previous forecast,[1] there appears to have been a reduction in the time taken for the ECJ to hear cases, down to 12 months for 177 references[2]

---

[1] *Annual Review,* 1996, p. 96.

[2] See, for example, Case C-307/96, Proceedings 24/97, p. 1, or Case C-5/97 Proceedings 35/97 p. 14.

and 5 months[3] for direct actions, although the average necessarily remains higher. The reduction is at the expense of cases delayed before the CFI, many as a result of the transfer of cases from the ECJ to the CFI.[4] Appeals from the CFI, however, may start pushing times back up.

Despite Amsterdam, there has been no radical shake up of the Court or its *modus operandi* as some feared might happen as a result of the IGC. Indeed, all the institutions were affected less than anticipated as the Member States failed to reach agreement on many of the institutional reforms considered necessary. Apart, therefore, from the Amsterdam changes proposed for the ECJ, which will extend and clarify its role in relation to the safeguarding of fundamental rights, action by the Union on asylum and immigration, and co-operation in police and judicial matters, it remains business as usual.

II. The Development of the Competence and the Powers of the EU and its Institutions

External Competence

After a few years in which the ECJ has been active with cases dealing with the rights and duties of the EU / EC or single institutions or Member States with the outside world, 1997 was very quiet. Only *Opel* v *Austria* [5] warrants mention. Unlawful retroactive action by the Council was held by the CFI to breach the public international law principle of good faith, held as binding on the Community. Good faith was regarded as being an element of the principle of legitimate expectations, a recognized EC general principle. The case concerned the granting of state aid by Austria to Opel to manufacture gearboxes, most of which would be exported to the EC under the Free Trade Agreement (FTA) between Austria and the EEC.[6] The Commission, however, regarded the grant as incompatible with the FTA and prepared a regulation withdrawing tariff concessions and imposing a 4.9 per cent import duty on Opel. This was adopted by the Council on 20 December 1993 in the full knowledge that on 1 January 1994 the European Economic Area (EEA) would come into force which provided for a prohibition of import duties between Austria and the EEC. To the CFI, that alone was sufficient to establish a breach of legitimate expectation and legal certainty in that EC law had created two conflicting legal regimes in respect of the import of gearboxes. However, that was not all. The CFI was satisfied from the facts that

---

[3] See, e.g., Case C-43/97, Proceedings 22/97, p. 40.
[4] For example, the case referred to the CFI now with designation T-159/94 first brought to the ECJ September 1991, heard on 18/12/1997, Proceedings 35/97, p. 44. On average, 3.5 years is not uncommon for the transfer cases but the CFI has ruled in 12 months in an Art. 173 action, Cases T-121/96 and 151/96, Proceedings 23/97, p. 27.
[5] Case T-115/94, *Opel* v. *Austria*, [1997] ECR II-39, [1997] 1 CMLR 733, [1997] 1 CMLR 347.
[6] *OJ* English Special Edition 1972, p. 3.

the Council had deliberately backdated the issue of the OJ in which the regulation was published from 11 January 1994 to 31 December 1993, thus again infringing legal certainty. Under the circumstances, the CFI had no hesitation in annulling the regulation. It was a blatant misuse of power.

Internal Competence

In March, the ECJ ruled on a French Art. 173 action[7] to annul a Commission communication which it was argued imposed new obligations on the Member States. The Member States, as privileged applicants under Art. 173, are granted automatic *locus standi*. However, this case concentrates initially on whether the communication challenged, which was published in the *OJ* 'C' series and was not a legislative act envisaged by Art. 189, was a measure which could be the subject of an Art. 173 annulment action. In keeping with established case law,[8] the ECJ stated that an action for annulment is available in the case of all measures adopted by the institutions, whatever their nature or form, which are intended to have legal effects. The ECJ considered the communication had 'imperative wording' the content of which was the same as a withdrawn draft directive dealing with the same matter, which had not received approval. It was an attempt to bring in via the back door rules refused entry at the front door. Hence, it held that the communication constituted an act intended to have legal effects on its own which imposed new obligations on the Member States which were neither inherent in the Treaty nor expressly granted by the Commission. The Act was annulled because the Commission had no competence to enact it. It is one of the few cases involving this substantive ground.[9]

Inter-institutional Relations

EP v. *Council*[10] is the latest case involving the prerogatives of the European Parliament (EP). An essential procedural requirement was infringed because the EP was not consulted a second time as it should have been under Art. 100c EC on a directive concerning EC visa requirements for nationals of third countries. An obligation to reconsult on essential text differences exists.[11] The legal position and right of the EP to have this upheld is not in doubt but one may start to question the sense in doing so. There was nothing substantive objected to by

[7] Case C-57/95, *French Republic* v. *Commission,* 20/3/97, [1997] ECR I-1627, [1997] CMLR 935.
[8] Case 22/70, *Commission* v. *Council* (Re: ERTA) [1971] ECR 363, [1971] CMLR 335. and Cases 8-11/66 Re: *Noorwijk's Cement Accord* [1967] ECR 75, [1967] CMLR 77.
[9] Case 9/56, *Meroni* v. *High Authority* [1957-8] ECR 133, Case C-327/91, *France* v. *Commission* [1994] ECR I-3641.
[10] Case C-392/95, *European Parliament* v. *Council of the European Union,* [1997] 3 CMLR 896.
[11] Following on from previous reconsultation cases, e.g. Case C-388/92, *EP* v. *Council* [1994] ECR I-2067, see *Annual Review 1994,* p.90, and Case C-303/94, *European Parliament* v. *Council* [1996] ECR I-2943, see *Annual Review,* 1996, p. 100.

the EP and, although annulled, the directive's effects were maintained whilst a new one was being adopted. A question might justifiably be raised whether the benefit of protecting every instance where the EP's prerogative may be injured outweighs the time and cost of all parties involved including the Court, and all courtesy of the European taxpayer. The principle is clearly established. The EP must regard it vital to allow no quarter, regardless of the cost.

III. Development of the Principles of Primary EC Law

In 1997, Art. 6 EC made an impression in three cases involving the requirement for non-nationals to pay deposits or costs securities into court, not similarly required of nationals.

In *Eckehard Pastoors*,[12] a deposit system levied by the Belgian authorities on non-residents wishing not to pay transport regulation breach fines immediately, was found to be indirect discrimination on the grounds of nationality, as it was liable to act more severely against non-nationals. Whilst in the case there was an objective justification to ensure enforcement of judgment, the amount demanded as deposit was found to be excessive and thus manifestly disproportionate and in breach of Art. 6 EC. In *Hayes* v. *Kronenberger*,[13] it was held that Art. 6 EC prohibited the statutory requirement[14] that security for judicial costs be required of Community nationals in proceedings connected with rights deriving from the Community legal order where the same conditions were not imposed equally on its own nationals having neither assets nor residence in that country. The final case[15] concerns the requirement of the Austrian Civil Code that foreigners who are plaintiffs must lodge a security before Austrian courts, unless resident in Austria or where the ruling is enforceable abroad. No similar requirement was imposed on Austrians living abroad. The ECJ held that, in principle, such procedural rules are matters for the state concerned, but it has consistently held, as in the above cases, that such provisions may not discriminate contrary to Art. 6 EC. These cases demonstrate with others that national procedural rules are required to take cognizance and bow to Community law.[16]

Articles 30–36 (non-tariff barriers to the free movement of goods).

This chapter of the Treaty continues to see cases reaching the ECJ which consist of factual and legal considerations seen countless times before and whose answer

[12] Case C-29/95, *Eckehard Pastoors et al.* v. *Belgian State* [1997] ECR I-285, [1997] CMLR 457.
[13] Case C-323/95, *D. Hayes and J. Hayes* v. *Kronenberger GmbH*, 20/3/97 [1997] ECR I-1711, confirming Case C-20/92, *Hubbard* [1993] ECR I-3777.
[14] §110 of the German Code of Civil Procedure.
[15] Case C-122/96, *Stephen Saldanha and MTS Securities Corporation* v. *Hiross Holding AG*, 2/10/97, Proceedings, 25/97, p. 17.
[16] See further comments in the concluding section to this review.

is obvious. As such, the cases bear witness to the persistence of the authorities of Member States in applying national legal measures to imported goods contrary to Art. 30. This particular case[17] concerns the import of frozen bread which contravened national statutory limits by having a moisture content exceeding 34 per cent, an ash content of less than 1.40 per cent and containing bran. France was unable to demonstrate a threat to public health and it was easy to reach the conclusion that, the national law constituted a quantitative restriction contrary to Art. 30 EC and not saved by Art. 36. National courts were reminded they should disapply on their own initiative, conflicting provisions of national law.

Case law in the *Cassis de Dijon–Keck* line continues to make its mark. The Austrian law prohibiting the offering of free gifts linked to the sale of goods was the basis for an Austrian publishers' suit[18] against a German magazine containing a prize crossword puzzle. The ECJ repeated its position established since *Keck*[19] that certain national rules would not breach Art. 30 unless imposing additional requirements. Austrian rules would constitute a hindrance to free movement if the content of the magazine had to be altered for the Austrian market. However, maintaining the diversity of the press was the legitimate public interest objective given by the authorities and accepted by the ECJ. It remains up to the national judge to determine whether the ban is proportionate, or whether less restrictive aims to reach the objective are available.

The perfume sector of the economy has generated a number of cases, many of which are concerned with the lawfulness of the various agreements they have developed to ensure that their products are distributed and sold in a manner they consider fitting the product. *Dior* v. *Evora* [20] involves perfume, the free movement of goods and the right to or not to exploit intellectual property. Art. 5 of the Trade Marks Directive[21] allows a proprietor to prevent third parties from using his or her trademark unless, in line with well-established case law and Art. 7 of the directive, the goods have been already been put into free circulation by that person or with their consent.[22] However, in situations where the proprietor considers the product is changed or impaired, further commercialization may be opposed. This case involves the sale of perfumes from 'chemists' shops'[23] which

---

[17] Case C-358/95, *Tommaso Morellato* v. *Unita Sanitaria Locale (USL) No. 11 di Pordenone* [1997] ECR I-1431.

[18] Case C-368/95, *Vereinigte Familiapress Zeitungsverlags- und vertriebs GmbH* v. *Heinrich Bauer Verlag,* [1997] 3 CMLR 1329.

[19] Case C-267/91, *Keck and Mithouard* [1993] ECR I-6097, [1995] 1 CMLR 101.

[20] Case C-337/95, *Parfums Christian Dior SA & Parfums Christian Dior BV* v. *Evora BV* [1998] 1 CMLR 737, but see also the IHT Case C-9/93 [1994] ECR I-2789 also concerned with exhaustion of trademarks in the *Annual Review 1994*, p.94.

[21] Directive 89/104, OJ 1989 L40/1.

[22] This is known as the 'exhaustion of right' and was considered also in the *Annual Review 1996*, pp. 100–01.

[23] Who had lawfully bought 'parallel imports' and their right to do so was not disputed in the case.

were not Dior appointed distributors. Dior objected to the advertising leaflets which carried pictures of the packages and bottles of certain Dior perfumes as not corresponding to the luxurious and prestigious image of the Dior marks and sought to prevent the further use of their trademarks. Firstly, the ECJ held that, once a product is lawfully put on the market, resellers have the right to use trademarks to further aid selling the product, unless within Art. 7(2) of the directive, damage is done to the reputation of the trademark. If the reseller advertises in a manner usual for such products this could not be opposed unless the proprietor could prove that the reseller's advertising seriously damages the reputation of the trademark. Whilst Art. 36 EC also allows for restrictions on the movement of goods to protect commercial property, the ECJ has consistently held that this does not override the exhaustion of rights doctrine.

Article 48 (free movement of workers)

With little movement in this area of law in 1997, an Art. 169 action, which does not normally generate significant developments in Community law, against Belgium,[24] serves to demonstrate how the continued lack of compliance by Member States still creates real barriers to the proper establishment of the fundamental freedoms. A Belgian rule providing for the automatic expulsion of Community national who had not found work after three months was held to be manifestly contrary to Art. 48 EC and the previous *Antonissen* ruling.[25] Furthermore, the documents issue delay, the limited duration residence permits and payment demanded in excess of that comparable for national identity cards, all breached Directive 68/360. So Belgium, despite being host to Community institutions and employing thousands of Community nationals, maintained these unlawful provisions.

Articles 52 and 59 (freedom of establishment and free movement of services)

Television broadcasting continues to give rise to cases in which the ECJ attempts to strike the correct balance between the free movement of persons and the effective regulation of broadcasting. In this context, Directive 89/552 has been subject to frequent investigation and interpretation.

Denuit[26] concerns the right of Member States to oppose the retransmission of programmes on its territory where they consider the programmes contravene Directive 89/552. The ECJ held that the directive determines that the state with jurisdiction over broadcasts is the state of establishment of the broadcaster. It is up to this state to monitor and be assured that the broadcasts are in conformity

---

[24] Case C-344/95 *Commission* v. *Belgium*, [1998] 2 CMLR 187, [1997] ECR I-1035.
[25] Case C-292/89, *Antonissen* [1991] ECR I-745, [1991] 2 CMLR 373.
[26] Case C-14/96, *P. Denuit* [1997] 3 CMLR 943.

with national law and the provisions of the directive.[27] Other Member States have no right to oppose transmission but, if not satisfied, they retain the right to take an Art.170 action or request the Commission to take an Art.169 action. The *VT4* case[28] also considers jurisdiction over broadcasters. The ECJ confirmed that this is the state where the broadcaster is established even if no services are provided in that home state and the only transmissions are those broadcast abroad. Additionally, it was held that if the broadcaster is established with offices in more than one state, it is the state with the centre of its activities that determines its establishment and state of jurisdiction. In the *Swedish Consumer Ombudsman* cases,[29] also concerning broadcasting from companies established in the UK, an action to prevent advertising was held to be acceptable under Directive 89/552 providing it did not prevent the retransmission of the broadcasts. Whilst such a prohibition on advertising amounted to a restriction on the freedom to provide services, the ECJ held that in the absence of harmonizing rules, Art. 59 does not prevent Member States from taking measures against an advertiser provided the national courts are satisfied that the measures are necessary, proportionate and could not be met by less restrictive measures. However, the ECJ ruled that a further national provision which stated that adverts must not be designed to attract the attention of children under 12 would not be acceptable, as Directive 89/552 already provided the broadcasting state authorities with provisions to protect minors from television advertising.

Partly as a result of this and other case law, and partly the result of general complaints and dissatisfaction with the 'Television without Frontiers' directive above, an amending Directive 97/36 has been enacted. In particular it further addresses questions relating to advertising and the protection of minors.[30]

Articles 85, 86 and 90 (competition law)

In a quiet year on competition, there was one case[31] of somewhat historic interest. The ECJ was asked about the status of competition agreements which were concluded prior to Regulation 17 and notified to the Commission prior to the deadline of 1/11/1962. Normally such agreements would carry provisional validity until the Commission had either given positive clearance or had taken a negative decision holding them to be contrary to EC law. Many agreements, similar to this one on retail price maintenance for books, have continued in legal

---

[27] This is the principle of equivalence for broadcasting. If acceptable in state A it must be accepted in all other states.

[28] Case C-56/96, *VT4 Ltd* v. *Vlaamse Gemeenschap* [1997] 3 CMLR 1225.

[29] Cases C34-36/95, *Konsumentomombudsmannen (KO)* v. *De Agostini (Svenska) Förlag AB & TV-Shop I Sverige AB* [1998] 1 CMLR 32.

[30] *OJ*, 1997 L220/60.

[31] Case C-39/96, *Koninklijke Vereeniging ter Bevordering van de Belangen des Boekhandels* v. *Free Record Shop BV, Free Record Shop Holding NV* [1997] ECR I-2303, [1997] 5 CMLR 521.

limbo ever since. The Commission is simply unable to investigate all of them and many are left without interference. The agreement in question, however, had been challenged as contrary to Art. 85 EC by a shop selling below the imposed retail price. Having lain dormant for so long, questions about the continued validity were raised by the national court. The ECJ held that until the Commission decides one way or the other the agreement remains provisionally valid even if it has been amended, but only insofar as the amendments render the agreement less restrictive. More restrictive amendments would end the validity unless these were severable from the original agreement.

Article 119 and related directives (equal pay and sex equality)

This area sees a steady flow of cases, some confirming positions previously reached, particularly in respect of part-time workers. For example, in *Gerster*, [32] the method by which the length of service of part-time workers was calculated as worth pro-rata only two-thirds that of full-time workers for the purposes of determining promotion breached Directive 76/207.

The *Barber* fall-out continues. This intensely complex area of law continues to provide cases to test concentration and understanding. When is a pension or retirement or redundancy benefit to be regarded as pay or part of the social security policy of the state and thus outside the prohibition of discrimination based on sex of Art.119? According to the ECJ in the *Evrenopoulos* case,[33] the clear criterion is that a benefit is pay if it is paid by reason of an employment relationship. Pensions, even if organized by the state, can also be pay if limited to certain categories of workers, directly related to length of service or calculated by reference to the last salary, and a survivor's pension also falls within Art. 119. Thus a scheme which subjected widowers' awards to conditions not imposed on widows was held to breach Art.119. In *Magorrian and Cunningham*,[34] the court reaffirmed[35] that the temporal limitation to the ruling in *Barber* and Protocol No. 2 to the TEU that parties are precluded from relying on the DE of Art. 119 in claims for equal treatment in pensions schemes, does not apply to conditions relating to access to such schemes. Further, in this case, limitation rules which impose a two-year period running backward from the date of claim so as to deprive the applicants of any rights in Community law does not conform with Community law. Hence, the limitation would not apply to a claim to receive

[32] Case C-1/95, *Hellen Gerster* v. *Freistaat Bayern* [1998] 1 CMLR 303.
[33] Case C-147/95, *Dimossa Epicheirissi Ilektrismou (DEI)* v. *Efthimios Evrenopoulos* [1997] ECR I-2057. [1997] 2 CMLR 407.
[34] Case C-246/96, *Magorrian and Cunningham* v. *Eastern Health and Social Services Board and Department of Health and Social Services*, 11/12/1997 Proceedings 34/97, p.18.
[35] C-57/93, *Vroege* v. *NCIV Instituut* [1994] ECR I-4541, [1995] 1 CMLR 881; Case C-128/93, *Fisscher* v. *Voorhuis hengelo BV* [1994] ECR I-4583 and previously Case 170/84, *Bilka Kaufhaus* v. *Karin Weber Van Harz* [1980] ECR 1607, [1986] 2 CMLR 701.

additional benefits from a scheme, the access to which was denied to part-timers, most of whom were women.

Other notable cases include *Draehmpaehl* v. *Urania*.[36] A job was advertised only to females, contrary to both Community and German law. In the consequent claim for damages due to discrimination, damages were limited to a maximum of three months' salary but dependent on proving fault on the part of the employer. If more than one plaintiff sued, the aggregate compensation payable was limited to six months' salary.[37] The ECJ, confirming its previous case law,[38] held that liability to compensate cannot be made dependent on fault, compensation itself must guarantee real and effective judicial protection, have a real deterrent effect on the employer and be adequate in relation to the damage suffered. Limits such as three months' salary are acceptable where the employer can prove that, notwithstanding the discrimination, a better qualified person was appointed and the complainant would not have been appointed in any event. However, an aggregate award ceiling regardless of the number discriminated against is not acceptable under Directive 76/207 as it might have the effect of dissuading applicants so harmed from asserting their rights. The problem with this latter aspect is that not every one could be appointed to the position, only one person. What if there were 50 male applicants who were discriminated against? Unfortunately, this aspect was not considered in the case itself. A further novelty in the case is that there was no mention of Art. 5 EC which begs the question as to whether it was decided on the basis of the directive alone and thus suggests the subtle introduction of horizontal direct effects or that it does follow *von Colson*,[39] but the ECJ simply failed to make it clear within the text of the judgment. Subsequent cases may clarify these points.[40]

In *Larsson* v. *Dansk Handel & Service*,[41] the opportunity to reconsider the position of dismissals for absences resulting from illnesses originating in pregnancy was given to the ECJ. The Court, however, confirmed its previous position in *Hertz*.[42] Directive 76/207 does not prevent such dismissals where the illness arose and continued during pregnancy and persisted afterwards. The directive only prevents dismissal during maternity leave.[43]

---

[36] Case 180/95, *Nils Draehmpaehl* v. *Urania Immobilienservice OHG*, 22/4/1997 [1997] ECR I-2195, [1997] 3 CMLR 1107.

[37] §61b ArbGG (Labour Courts Statute).

[38] Case C-177/88, *Dekker* v. *Stichting VJV Centrym* [1988] ECR I-3941.

[39] Case 14/83, *Von Colson & Kamann* [1984] ECR 1891, [1986] 2 CMLR 430.

[40] A full case comment can be found by E. Steindorff in 34 CMLR 1997, pp. 1259–77.

[41] Case C-400/95, *Handels- og Kontorfunktionaererernes Forbund I Danmark, acting for Helle Larsson* v. *Dansk Handel & Service, acting for Fotex Supermarked A/S* [1997] 2 CMLR 915.

[42] Case C-179/88, *Handels-og Kontorfunktionaererernes Forbund i Danmark (Hertz)* v. *(Aldi) Dansk Arbejdsgiverforening* [1991] ECR 1-3979.

[43] At the time of the facts of this case, Directive 92/85 (the Pregnancy and Maternity Directive) had not been adopted but arguably would not have helped as this also only protects dismissal for the beginning of pregnancy to the end of maternity leave. Absences due to illnesses thereafter are treated in the same way as any other any and constitute grounds for dismissal according to provisions of national law.

Positive discrimination was considered in *Marschall*,[44] involving an application for a teaching post by a qualified man, which was rejected by the local authority in accordance with a law providing that women should be given priority in the event of equal suitability. Previously,[45] the ECJ had ruled that a national rule discriminated on the grounds of sex which provided that, where equally qualified men and women were candidates for a position with fewer women, women are automatically to be given priority. Directive 76/207 Art. 2(4) provides that the prohibition of discrimination on the grounds of sex is without prejudice to measures to promote equal opportunity by removing, for example, inequalities in the area of promotion. In the present case the existence of a 'saving clause', providing that if a particular male candidate has grounds which tilt the balance in his favour, women are not to be given priority, enabled the ECJ to reach the conclusion that the provision was one which could fall within the scope of Art. 2(4) of the directive and did not offend the prohibition of discrimination. There were, however, two safety mechanisms which should be set up; the first to avoid discrimination against men and the second to stop the pendulum from swinging back against women. The ECJ considered such clauses are acceptable provided the candidates are objectively assessed to determine whether there are any factors tilting the balance in favour of a male candidate but that such criteria employed do not themselves discriminate against women. Somewhat convoluted but it gets there.

In *Sutton*,[46] it was held that, in contrast to the position taken in *Marshall II*,[47] Art. 6 of Directive 79/7, which is almost identical to Art. 6 of Directive 76/207, does not oblige the Member State to pay interest on the payment of benefits when the delay was the result of unlawful discrimination. The reason given was that the payments are made under social security benefits and not compensation for damage sustained. The ECJ did hold however that, post-*Francovich*, a Member State must make good any loss to an individual that results from a breach of Community law, but that it was up to the national courts to decide that question. In other words, this would encourage more litigation to determine the question. To assist future litigants in cases involving sex discrimination, a new directive has been adopted on 17/12/1997[48] with a three-year implementation period, on the burden of proof in cases of discrimination. The directive is largely a consolidation of case law and may serve as an example of the evolving maturity

[44] Case C-409/95, *Hellmut Marschall* v. *Land Nordrhein-Westfalen* [1998] 1 CMLR 547.
[45] Case C-450/93, *Kalanke* v. *Freie Hansestadt Bremen* [1995] ECR I-3051, [1996] 1 CMLR 175, see also *Annual Review 1995*, pp. 94–5.
[46] Case C-66/95, *The Queen* v. *Secretary of State for Social Security, ex parte: Eunice Sutton* [1997] ECR I-2163, [1997] 2 CMLR 382.
[47] C-271/91, *Marshall* v. *Southampton and South West Hampshire Area Health Authority* [1993] ECR I-4367, [1993] 3 CMLR 293.
[48] A similar proposal for such a directive was vetoed in 1989 by a minister from the Thatcher Government.

of the Community legal system by the codification of procedural law from case law.

IV. Enforcement and Effectiveness of Community Law

Individual Enforcement

The waves emanating from the *Francovich*[49] ruling spread wider, and in the wake of 10 July 1997 is a trio of cases from Italy also involving claims by redundant employees against the Italian authorities for failure to implement Directive 80/987. *Francovich* established that a Member State can be held liable in damages for the loss it has caused to individuals by its breach of a Community law obligation.[50] *Bonifaci*[51] considered the particular question of conditions governing the extent of compensation. The Italian legislation established after the *Francovich* ruling only permitted back-dated claims 12 months prior to implementation on 5 April 1985 and not back to 20 October 1983, when the directive was to have come into force, thus excluding the particular claims by *Bonifaci* and others. The ECJ held there should be full retroactive application of the measures implementing the directive. Furthermore, if the loss sustained included supplementary loss by reason of the delayed implementation and inability to claim, this must also be compensated.[52]

Palmisani[53] questioned whether a limitation period of one year from the date of the belated transposition of the directive was compatible with Community law. The ECJ repeated the criteria for establishing liability from the rapidly increasing line of cases under *Francovich* and stated that time limits under national law must not be less favourable than under comparable domestic claims and must not make it virtually impossible or excessively difficult to make a claim. In this case the ECJ thought the one-year limit could not be regarded as making it excessively difficult. The comparability with national rules could not be undertaken by the ECJ as it did not have the information to hand in the case and held that this must be left to the national court to determine. If the national court had supplied details on its limitation periods, which future courts would now be aware they could do, this suggests the ECJ would be willing to draw the appropriate conclusions to develop these quasi Community-national procedural rights.

[49] Case 6,9/90, *Francovich* v. *Italian State* [1991] ECR I-3633, [1993] 2 CMLR 66.
[50] In this respect, see also the *Sutton* case noted above and the previous developments noted in *Annual Review 1996*, pp. 105–6.
[51] Cases C-94/95 and C-95/95, *Danila Bonifaci et al.* v. *Instituto Nazionale della Previdenza Sociale (INPS)*, [1998] 1 CMLR 257.
[52] The case of *Maso* was decided similarly. Case C-373/95, *Federica Maso et al.* v. *INPS* [1997] 3 CMLR 1356.
[53] Case C-261/95, *Rosalba Palmisani* v. *INPS* [1997] 5 CMLR 364.

The case of *AssiDomän*[54] is a successful Art.173 annulment action which also considers the obligation imposed by Art.176 EC. Companies fined by the Commission in the *Wood Pulp* decision but who had not contested this and had paid their fines instead, sought to have the Commission reconsider their fines when the ECJ annulled, in part, the original decision.[55] The Commission rejected their application by letter on the grounds that it was not obliged or entitled to refund the fines. The applicants pleaded that the Commission had breached Art.176, requiring the Commission to take the necessary measures to comply with the previous judgment. Although this was held by the CFI not to extend automatically to circumstances beyond the immediate judgment, it should apply in the interests of good administration in this case and the Commission should have reviewed its previous decision insofar as it related to the applicants. The CFI held that nothing prevented repayment, instead an obligation to review arose under the general principles of legality and good administration. The Commission letter stating it could not review the fines was held to be a decision containing an error in law and was consequently annulled.

1997 saw some interesting cases arising from the Art.177 preliminary ruling procedure whereby national courts refer a question to the ECJ for guidance on the interpretation or validity of EC law. The first two cases consider the reference procedure. In *Dorsch*,[56] the ECJ returned to an old question in Community law as to what constitutes a court for the purposes of Art.177 and which questions could be referred. The case is instructive as the ECJ summarized guideline questions for national courts to pose. These are: whether the body is established by law, whether it is permanent, whether its procedure is *inter partes*, whether it applies rules of law and whether it is independent. The body in the case was the Federal Public Procurement Awards Supervisory Board (FPPASB). The ECJ held that the FPPASB satisfied these criteria despite the contrary opinion of the Advocate General. In *Krüger*,[57] the ECJ confirmed[58] the circumstances by which a national court can order the suspension of national law based on Community law. There must be serious doubt as to the validity of the Community Act and, if not already before the ECJ, a reference must be made. The national court must consider the matter to be urgent and suspension be considered necessary to avoid serious and irreparable damage being caused, but it must take

---

[54] Case T-227/95, *AssiDomän Kraft Products AB et al.* v. *Commission,* 10/7/97, Proceedings 21/97, p.28, which could also have been considered under the individual rights section below.
[55] Cases C-89, 104, 114, 116-7, 125-129/85 *Ahlström Osakeyhtiö et al.* v. *Commission* [1993] ECR I-1307, [1994] 4 CMLR 407.
[56] Case C-54/96, *Dorsch Consult Ingenieurgesellschaft mbH* v. *Bundesbaugesellschaft Berlin mbH,* 17/9/97 Proceedings 23/97, p.9.
[57] Case C-334/95, *Krüger GmbH & Co. KG* v. *Hauptzollamt Hamburg-Jonas* [1998] 1 CMLR 520.
[58] Cases C-143/88 and C-92/89, *Zuckerfabrik Süderdithmarschen* and *Zuckerfabrik Soest,* and Case C-465/93, *Atlanta Fruchthandelsgesellschaft et al.* [1995] ECR I-3761, [1996] 1 CMLR 575, see *Annual Review 1995,* p. 97 and *Annual Review 1996,* p. 107.

account of the Community interest and the rulings on the CFI or ECJ on the question. In *Eurotunnel* v. *SeaFrance*,[59] Eurotunnel sought to challenge the right of a ferry operator to sell duty-free goods on board using the argument that the EC directive law which authorized tax-free sales was invalid, thus subsidizing transport costs unlawfully. Although the substantive issues were not proved, the case revives an interesting procedural question, whether individuals who had not commenced Art.173 annulment proceedings against the directive could do so before a national court using the Art.177 preliminary ruling procedure. In simple terms, the ECJ answered that an individual may challenge the provisions of a directive before a national court and need not challenge them via Art. 173. In its view, the ECJ is simply responding to a court which considers that a ruling on Community law is necessary for it to reach a judgment. The judgment complements previous case law[60] so that where of direct concern, Art.173 would seem to be appropriate, where not, Art.177 is acceptable. When not the specific subject of a Community legislative Act, it is rarely obvious that a Community Act is of direct concern to the applicant and only the CFI or ECJ can state if this is the case. A further rewidening of the use of Art.177 may help to clarify matters.

In *Leur-Bloem*,[61] concerning taxation, the Advocate General recommended the ECJ should decline jurisdiction over an entirely domestic situation. But in an unusual departure from the generally understood view of Art. 177, the ECJ considered an interpretation of national law was warranted because it was based entirely on EC law and in the Community interest to ensure the uniform application of EC law. The ECJ stressed that it was up to national courts to determine whether EC law is relevant and, if they considered it to be the case, the ECJ is obliged to give a ruling. Does it matter that EC law would apply differently to domestic situations provided it applies in the same way in a Community context throughout the EC?

Enforcement by the Commission

The Treaty on European Union (Maastricht) amended Art.171 EC so that continued breaches of Community law by Member States could be fined by the ECJ. A penalty calculation system has been established by the Commission[62] whereby it will state what penalty, if any, it considers appropriate. The basic penalty is fixed at 500 ECU per day times factors reflecting the gravity and duration of non-compliance and the financial situation of the Member State. During 1997, the first daily penalties were sought, ranging from 26,400 to

---

[59] Case C-408/95, *Eurotunnel et al.* v. *SeaFrance*, 1/11/1997, Proceedings 30/97 p. 7.
[60] Case C-188/92, *TWD Textilwerke Deggendorf GmbH* v. *Germany* [1994] ECR I-833, [1995] 2 CMLR 145, as noted in *Annual Review 1994*, p. 101.
[61] Case C-28/95, *A. Leur-Bloem* v. *Inspecteur der Belastingdienst/Ondernemingen Amsterdam 2*, [1998] 1 CMLR 157.
[62] Commission Memorandum, *OJ* 1997 C63/2.

264,000 ECU, in cases against Germany and Italy. Following notification the Member States complied, except in one action against Germany[63] for failure to transpose fully the surface water directives in which a fine of 158,400 ECU per day was requested. The penalty will apply from the date of judgment in the action and not from the date of original non-compliance. Hence Member States have a chance to minimize the penalty. A further Art.171 action was initiated against Greece.[64]

The Commission has taken an Art.169 action against *France*[65] under Art.5 in conjunction with Art.30 EC for a breach of the state's obligation caused by not taking action to ensure the free movement of goods when French farmers protested against agricultural products imported from other Member States.[66] Would the ECJ accept this argument? The ECJ held that Art.30 also applies where a Member State has failed to take action to remove obstacles to the free movement of goods, even though not caused directly by the state but which omission allowed others to hinder the free movement of goods. The facts accepted by the ECJ were that acts of violence, which had persisted for more than ten years, against products emanating from other Member States were clear obstacles to free movement. Despite numerous warnings from the Commission, the French Government did not eliminate this form of restriction. The ECJ recognized that in the areas of public order and internal security, the Member States have exclusive competence and this provides a margin of discretion in how they should act, but act they should, and it held that the action taken previously was manifestly inadequate to ensure freedom of intra-community trade.

Although the French state has already announced its responsibility for the loss caused, the ruling will nevertheless open the door further and certainly far more clearly for *Francovich*- type compensation claims against the French state in the national courts. Many claimants may well prefer actions for damages rather than the protracted and rarely successful administrative compensation procedures currently available. It might have been asked whether EC law is a suitable vehicle to resolve disputes of this nature but then again, it appears to have produced results otherwise not politically forthcoming.

---

[63] Case C-122/97, *Commission v. Germany,* Proceedings 12/97, p.19 based on Case C-58/89, *Commission v. Germany* [1991] ECR I-4983.
[64] Case C-387/97, Proceedings 33/97, p. 18.
[65] Case C-265/95, *Commission v. France,* 9/12/1997 Proceedings 34/97, p. 1.
[66] Not dissimilar to protests which have taken place in Britain in late 1997 and early 1998.

V. Protection of Individual Rights

Individual Rights of Redress against Community Institutions

Generally, 1997 has seen more successes by individuals in annulment and damages actions under Arts 173 and 215 although, in the damages cases, they centre on mistakes in the attempt to reduce milk overproduction.

Judicial Review (locus standi of the non-privileged applicants under Art. 173 EC)

The Art.173 action[67] by the *WWF* concerns the 1994 Commission decision on public access to Commission and Council documents[68] (transparency). This provides a code of conduct on the procedure by which access to official documents should be requested. The procedure was followed to request information on a Commission investigation of a project in Ireland which may have misused Community structural funds. The Commission rejected the requests for documents and WWF UK challenged this rejection, relying on Decision 94/90. The CFI held that, whilst the code of conduct was capable of conferring legal rights on third parties, exceptions existed to those rights on the grounds of the protection of the public interest involving security, international relations, monetary stability, court proceedings and investigations, provided the Commission demonstrates that these circumstances exist. The Commission has the discretion to refuse access to protect confidentiality also, but must strike a genuine balance. That discretion has been exercised, cannot simply be stated. In the case, which might have led to Art.169 proceedings, the Commission should have indicated at least the categories of documents which related to the possible proceedings. The CFI held the Commission had not given sufficient reasons in its decision not to release documents or stated which categories of documents related to which exception and had thus breached Art. 190, hence the refusal decision was annulled.[69]

Related Art. 173 and damages actions under Article 215 EC

The *Mulder* cases,[70] in which the claimants succeeded in getting regulations concerned with milk surpluses annulled and later in obtaining damages for losses

---

[67] Case T-105/95, *WWF UK* v. *Commission* [1997] ECR II-313, [1997] 2 CMLR 55. Transparency cases are also creating a trend, see *Annual Review 1996*, pp. 109–10.
[68] Decision 94/90 of 8 February 1994 (*OJ* 1994 L46/1) as amended by Decision 96/567 (*OJ* 1996 L247/4).
[69] The Amsterdam Treaty amends the TEU to provide a right subject to similar conditions outlined above but yet to be finalized by each institution for citizens to obtain access to Community documents. See proposed Art. 191a.
[70] Case 120/86, *Mulder* v. *Minister van Landbouw en Visserij* [1988] ECR 2321 and Cases C-104/89 and 37/90, *Mulder et al.* v. *Council and Commission* [1992] ECR I-3061.

sustained have been followed now by a number of cases. Whilst none of these makes for exciting reading, they are reviewed mainly because they have further increased the success rate under Art. 215, though admittedly from a very low base.

In *Connaught*[71] and *Saint and Murray*[72] applications for annulment of the regulation governing compensation (2187/93) were found not to be admissible but provide the necessary background information to understand the Art. 215 actions. In 1977, regulations were enacted which provided a premium for milk producers willing not to produce milk for five years or instead to convert their herds. Further measures to penalize overproduction in 1984 were Regulations (857/84 and 1371/84) which introduced a levy on those producing more than their reference quantity which itself was determined by a previous reference year. The problem was that the Council had failed to take into account those who had agreed not to produce but who wished to re-enter production after the five-year period. This situation led to the original *Mulder* case and the successful application for the annulment of the 1984 regulations and subsequently damages. In view of large numbers of potentially successful claimants, the Council and Commission published a communication and then a Regulation (2187/93) to govern the compensation claims. The present applicants objected to Arts 8 and 14 of the regulation, which introduced a five-year time bar and a condition that, if accepting compensation, all other claims arising from these facts be relinquished. The CFI held that the regulation did not remove their right to pursue damages under Art. 215, but constituted an offer as an alternative to judicial resolution so that compensation could be achieved without bringing an action. It was a measure having no legal effect for the producers and thus not open to challenge for annulment.

Actions for damages were successful, as shown by two cases: *Saint and Murray*, and *Hartmann*.[73] The successful *Mulder II* claim for damages acted, if not as a legal precedent, certainly as a factual precedent for the Court to establish liability without argument on the part of the institutions. The contentious issues remaining in these cases related to the determination and limitation of the period for which compensation was payable. The CFI held that, under the limitation period, time ran from the date when they were refused reference quantities, thus either from the date of entry of the 1984 Regulation or, if later, following expiry of the non-marketing period. However, Art. 43 of the statute of the Court of Justice imposes a time bar for the backdating of claims to five years prior to the cut-off date. That was the Commission communication in August 1992, but in

---

[71] Case T-541/93, *Connaughton et al.* v. *Council* [1997] ECR II-549, [1997] 2 CMLR 553.
[72] Case T-554/93, *Saint & Murray* v. *Council*, 16/4/1997 [1997] ECR II-563, [1997] 2 CMLR 327.
[73] Case T-20/94, *Hartmann* v. *Council*, 16/4/1997 [1997] ECR II-595. Further cases seeking damages include Cases T-195/94 and T-202/94, *Quiller and Heusmann* v. *Council*, and Commission 9/12/1997, Proceedings, 34/97, p. 22, the particularly individual details of which will not however, be rehearsed here.

Saint and Murray the real event putting an end to the damage was when the correcting Regulation 764/89 entered into force in March 1989, thus limiting their period to 18 months. In *Hartmann* similar arguments reduced the period to 22 months. Given the degree of error on the part of the Council and the complexity of the Community legal regime and especially limitation period rules, the applicants can feel justifiably aggrieved. Understandably, the CFI held that the Art. 215 actions extinguished any claims under the compensation Regulation 2187/93.

State Aid Procedures

Rheinland Pfalz v. *Alcan Deutschland*[74] concerns national procedural rights of legitimate expectations and legal certainty which acted in support of resisting a claim for the repayment of state aid. According to the national court, legal certainty was breached when the one-year period in which recovery could take place under national law was exceeded by the final decision of the Commission. Legitimate expectation would then normally prevent a company having to return aid even if granted unlawfully. However, according to the ECJ, they could not apply where the grant of aid was unlawful according to Community law. Any discretion in national law is absent when the national authorities are merely acting as agents of the Commission. The Community interest is that aid granted unlawfully is recovered. The ECJ considered that any question of a breach of good faith by the authorities was a question of national law to be left to the national courts to decide. This serves as a further example of the ECJ being engaged with national procedural rules.

And finally, in a case involving mineral water,[75] it was held by the ECJ that in order to be classified as mineral water under Community law, it need not have to possess properties favourable to health.[76] So now you know!

VI. Overall Evaluation and Conclusion

1997 has seen a consolidation and marginal expansion or explanation of positions previously reached in a number of areas including free movement of goods, free movement of persons and particularly in equal treatment. An increasing trend[77] is the number of cases where national procedural law has been subjected to the scrutiny of the ECJ or CFI. Where a Community law right is involved, national procedural law must not deprive a litigant of their rights under

---

[74] Case C-24/95, *Rheinland Pfalz* v. *Alcan Deutschland* [1997] ECR I-1591, [1997] 2 CMLR 1034.
[75] Case C-17/96, *Badische Erfrischungs-Getränke GmbH & Co, KG* v. *Land Baden-Württemburg* [1998] 1 CMLR 341.
[76] Which were the requirements in Germany.
[77] Also observed previously in the *Annual Review 1995*, p. 96.

Community law and Community nationals should be treated no less favourably than nationals, so that the general principle of Art. 6 is not breached. See for examples the cases above: *Eckehard Pastoors, Hayes* v. *Kronenberger, Stephen Saldanha* and *MTS Securities Corporation, Magorrian and Cunningham* and *Rheinland Pfalz* v. *Alcan Deutschland.* If national procedural law is the legitimate target of EC law scrutiny, so as not to undermine rights anchored in EC law, then logic would suggest that procedural rules in different Member States must be harmonized so that the same rules apply throughout the EC. With the expansion of the *Francovich* actions, the ECJ appears to be embarked on a twin approach to the enforcement of Community law.

References

Cardiff University of Wales European Access: http://www.cf.ac.uk/uwcc/liby/edc/euracc/

Employment and social policy: http://europa.eu.int/en/eupol/socdim.html

Free movement of persons: http://europa.eu.int/en/agenda/frmov.html

On *Francovitch* http://www/unimaas.nl/~egmilieu/dossier/francovi.htm

The single market: http://europa.eu.int/en/agenda/sm/index.html

Social policy: http://www.cec.org.uk/pubs/facts/social/index.htm

Tritton, G. (1997) *Parallel Imports in the European Community* (London: Intellectual Property Institute).

Journal of Common Market Studies

Volume 36, Annual Review
September 1998

Developments in the Economies of the European Union

ANDREW SCOTT

University of Edinburgh

I. Overview

The economy of the European Union (EU) continued to recover strongly in the course of 1997. Against a background of a strong expansion in world output of 4.3 per cent, the European Union recorded a growth of GDP of 2.6 per cent in 1997, confirming that the economic recovery which had faltered in mid-1995 had recommenced, and had become more solidly based. The current positive output trend is expected to continue, with GDP growth for the EU as a whole of 3 per cent forecast for 1998, rising slightly to 3.1 per cent in 1999. Whilst this remains lower than GDP growth in the USA, which stood at 3.6 per cent in 1997, it is expected that EU growth will move ahead of marginally slowing US growth (to 2.6 per cent) during 1998. The rate of economic growth in the EU is above that in Japan, where increases in consumption taxes had the effect of slowing markedly the expansion in the economy. In 1997 GDP increased by only 1.3 per cent, although some strengthening in the economy is anticipated in 1998.[1]

The economic performance and the medium-term prospects of the EU economy are, therefore, reasonably buoyant in the context of both recent performance and international comparison. Moreover, with growth in the global economy forecast to remain robust, the medium-term economic prospects

---

[1] It is worth noting that the overall strength of the global economy is forecast despite the weakening of the Japanese and dynamic Asian economies following recent financial turbulence affecting those areas. This is accounted for by a stronger than expected performance in the NAFTA countries.

remain good. The current health of the global economy is founded upon three elements. First, indicators of underlying economic tensions are very weak. Inflation rates globally are low and there are no signs of this changing; fiscal imbalances are being corrected and this is lowering interest rates and keeping inflation expectations in check; and exchange rates between the main economies are fairly stable. This stability in underlying conditions not only raises investor and consumer confidence, it prevents significant swings in economic policy and the resultant disturbances and uncertainties within the private sector that sudden and large policy changes can generate. Second, the current economic recovery is not likely to be constrained by capacity shortage or other supply bottlenecks in the medium term. The effects of the cyclical downturn – particularly in the EU – were such as to generate substantial spare productive capacity with the result that there is considerable scope for non-inflationary expansion in real activity over the foreseeable future. Third, world trade, investment and so economic growth are being boosted by progressive economic reforms being undertaken in the transition countries of central and eastern Europe, a particularly important source of growth for the EU Member States both in terms of new markets and new investment opportunities. Together, these three factors point to the likelihood of an historically high sustainable rate of economic growth being achieved within the global economy. Indeed, international forecasting agencies are predicting trend rates of growth of world GDP of over 4 per cent annually into the early years of the new millennium.

The continued strength of global economic growth is a key element in the medium-term prospects for the EU economies in that export demand is forecast to remain the driving force of EU economic growth in the immediate future. During 1997, exports of goods and services from the EU increased by 7.9 per cent, compared to less that 5 per cent growth in 1996, and the growth in exports is expected to remain around this higher rate in both 1998 and 1999. Whilst partly reflecting the general strength of the global economy, EU exports in world markets have gained substantially from the considerable appreciation in the US dollar against EU currencies since mid-1995. At the same time, the broader-based nominal effective exchange rate for the EU countries (EUR15) has depreciated by almost 10 per cent in the course of 1996–97 (by 5.5 per cent in 1997 alone), enhancing further the competitiveness of EU exports in global markets.[2] These favourable (to EU exports) currency movements reflect the considerable easing of monetary conditions that has occurred in continental Europe since the currency turmoil in the spring of 1995, with short- and long-

---

[2] For the principal EU economies (except the UK and Italy), real effective exchange rates have also depreciated over the period since 1995, reflecting the ability of these countries to maintain a firm grip over domestic inflation forces. For the UK, the appreciation in the real effective exchange rate is a consequence of the dramatic appreciation in the pound in global currency markets rather than high domestic inflation.

term interest rates in both France and Germany having fallen over that period. In part, this reflects the significant progress achieved in consolidating the EU's public finances, with a marked decline in budget deficits having been recorded in all Member States since the peak was reached in 1993.

However, the improving situation in the EU economy, including the easing in EU-wide monetary conditions, is also related to the continued success recorded in controlling domestic inflationary forces. In part, this is linked to the readiness of EU governments to move speedily to check inflationary forces when these have appeared by appropriate macroeconomic adjustments in line with a stability-oriented monetary–fiscal policy mix. However, beyond that, the success in curtailing inflation (and promoting global competitiveness) reflects a significant element of wage moderation on the part of labour. Inflation (measured by the deflator of private consumption) fell from 2.6 per cent in 1996 to 2.1 per cent in 1997, and only a very slight increase in inflation rates is expected over the forecast period. Underpinning this low rate of inflation has been a moderate growth in unit labour costs of only slightly above 1 per cent in 1997 (and expected to be only marginally higher in 1998). Some caution is necessary, however, in that the depreciation in the EU currencies referred to above will tend to push imported prices higher adding slightly to inflationary forces in the medium term. In addition to a general lowering in inflation, the data also show a continuation of the trend towards convergence between EU national inflation rates around these lower rates. Among 13 EU countries, the inflation differential was less than one percentage point in 1997[3] and the differential is expected to fall even further in 1998 ahead of the start of EMU and the adoption of the euro.

Unit labour costs have also been kept low by higher labour productivity (GDP per person employed). After decreasing from an annual increase of 3.3 per cent in 1994 to only 1.5 per cent in 1996, in 1997 EU-wide labour productivity increased by 2.1 per cent, and this is expected to continue into 1998 and 1999. In fact, this rate of growth of productivity conforms closely to the EU trend of 2 per cent per annum over the period since 1974, although that was well below the trend rate of 4.4 per cent recorded in the earlier 1961–73 period. Nonetheless, the moderation in wage rates coupled with the increase in the rate of productivity provides a sound basis for a subsequent period of non-inflationary growth for the EU as a whole. It is worth noting that productivity in the EU remains well above that in the USA which has averaged only at 0.7 per cent per annum over the period since 1974.

Although the economic recovery which gathered force in 1997 was triggered initially by an increase in external demand (i.e. exports from the EU), by the end of the year it was clear that domestic elements of demand were also picking up in sufficient measure to usher in a period of self-sustaining economic growth.

---

[3] Greece (6 per cent) and the UK (2.4 per cent) being the exceptions.

Despite the continued existence of some spare productive capacity, domestic demand showed signs of recovery in the course of 1997 with both investment and consumption levels beginning to rise relatively strongly. This reflects two factors: first, the lowering of EU interest rates; and, second, an increasing recovery of consumer and business confidence across the EU.

Whilst short-term interest rates across the EU remained broadly constant for the first nine months of 1997, the fillip to domestic demand provided by earlier interest rate reductions began to appear in the course of the year. In particular, the sharp reduction in German short-term interest rates over the 12 months from spring 1995 boosted both demand and confidence. Short-term rates in most EU countries remained broadly constant during 1997, although rates began to move upward in October with the decision by the Bundesbank to raise its key money market rate by 30 basis points from 3 per cent to 3.30 per cent. This move was immediately followed in Belgium, Denmark, France, the Netherlands and Austria, leading to a general rise in short-term rates for the first time since mid-1996. However, the stability in German interest rates since 1996 had, by the last quarter of 1997, permitted short-term rates in Italy to fall significantly (from 11 per cent in the spring of 1995 to 6.5 per cent in October, 1997), as also was the case in both Spain and Portugal. Consequently, the spread of short-term rates declined across the EU during 1997, partly in anticipation of EMU by participants in financial markets (the differential between the lira and the deutschemark narrowed from 6 per cent to 3 per cent over the period 1995–97). The sole exception to the EU trend was the UK, where fear of an overheating in the economy fuelled by buoyant domestic consumption led to five base rate rises, each of 0.25 per cent, being implemented during 1997. As a result, UK short-term interest rates stood at 7.25 per cent by the end of the year.[4] Long-term interest rates in the EU also fell in the course of 1997, once again boosting investment activity and confidence generally. As expected, the largest falls occurred in those countries with high long-term rates (e.g. in Italy long-term rates fell by 100 basis points in 1997; in Germany only by 20 basis points), leading to a convergence in long-term rates as market confidence in the realization of a broadly-based EMU (i.e. one which included Italy, Spain and some other traditionally 'weaker' economies) grew.[5] At the same time, a reduction in long-term rates in the USA greatly facilitated an easing of long rates in the EU.

Although an imprecise predictor of future economic performance, indicators of business and consumer confidence showed a significant upturn in 1997. This tends to confirm the view that the elements of a period of sustained economic growth are in place, and that both businesses and consumers are willing to increase levels of domestic spending as a result.

[4] It is clear that the UK business cycle is further advanced than is the case elsewhere in the EU.
[5] This narrowing of long-term yields reflects the increasing substitutability between currencies and long-term debt instruments driven by the expectation that most EU Member States will join EMU in the first wave.

Despite the generally positive economic outlook for the EU, and regardless of the upturn in activity during 1997, high levels of unemployment persist. For the EU as a whole in 1997 the rate of unemployment stood at 10.7 per cent (approximately 18 million persons), down only marginally on the 1996 level of 10.9 per cent. Moreover, notwithstanding the increase in economic growth forecast over the next few years, unemployment is expected to remain high, falling only slightly in 1998 to 10.3 per cent and again in 1999 to stand at 9.7 per cent. As has been the case since the mid-1970s, unemployment in the EU compares unfavourably with unemployment rates in the USA and Japan (5.3 per cent and 3.2 per cent respectively in 1997). The problem of persistent unemployment in the EU has been thrown into sharp relief with the impending move to EMU. Indeed, the question of employment generally formed a central element in the negotiations leading up to the revisions to the TEU that were agreed upon at the June European Council in Amsterdam, but which have yet to be ratified. The revised Treaty provides for the inclusion of a new Employment Title (Title VIII, Arts 125–130), which introduces the objective of realizing a 'high level of employment' explicitly to the Treaty.[6] This requires the consequences for employment to be taken into consideration ' in the formulation and implementation of Community policies and activities' (Art. 127(2), Amsterdam). Although the revised Treaty expressly avoids all mention of common actions that should be adopted to meet the general employment objective, instead regarding this as a matter of national competence, this does not, of course, preclude common policies being developed subsequently should this gain the consent of all Member States.

The issue of EU labour market flexibility continued to dominate political and academic debate in 1997. In addition to ongoing deliberations over the causes of, and cures for, the persistence of unemployment in the EU (with structural unemployment estimated to be one-half of all unemployment), increasingly attention was focused on the possibility that higher levels of unemployment may arise as a consequence of EMU.[7] The core issue here is the extent to which comprehensive labour market reforms are necessary not only to reduce structural unemployment across the EU, but also to equip a single currency EU with the degree of flexibility required to enable Member States to adjust more rapidly to adverse economic disturbances, including those arising from asymmetric shocks or events that have asymmetric effects. As is well understood, the transition to EMU reduces the instruments available to the national authorities to tackle disturbances that affect their economies, particularly where the impact differs

---

[6] Although this was already incorporated under Art. 2, TEU, the Amsterdam revision promotes the ranking of the employment objective in a revised Art. 2, as well as introducing the new Employment Title.
[7] Two reviews of the 'flexibility' debate are Siebert (1997) and Nickell (1997). See also Feldstein (1997) on EMU and unemployment.

from one Member State to another.[8] No longer will it be possible for countries to dampen the impact of shocks by nominal exchange rate changes, raising the question of how the required adjustment will be made. One possibility is via labour mobility. However, it is unlikely that intra-EU labour mobility will be sufficient to ease the adjustment process – i.e. labour displaced by external shocks simply moves elsewhere in search of employment. Consequently, policy-makers have tended to focus once more on labour market reforms. The objective is to make European labour markets more 'flexible' in order that both the employment created by episodes of economic upturn increases and that the job losses arising from external disturbances are minimized.

In this context, it is not surprising that a large part of the European Commission's report on the economic situation in the EU during 1997 (CEC, 1998) focuses on unemployment. To this end, the Commission advocates a supply-side strategy focusing on investment in human capital and employment creation against a background of macroeconomic stability based on three elements:

- a stability-oriented monetary policy;
- sustained efforts to consolidate the public finances in most Member States consistent with the objectives of the Stability and Growth Pact;[9]
- nominal wage trends consistent with the price stability objective.

However, rather than viewing EMU as posing a potential difficulty for Member States with regard to employment, the Commission regards the macroeconomic context of EMU as beneficial to job creation. From the perspective of the Commission, the realization of EMU enhances the prospects of avoiding the three obstacles that have persistently interrupted EU growth and employment generation, namely;

- exchange rate turbulence, which can no longer arise within EMU countries or, although to a lesser extent, non-EMU countries that participate in the ERM2;
- stability 'conflicts' between fiscal and monetary policies, which will be avoided given that the Stability Pact requires EMU countries to continue to observe the excessive deficit fiscal criteria set out in the TEU after EMU has begun;
- an inflationary environment which, assuming that the single currency area will be one characterized by low inflation and macroeconomic stability, will no longer arise with the result that investment and growth will occur within a more stable and confidence-enhancing framework.

[8] Whilst clearly true in the case of monetary policy, under EMU national fiscal policy too will be subject to constraints as agreed upon under the Growth and Stability Pact signed at the Amsterdam Council in June.
[9] European Council (1997). Ten EMU countries are permitted to run an 'excessive deficit' if the annual fall in GDP exceeds 2 per cent, whilst a fall of GDP of between 0.75 and 2 per cent may be enough to justify an 'excessive deficit' being incurred.

It is, of course, premature to comment upon the extent to which the new monetary authorities will be able to maintain a low-inflation environment. Undoubtedly a continuation of the trend towards a convergence of Member State inflation rates in a downward direction, along with the Treaty-resident obligations to deliver price stability which rest with the European Central Bank, will make this task easier. However, doubts remain regarding the ability of some Member States to continue to observe the exacting fiscal conditions now incumbent upon EMU countries. Indeed, for a number of countries (particularly Belgium and Italy) considerable progress is required before they come close to the debt-to-GDP criteria defined in the TEU, although this will not prevent them being part of the first wave of EMU countries. The fear is, however, that the commitment to the fiscal conditions embedded in the Stability Pact will result in an unduly restrictive fiscal stance being adopted in some countries with the attendant risk of curtailing the capacity of that country to implement counter-cyclical economic policies. Should such a conflict arise then, other than in exceptional circumstances, the danger is that EMU will weaken the stabilization role of fiscal policy and generate higher rather than lower unemployment.

In the course of 1997 further progress was made in bringing Member State budgetary positions within the TEU convergence criteria. For the EU as a whole, net borrowing by governments fell from 4.2 per cent of GDP in 1996 to 2.7 per cent of GDP in 1997, bringing it within the 3 per cent ceiling for the EU as a whole. This is a significant achievement for the EU, as this represents a decline in the ratio from 6.1 per cent of GDP in 1993 to the present position. The overall figure for outstanding debt is less impressive, however. For the EU as a whole the ratio of debt to GDP stood at 72.3 per cent in 1997, down only slightly from the previous year (73 per cent) and still well above the levels recorded at the beginning of the 1990s (e.g. 55.3 per cent in 1990). And whilst net borrowing for the EU as a whole is forecast to decline to only 1.8 per cent of GDP by 1999, the debt-to-GDP figure will remain high, at just under 70 per cent in 1999. From the data, it is clear that the lowering in Member States' net borrowing has been achieved through a contraction in the level of total expenditures in GDP and not as a result of higher taxation. Indeed, the ratio of total expenditure to GDP for the EU 15 fell from 52.4 per cent in 1993 to 48.7 per cent in 1997 over which period the overall tax pressure remained practically constant – at 46.3 per cent of GDP in 1993 and 46 per cent of GDP in 1997. This outcome is consistent with the objectives set out in the EU's Broad Economic Guidelines which sought to secure reductions in budget deficits via expenditure restraint rather than tax increases. The doubts that remain in the minds of some EMU critics revolve around the degree of manoeuvrability implicit in the 3 per cent and 60 per cent fiscal ceilings that are to remain with respect to the ratios of net government borrowing and national debt to GDP. In the event of a cyclical downturn, or in the context of an external shock whose impact is unevenly spread across the area, will these ceilings be sufficient to prevent a transient rise in unemployment which may quickly become permanent? It is because of this concern that the Commission continues to urge Member States to bring about a balance – or even modest surplus – in national budgetary positions. This, it is argued, should provide individual countries sufficient latitude in fiscal policy to implement those offsetting elements of automatic and discretionary policies that arise following negative demand shocks that otherwise may lead to a full-blown recession.

II. Main Economic Indicators

Economic Growth

Indicators point to a strengthening economic recovery in the EU generally, and it is anticipated that this will give rise to a period of sound and self-sustaining economic growth. The EU-wide rate of economic growth in 1997 was 2.6 per cent, and this will rise to 3 per cent in 1998. Although initially fuelled by an increase in export demand, increasingly the economic upturn will be driven by a recovery in domestic elements of demand – with both consumer and investment spending recovering in the course of 1997 and expected to grow further over the next two years. Moreover, the economic policy background is regarded as conducive to a sustained period of economic growth over the medium term, characterized as it has been both in 1996 and 1997 by an easing of national monetary policies in the context of greater budgetary consolidation. In 1997, and driven by a strengthening of economic performance in the global economy, EU exports of goods and services increased by 8.5 per cent. This is a significant improvement on the 1996 growth of 4.8 per cent, and exports are forecast to grow by 7.5 per cent in 1998 and 1999. Private consumption grew at 2.1 per cent in 1997, similar to the rate for the previous year, although this is expected to accelerate to 2.5 per cent in 1998 and 2.6 per cent in 1999. Investment spending has been encouraged by a combination of lower interest rates and higher profitability with the continuance of moderation in wage demands. Total investment in the EU increased by 2.5 per cent in 1997, and this is forecast to rise strongly in both 1998 and 1999 to 4.3 per cent and 5.5 per cent respectively.

It can be seen from Table 1 that most countries achieved growth rates above the EU average in 1997, significantly so in the case of both Ireland and Finland, although Austria and Italy both under-performed compared to the EU average. In 1998–99, a more uniform cyclical movement is expected. However, Ireland is forecast yet again to outperform all other countries, maintaining the trend over the 1990s as a whole. Although the UK recorded a growth rate of 3.3 per cent in

Table 1: Gross Domestic Product (Annual Average % Change, 1991–99) Private

	1991	1992	1993	1994	1995	1996	1997	1998*	1999*
Austria	n.a	2.0	0.4	3.0	1.5	1.6	1.9	2.8	3.3
Belgium	3.4	1.7	−1.4	2.3	2.1	1.5	2.4	3.0	3.1
Denmark	1.4	0.2	1.5	4.4	2.6	2.7	3.5	3.3	3.2
Finland	n.a	−3.6	−1.2	4.4	5.1	3.3	4.6	4.0	3.6
France	2.5	1.2	−1.3	2.8	2.1	1.5	2.3	3.1	3.1
Germany	5.7	2.2	−1.1	2.9	1.9	1.4	2.5	3.2	3.3
Greece	−1.0	0.4	−1.0	1.5	2.0	2.6	3.3	3.5	3.6
Ireland	7.8	4.6	3.7	7.3	11.1	8.6	8.6	8.1	7.6
Italy	2.1	0.6	−1.2	2.1	2.9	0.7	1.4	2.5	2.8
Luxembourg	3.2	1.9	0.0	3.3	3.8	3.0	3.4	3.8	4.0
Netherlands	4.1	2.0	0.8	3.4	2.3	3.3	3.1	3.6	3.3
Portugal	4.3	1.1	−1.2	0.8	1.9	3.3	3.5	3.7	3.7
Spain	3.7	0.7	−1.2	2.1	2.8	2.3	3.3	3.5	3.6
Sweden	n.a	−1.4	−2.2	2.6	3.6	1.1	2.1	2.9	3.3
UK	0.4	−0.5	2.2	3.8	2.5	2.3	3.3	2.1	2.3
EUR12/15	3.0	0.9	−0.5	2.8	2.4	1.8	2.6	3.0	3.1

Source: CEC.
* Forecast.

1997, above the EU average, activity there is expected to slow down relatively sharply in 1998 and 1999. This reflects the fact that the economic cycle in the UK continues to be out of phase with that in the majority of other Member States, rather than any underlying weakness in the UK economy. At the same time, however, the considerable appreciation in the external value of sterling is causing real concerns over the prospects for UK exports, and by extension future rates of economic growth. What is particularly notable from Table 1 is the extent to which the four 'cohesion' countries (Greece, Spain, Portugal and Ireland) achieved rates of economic growth which are above the EU average in 1997, a feature that is expected to continue over the forecast period. The consequence of this is that national per capita income disparities across the EU will fall, leading to a greater measure of economic and social cohesion than previously.

Unemployment

As Table 2 shows, the average level of unemployment in the EU fell marginally in 1997, with this gradual downward trend expected to continue in 1998 and 1999. In large measure this reflects the expected lagged response of employment

Table 2: Unemployment (as % of the Civilian Labour Force, 1991–99)

	1991	1992	1993	1994	1995	1996	1997	1998*	1999*
Austria	n.a	3.6	4.1	3.8	3.9	4.4	4.4	4.2	3.9
Belgium	8.6	7.6	7.3	8.9	9.9	9.8	9.7	8.8	8.0
Denmark	8.9	9.2	10.1	8.2	7.2	6.9	6.0	5.4	5.1
Finland	n.a	13.1	17.9	18.4	16.3	15.4	13.8	12.6	11.7
France	9.0	10.4	11.7	12.3	11.7	12.4	12.5	12.3	11.9
Germany	4.8	6.6	7.9	8.4	8.2	8.9	10.0	9.8	9.1
Greece	7.0	7.9	8.6	8.9	9.2	9.6	9.5	9.3	9.2
Ireland	14.5	15.4	15.6	14.3	12.3	11.8	10.8	9.5	7.9
Italy	10.0	9.0	10.3	11.4	11.9	12.0	12.1	11.9	11.8
Luxembourg	1.7	2.1	2.7	3.2	2.9	3.3	3.6	3.8	3.9
Netherlands	7.5	5.6	6.6	7.2	6.9	6.3	5.5	4.8	3.9
Portugal	4.6	4.2	5.7	7.0	7.3	7.3	6.8	6.7	6.3
Spain	6.2	18.5	22.8	24.1	22.9	22.1	21.0	19.8	18.7
Sweden	n.a	5.8	9.5	9.8	9.2	10.0	10.4	9.9	9.3
UK	7.0	10.1	10.4	9.6	8.7	8.2	6.4	5.8	5.5
EUR12/15	8.3	9.4	10.9	11.3	10.8	10.9	10.7	10.3	9.7

Source: CEC.
* Forecast.

with respect to the pick-up in the level of EU economic activity. Estimates provided by the European Commission suggest that in 1997 employment levels across the EU increased by 0.5 per cent, equivalent to approximately 700,000 jobs. The increase in employment is expected to strengthen in 1998 and 1999 with employment growth of 0.8 per cent (1.3 million) and 1.3 per cent (1.8 million) respectively being forecast. This increase in job creation will not significantly lower the level of unemployment because of the cyclical increase in productivity. Consequently, unemployment will remain around 10 per cent of the labour force to the end of the decade.

Despite the lowering in the EU average rate of unemployment in 1997, in five Member States the level of joblessness actually increased, particularly in Germany and Sweden. This is explained principally by the relatively low rates of economic growth of both countries over the past two years. The rate of unemployment in 1997 was lowest in Austria, the Netherlands, Denmark, the UK and Portugal. In each of these countries employment growth is forecast to continue and their average unemployment rate (below 6 per cent) is expected to be significantly lower than the EU average over the next few years. The poorest performing countries in terms of unemployment remain Spain (21 per cent),

Finland (13.8 per cent), France (12.5 per cent) and Italy (12.1 per cent). In each case, the rate of unemployment is expected to fall more or less proportionately to the rate of economic growth being forecast over the next two years.

Inflation

As can be seen from Table 3, the EU-wide rate of inflation (as measured by the deflator of private consumption) fell from 2.6 per cent in 1996 to 2.1 per cent in 1997. Moreover, the immediate outlook is one of continuing low rates of inflation with only a slight increase to 2.2 per cent for each of 1998 and 1999 being forecast. Although a trade-weighted average depreciation of EU currencies amounting to 5.5 per cent has been estimated, the resulting increase in import prices is not expected to fuel EU inflation. This is due to both the continued existence of spare productive capacity across the EU and the offsetting effects of moderate unit labour cost developments. Unit labour costs increased in the EU as a whole by about 1 per cent in 1997, and this trend is forecast to continue in 1998 and 1999. Further, control over domestic inflation now represents the

Table 3: Inflation (Private Consumption Deflator: % Change on Preceding Year, 1993–99)

	1993	1993	1994	1995	1996	1997	1998*	1999*
Austria	3.4	3.0	2.3	1.4	2.5	1.9	2.1	2.2
Belgium	2.1	3.0	3.2	1.7	2.3	1.7	1.8	1.8
Denmark	0.3	1.7	2.1	2.0	2.1	2.1	2.5	2.7
Finland	4.2	1.4	0.2	0.3	1.6	1.3	2.0	2.0
France	2.2	2.1	1.7	1.6	1.9	1.3	1.5	2.0
Germany	3.9	2.7	1.9	1.9	1.8	2.1	2.2	2.2
Greece	13.7	10.8	9.3	9.3	8.5	6.0	4.5	3.5
Ireland	1.9	2.6	2.0	2.0	1.1	1.4	2.5	3.0
Italy	5.4	4.6	5.8	5.8	4.3	2.2	2.2	2.0
Luxembourg	7.0	2.4	2.0	0.7	1.4	1.6	1.7	1.8
Netherlands	2.1	2.7	0.9	1.5	1.3	2.1	2.4	2.6
Portugal	7.1	4.8	4.2	4.2	3.3	2.2	2.1	2.3
Spain	5.5	4.9	4.7	4.7	3.4	2.1	2.1	2.3
Sweden	5.7	3.1	2.7	2.4	1.2	1.8	2.0	2.3
UK	3.5	2.5	2.6	2.6	2.6	2.4	2.4	2.3
EUR15	4.1	3.3	3.0	3.0	2.6	2.1	2.2	2.2

Source: CEC.

* Forecast.

central plank in the macroeconomic policy in all EU Member States, ensuring that inflationary pressures will remain subdued.

Of the individual Member States, only Greece (6 per cent) recorded an inflation rate significantly above the EU average in 1997, whilst in the UK the more advanced nature of the cyclical upturn is generating only a slight intensi-fication of inflationary pressures. In Ireland, however, the high rates of economic activity forecast over the next few years are expected to generate inflation, with the rate expected to double from 1.4 per cent in 1997 to 3 per cent in 1999. It is expected that inflation rates in Denmark and the Netherlands will also rise due to the higher than average growth rates forecast for these countries. Despite these exceptional cases, however, a substantial convergence in inflation rates across the EU has been achieved during the past few years. Inflation differentials among 11 countries are expected to be no bigger than half a percentage point in 1998 (within the range 2–2.5 per cent) and 1999 (1.8–2.3 per cent), with inflation rates in all Member States in 1997 (except Greece) at or below 2.5 per cent.

Public Finances

Tables 4 and 5 present data on the state of public finances across the EU; Table 4 shows the annual government deficit/surplus in relation to GDP, and Table 5 shows the total level of public debt in relation to GDP. As is well known, the convergence criteria set out in the TEU required that these ratios should be at, or close to, 3 per cent and 60 per cent respectively for countries intending to move to stage III of EMU on 1 January 1999. With the agreement reached under the Growth and Stability Pact, members of EMU are obliged to continue to observe these ratios after that date, other than under clearly defined 'exceptional' circumstances.

It is clear from Table 4 that there has been a dramatic lowering in the EU average ratio of annual budget to GDP in the latter half of the 1990s. By 1997, that ratio stood at 2.7 per cent, down from 4.2 per cent the previous year. Moreover, it is expected to remain comfortably inside the 3 per cent ceiling over the next two years – these forecasts being based on budget figures presented by Member State governments. Two forces have influenced this improving situa-tion. The first is the onset of a cyclical recovery in the EU, assisted by lower interest rates and moderate wage claims. Not only has this reduced expenditure that arises during periods of recession, at the same time government revenues begin to rise as economic activity recovers. The second has been a significant reduction in the share of government expenditure in GDP, one element of which is lower debt service charges with the recent fall in interest rates. Between 1995 and 1999 the share of government expenditure in GDP for the EU as a whole will have decreased by about 4 percentage points. This trend change in the share of

Table 4: General Government Financial Balances, Surplus (+) or Deficit (–) as % of Nominal GDP, 1992–99

	1992	1993	1994	1995	1996	1997	1998*	1999*
Austria	n.a	–4.2	–4.4	–5.0	–3.8	–2.8	–2.6	–2.4
Belgium	–6.5	–7.5	–5.1	–3.9	–3.2	–2.6	–2.3	–2.2
Denmark	– 2.1	–3.9	–3.5	–2.4	–0.8	1.3	1.9	2.4
Finland	n.a	–8.0	–6.2	–5.0	–3.1	–1.4	–0.2	0.5
France	–3.9	–5.6	–5.6	–5.0	–4.1	–3.1	–3.0	–2.6
Germany	–2.9	–3.5	–2.4	–3.3	–3.4	–3.0	–2.6	–1.7
Greece	–11.8	–14.2	–12.1	–9.8	–7.6	–4.2	–3.0	–2.7
Ireland	–2.2	–2.4	–1.7	–2.1	–0.4	0.6	1.2	2.1
Italy	–9.5	–9.6	–9.0	–8.0	– 6.8	–3.0	–3.7	–3.6
Luxembourg	n.a	1.7	2.6	2.0	2.6	1.6	1.0	0.5
Netherlands	–3.8	–3.2	–3.4	–4.0	–2.3	–2.1	–1.9	–1.5
Portugal	–3.8	–6.9	–5.8	– 5.8	–3.2	–2.7	–2.4	–2.2
Spain	–4.2	–6.8	–6.3	–7.3	–4.7	–2.9	–2.4	–2.2
Sweden	n.a	–12.3	–10.8	–7.1	–3.7	–1.9	–0.2	0.2
United Kingdom	– 6.2	–7.8	–6.8	–5.5	–4.9	–2.0	–0.6	–0.3
EUR12/15	n.a	–6.5	–5.4	–5.1	–4.2	–2.7	–2.2	–1.8

Source: CEC.
* Forecast.

GDP accounted for by government spending is reflected in data on government borrowing after adjusting for the effects of the economic cycle. This shows a fall in the ratio of 5.5 per cent in 1992 to only 2.1 per cent in 1997. In some Member States, however, the deficit-to-GDP ratio remained relatively high in 1997 – Greece (4.2 per cent), France (3.1 per cent), Germany and Italy (3 per cent) and Spain (2.9 per cent). However, with the exception of Italy, where the deficit is expected to rise in 1998 and 1999 (at 3.7 and 3.6 per cent respectively), in each case the ratio will fall below the 3 per cent threshold in 1998.

Similarly, the burden of public debt has been lowered by a favourable development of public deficits in most Member States. The EU average debt ratio fell to 72.4 per cent in 1997 from 73 per cent in 1996, and is expected to follow this downward trend over the forecasting horizon (71.4 per cent in 1998; 69.8 per cent in 1999). As can be seen in Table 5, in 10 out of the 11 Member States with debt to GDP ratios above 60 per cent in 1997, the ratio will fall in 1998. Germany is the sole exception, where the ratio will remain roughly constant. It is clear that Italy, Belgium and Greece continue to have debt ratios which are significantly above the 60 per cent threshold, although in each case

Table 5: Gross Public Debt as % of Nominal GDP, 1992-99

	1992	1993	1994	1995	1996	1997	1998*	1999*
Austria	58.3	62.8	65.1	69.3	69.5	66.1	65.6	64.8
Belgium	130.6	137.0	135.0	131.2	126.9	124.7	121.3	117.7
Denmark	68.7	80.1	76.0	73.8	71.6	67.0	62.2	57.0
Finland	41.5	57.3	59.5	58.1	58.0	59.0	57.3	55.8
France	39.6	45.6	48.4	52.5	55.7	57.3	58.2	58.2
Germany	44.1	48.2	50.4	58.0	60.4	61.7	61.4	60.0
Greece	99.2	111.8	110.4	111.3	112.6	109.3	106.4	104.2
Ireland	92.0	94.5	87.9	82.2	72.7	65.8	59.2	52.3
Italy	108.5	119.3	125.5	124.4	123.8	123.2	121.9	120.0
Luxembourg	5.2	6.2	5.7	5.9	6.6	6.7	6.9	7.6
Netherlands	79.6	80.8	77.4	79.1	77.2	73.4	71.5	69.4
Portugal	63.3	68.2	69.6	66.5	65.6	62.5	60.8	59.5
Spain	48.4	60.5	63.1	65.3	70.1	68.1	66.5	64.8
Sweden	67.1	76.0	79.3	78.2	77.8	77.4	75.3	71.2
United Kingdom	41.9	48.5	50.4	53.8	54.4	52.9	51.5	49.8
EUR12/15	60.4	66.1	68.1	71.0	73.0	72.4	71.4	69.8

Source: CEC.
* Forecast .

slow progress is being recorded in lowering the extent of the debt. Recent – and prospective – falls in long-term interest rates should contribute further to lowering the debt in these countries.

III. Economic Developments in the Member States

Germany

In Germany, the rate of economic growth for 1997 was 2.5 per cent, a significant improvement on the 1996 rate of 1.4 per cent. Much of this improved perform-ance was a result of stronger export growth with domestic components of demand lagging somewhat. Nonetheless, with continued wage moderation coupled to lower interest rates and external price competitiveness (with the full effects of the recent appreciation of the dollar yet to be felt), growth is forecast to rise to 3.2 per cent in 1998 and 3.3 per cent in 1999. Whilst a stronger recovery in domestic demand is expected, public consumption in 1997 was constrained by continuing efforts at fiscal consolidation, a feature that will persist through the forecast period, particularly in the context of German unemployment levels.

Domestic policy remains focused on achieving fiscal convergence and controlling inflationary pressures in the economy. In June, the German Finance Minister, Theo Waigel, announced the immediate enforcement of a budget freeze to tighten the control on government spending further. Under this budget freeze, expenditures above 1 million DM require the explicit approval of the Finance Minister, although in practice the effect of the freeze was limited, producing savings of only 0.1 per cent of GDP. In October, the Deutsche Bundesbank raised the repurchase rate from 3 per cent to 3.30 per cent to counter concerns over inflationary pressures. At the same time, the budget freeze noted above was tightened in an attempt to further control public spending. It is clear that, while economic performance improved in the course of 1997, considerable problems will continue to confront the Government. It has to maintain public expenditure within the ceilings consistent with membership of EMU whilst, at the same time, tackling the deep-seated problem of unemployment. In the light of this, it is clear that much will depend on the continued competitiveness of the economy in the broader global economy.

France

Economic growth in France during 1997 stood at 2.3 per cent, slightly below the EU average. However, this marks a considerable improvement over the 1996 figure and it is expected that this improvement will continue through 1998 and 1999. It is clear that exports played an important role in France's economic performance in 1997, with both domestic demand and investment remaining sluggish – features largely attributable to weak consumer confidence. This lack of confidence reflects, in part, the continuing high level of unemployment of 12.5 per cent in 1997. As unemployment is forecast to decline only marginally in 1998 and 1999, and against the background of continuing problems in achieving the fiscal ceilings required, much of the additional growth being forecast for 1998 and 1999 will depend on external economic factors, particularly the stability and growth of the US economy.

Monetary policy in France was loosened marginally at the beginning of the year with short-term rates being lowered to 3.1 per cent in January. However, in response to the increase in German rates, this cut was reversed in October when rates were raised to 3.3 per cent. Nonetheless, by the end of 1997 short-term rates in France were 3 percentage points lower than in January, 1995. The Government continued to wrestle with the budget deficit in the course of 1997 as they strove to meet the convergence criteria. A number of expedient measures were implemented in the spring with a view to offset potential expenditure slippages or revenue shortfalls, although in the summer the government adopted a package of immediate measures to boost employment and consumption amounting to 0.1 per cent of GDP. In the event, the primary deficit stood at 3.1 per cent for 1997, slightly above the ceiling set for membership of EMU, although this is unlikely to prevent French participation from January 1999, in the light of an anticipated fall in the deficit to GDP ratio in both 1998 and 1999.

Italy

Economic growth in Italy was only 1.4 per cent in 1997, significantly below the EU average for the year. Two factors are responsible for this relatively low rate of economic growth. First, monetary policy remained fairly tight throughout the year with a view to combating inflationary forces and, following the decision of 25 November 1996, the lira re-entered the Exchange Rate Mechanism. Although the Central Bank lowered the discount rate to 6.75 per cent in January, 1997, this was the only reduction during the year and maintained Italian interest rates well above rates in Germany and France. Despite this, however, by the end of the year rates were still almost 4 percentage points lower than had been the case in 1995. Second, the paucity of growth reflected the Government's continued attempts to achieve a greater measure of fiscal consolidation. In December 1996, agreement had been reached on deficit-cutting measures amounting to approximately 3.5 per cent of GDP, with further cuts being introduced in March 1997, equivalent to a further 0.8 per cent of GDP. As a result of these measures, the budget deficit fell dramatically in 1997 to stand at only 3 per cent of GDP, down from 6.8 per cent in 1996. However, as many of the deficit-cutting measures implemented in 1997 were one-off measures, the public consumption element in domestic demand is expected to recover somewhat in 1998, boosting the rate of economic growth to 2.5 per cent. Despite this, however, unemployment is unlikely to fall significantly from its 1997 level of 12.1 per cent over the forecast period.

United Kingdom

Economic growth in the UK was 3.3 per cent in 1997, well above the EU average for the year. Indeed, 1997 represented the UK's fifth successive year of economic growth following the economic recovery that began in 1992. In this respect, the UK is ahead in the economic cycle than the majority of EU Member States, and this is reflected in the forecast for slower growth in the UK in the next two years. Consumer spending in the UK remained buoyant throughout 1997, and the attendant fear of fuelling inflationary forces in the economy led the Bank of England to raise short-term rates progressively throughout the year from 6 per cent in January to 7.25 per cent in December 1997. As a result, short-term rates have fallen only slightly (0.8 percentage points) over the course of the past three years. One of the main economic developments during 1997 was, of course, the dramatic surge in the external value of sterling, raising deep-seated concerns over export performance in the course of 1998 and 1999. Since mid-1996 it is estimated that the real effective exchange rate for sterling has appreciated by over 20 per cent, all of which is explained by an appreciation in the nominal exchange rate (as opposed to a better inflation performance). Consequently, the combined impact of high nominal and real short-term interest rates, along with such a strong value of sterling, is expected to produce a lower rate of growth in 1998 and 1999 in the context of a stable rate of inflation which will continue to lie well inside the Government's upper limit of 2.5 per cent.

It is also significant to record that, in his speech to the House of Commons on 27 October, the Chancellor of the Exchequer effectively ruled out UK participation in EMU during the first phase. He did make clear, however, that in the final instance the Government's view on UK participation in EMU would be influenced solely by economic considerations rather that constitutional matters. To this end, he set out five economic criteria that, if met, would indicate that UK membership of EMU would be advisable.

Significant Developments in Other Member States

Austria. Economic growth in Austria increased on the previous year to stand at 1.9 per cent, and is forecast to increase further to 2.8 per cent and 3.3 per cent in 1998 and 1999 respectively. The below average rate of growth in Austria reflects the greater share of intra-EU exports in total Austrian exports than for some other Member States, with the result that Austrian economic recovery is closely tied to economic recovery in other EU countries. Nonetheless, Austria remains one of the EU's best performing Member States with respect to unemployment, and the rate of 4.4 per cent in 1997 is the best of all Member States other than Luxembourg. Although exceeding the debt ratio of 60 per cent, Austria's deficit ratio for 1997 was well within the 3 per cent ceiling.

Belgium. At 2.4 per cent, economic growth in Belgium remained close to the average for the EU, with forecasts suggesting this will continue in the future. Unemployment remains slightly below the EU average at 9.7 per cent, and is expected to fall to 8 per cent by 1999. The key economic problem for Belgium remains controlling the total stock of debt which, although falling slowly, stood at almost 125 per cent of GDP in 1997. However, this is unlikely to prevent Belgium moving to EMU in the first wave.

Denmark. The Danish economy is showing signs of solid economic recovery with growth at 3.5 per cent in 1997. This has occurred within the context of falling unemployment (6 per cent in 1997), reasonably stable prices and continued fiscal consolidation. With the general recovery in the economies of the EU, the current trends are expected to continue.

Finland. With economic growth at 4.6 per cent in 1997, the Finnish economy is among the best performing EU Member States. The main difficulty facing the economy is the high level of unemployment (13.8 per cent) although the situation is expected to improve to some degree over the next two years in which the rate of economic growth is forecast to be above the EU average.

Greece. In Greece, the economy expanded by some 3.3 per cent in 1997 prompting a slight decline in the rate of unemployment from 9.6 per cent in 1996 to 9.5 per cent in 1997. The main economic problem, however, remains the relatively high rate of inflation fuelled in part by a relatively strong growth of domestic consumer demand in 1997. Inflation stood at 6 per cent in 1996, and whilst this is lower than the previous year (8.5 per cent) remains well above the EU average. At the same time, the deficit to GDP ratio in 1997 was 4.2 per cent and the debt ratio was 109.3 per cent, both well in excess of the EMU ceilings. Although it has been accepted that Greece will not be in the first wave of EMU, the recent re-entry of the drachma to the ERM signals the Government's wish to seek inclusion in the single currency area over the medium term.

Ireland. The Irish economy continues to grow very strongly, with output expanding by 8.6 per cent in 1997. Indeed, this continues the trend of above-average growth that has been a feature of the Irish economy throughout the 1990s. Despite strong economic growth, which is being driven by domestic demand (particularly by double-digit investment rates), unemployment remains close to the EU average although is expected to dip below this in the next two years.

The Netherlands. Economic growth in the Netherlands was 3.1 per cent in 1997, reflecting in particular a buoyant demand for exports. At the same time, unemployment fell for the third year in succession to 5.5 per cent, and this trend is expected to continue. Inflationary forces remain low, and the process of fiscal consolidation has achieved a deficit ratio of only 2.1 per cent. And although the debt ratio lies outside the EMU ceiling, this is unlikely to be an obstacle to guilder participation in EMU.

Portugal. Economic growth in Portugal was 3.5 per cent in 1997, above the EU average and thus promoting convergence in national living standards within the EU. In large part this strengthening of the economy reflects robust domestic investment levels, no doubt linked to expectations of EMU participation from the outset. Despite the upturn in domestic demand, which has seen unemployment falling to 6.8 per cent of the labour force in 1997, inflation remains at the EU average of just over 2 per cent.

Spain. Unemployment continues to represent the single biggest economic problem confronting the Spanish economy. Despite achieving economic growth of 3.3 per cent in 1997, the rate of unemployment was 21 per cent, by far the highest rate across the EU. Even with two years of comparatively rapid economic growth being forecast, principally on the basis of a high level of domestic investment, by 1999 unemployment is still expected to remain almost 19 per cent of the labour force.

Sweden. Sweden recorded a rate of economic growth of 2.1 per cent in 1997, somewhat lower than the EU average. Despite the fact that Sweden would almost certainly achieve the convergence criteria for EMU membership from the outset (the deficit ratio was 1.9 per cent in 1997; the debt ratio 77.4 per cent), on 10 October the Government proposed that Sweden should not introduce the single currency on 1 January 1999. However, it also made clear that this did not preclude membership in the future, but that this would be a matter to be decided upon by the Swedish population.

References

Commission of the European Communities (1998) *Growth and Employment in the Stability-Oriented Framework of EMU* (Brussels: CEC).

European Council (1997) 'Resolution of the European Council on the Stability and Growth Pact' (Amsterdam, 17 June), *Official Journal of the European Communities,* C236, pp. 1–2.

Feldstein, M. (1997) 'The Political Economy of the European Economic and Monetary Union: Political Sources of an Economic Liability'. *Journal of Economic Perspectives,* Fall, pp. 23–42.

Nickell, S. (1997) 'Unemployment and Labor Market Rigidities: Europe versus North America'. *Journal of Economic Perspectives,* Summer, pp. 55–76.

Siebert, H. (1997) 'Labor Market Rigidities: At the Root of Unemployment in Europe'. *Journal of Economic Perspectives,* Summer, pp. 37–54.

Journal of Common Market Studies

Volume 36, Annual Review
September 1998

Justice and Home Affairs

JÖRG MONAR
University of Leicester

I. Introduction

In future years, 1997 might well be regarded as a watershed year for the development of EU justice and home affairs: not only was substantial progress achieved in several of the policy areas covered by the third pillar, but the Member States also agreed in the final stage of the IGC on an overhaul of the treaty provisions on justice and home affairs which dwarfed any other reforms introduced by the Treaty of Amsterdam. Yet the balance sheet for 1997 also has its negative side: on some important issues – such as a common definition of 'organized crime' – consensus among the Member States proved again to be elusive, and the progress achieved in the new Treaty was bought at a hefty price in terms of persisting deficits and increased risks of fragmentation.

II. Developments in Individual Policy Areas

Asylum and Immigration

During 1997, the Union had again to face a considerable pressure on the asylum systems of the Member States and large numbers of refugees and immigrants, especially from Albania, Iraq, the Kurdish regions of Turkey and Northern Africa. The influx of asylum seekers and immigrants continued to cause political debates and tensions in some of the Member States, in particular France, Germany and Italy.

In the sphere of asylum policy, progress was achieved at the Union level by the entry into force of the Dublin Convention on 1 September 1997, the most substantial legal instrument adopted in this area so far. Signed as long ago as 15 September 1990 but delayed due to long national ratification procedures, the Dublin Convention establishes a comprehensive set of rules for determining the state responsible for examining applications lodged in one of the Member States. Its main rationale is to prevent multiple applications for asylum in several Member States, simultaneously or successively, and an uncontrolled circulation of asylum seekers within the European Union. The Convention sets out the criteria for determining the Member State responsible for examining an asylum application (place of application, family links, issuing of a visa or residence permit, special ties with the applicant or humanitarian reasons) and establishes a number of obligations of the responsible Member State in terms of taking charge of an applicant, examining the application and the expulsion of asylum seekers refused status. The Convention is likely to reduce the administrative burden on the national asylum systems and their abuse by 'asylum shoppers'. Yet it also reinforces the restrictive tendency of harmonization of national asylum policies at the European level by providing asylum seekers with only one chance of obtaining asylum in any of the EU countries and by tightening expulsion procedures. It should also be noted that the Convention does not provide for any harmonization of national asylum standards and procedures.

In March 1997, the Commission made a move towards harmonization by proposing a Joint Action providing for minimum rights and duties of displaced persons enjoying temporary protection in the Member States. This proposal was supported by the European Parliament but encountered major difficulties in the Council. The Commission proposed, for instance, the introduction of a right to family reunification (limited to the nuclear family) although no such right exists in most Member States. The Commission's proposal also provides for the granting of permission to engage in gainful activity to temporary protection beneficiaries, although most Member States so far apply various restrictive practices as regards the access of such beneficiaries to employment or self-employment. On 22 July the Member States agreed, however, to finance a number of projects in favour of persons under temporary protection, asylum seekers and refugees which include measures of education, vocational training and the improvement of administrative facilities.

The Council was also able to agree on a draft Convention concerning the establishment of the Eurodac electronic system for the comparison of fingerprints of applicants for asylum which is of some importance for the effective implementation of the Dublin Convention. In December 1997, however, the

European Parliament asked for a number of changes to the draft text which were aimed at strengthening the roles of the Commission and of the European Court of Justice and at increased data protection.

In the sphere of immigration policy, the Commission took an even more far-reaching step in July 1997 by adopting a proposal for a Convention on rules for the admission of third-country nationals to the Member States. For at least three reasons this proposal must be regarded as a major new political initiative. First, because it combines common rules for the initial admission of third-country nationals for the purposes of employment, self-employed activity, study and training, non-gainful activity and family reunification with the definition of basic rights for long-term residents, including provisions related to the possibility of accepting employment in another Member State. This makes it the first formal proposal ever made to the Council which takes a broad approach on the harmonization of national immigration admission and residence policies. Second, the proposal is clearly aimed at surmounting the Member States' so far dominating practice of adopting only legally non-binding texts on migration issues which leave a wide margin of discretion to the Member States in terms of interpretation and implementation. Third, the proposal can be taken as a sign of a new political assertiveness of the Commission in this area of intergovernmental policy-making, an assertiveness which may have been boosted by the prospect of communitarization of major parts of asylum and immigration policy after the entry into force of the Treaty of Amsterdam (see below). Not surprisingly, the proposal met a host of objections in the Council, and even the prospects for only parts of it being adopted during the next few months seemed remote at the end of 1997. For the time being the Member States continued to seek progress on a more modest line by adopting on 4 December 1997 a non-binding resolution on measures deterring marriages of convenience for the purpose of circumventing rules on entry and residence of third-country nationals. Yet the Commission proposal of July 1997 has sent a provocative signal of a new approach to immigration problems at the EU level which cannot be ignored by the Member States.

External Border Controls and Customs Co-operation

Only very limited progress was made during 1997 on the draft Convention on the crossing by persons of the external frontiers of EU Member States, which remains blocked by the question of its territorial application to Gibraltar and a number of unresolved issues of implementation. Yet in the Council Resolution of 18 December on priorities for co-operation in justice and home affairs, the Member States reaffirmed their commitment to the Convention and agreed on the objective of increased operational co-operation between authorities carrying out checks at external frontiers. In the absence of a comprehensive legal basis, operational co-operation seems indeed the only way to achieve practical progress as regards external border controls, and the Commission followed this logic by proposing in July a joint action on a programme of training, exchanges and co-operation ('Odysseus Programme') which targets a number of issues relating to external border controls.

In the area of customs co-operation – closely related both to external border controls and police co-operation – the Union was more successful. The Member States signed on 18 December the so-called Naples II Convention on mutual assistance and co-operation between customs administrations. It provides for the establishment of national central co-ordinating units, the possibility of appointing liaison officers and contains detailed regulations on requests for information, surveillance and enquiries. The Convention also places customs authorities under an obligation of spontaneous assistance (i.e. assistance without prior request) and provides for the possibility of officers of the applicant authority in specific cases (such as illicit traffic in drugs or weapons and cases of tax evasion) to engage in activities in the territory of the requested Member State, with the approval of the requested authority. It also contains comprehensive provisions on hot pursuit, cross-border surveillance measures and covert investigations. Although cross-border operations remain subject to a number of major limitations – officials of one Member State continue to have no right to apprehend in the territory of another Member State – Naples II represents a substantial step forward for regular investigative and operational co-operation between national customs authorities which is of considerable relevance to the fight against organized crime and drug trafficking. As with all Conventions concluded under Title VI TEU, however, Naples II will only fully enter into force after ratification by all Member States, which could well take two years.

Police Co-operation and the Fight against Drug-trafficking

Following the decisions taken at the Dublin European Council of December 1996 a High Level Group on organized crime was set up at the beginning of 1997. The Group met six times before it submitted a comprehensive Action Plan to Combat Organized Crime which was formally adopted by the Council on 28 April. In its political guidelines section, the Action Plan provides, *inter alia*, for a move towards greater approximation or harmonization of national laws against organized crime, a 'Pre-Accession Pact' with the candidate countries of central and eastern Europe on co-operation against crime, the establishment of a permanent Multidisciplinary Working Party (MDW) on organized crime within the Council, a strengthened role for Europol and extended measures on the confiscation of the proceeds of money laundering and organized fiscal fraud. The Action Plan also contains a detailed list of individual measures which are linked to target dates till the end of 1999. These comprise, for instance, the establishment of a Contact and Support Network for the collection and analysis of data on organized crime, measures to shield certain vulnerable professions (such as notaries, lawyers and accountants) from influences of organized crime, the designation of central national contact points for law enforcement co-operation and the creation of a legal basis for as broad as possible a range of powers of investigation into money laundering. The Action Plan tries for the first time effectively to bundle together the so far rather fragmented co-operation between the Member States in this area and to place all measures taken in the context of strategic guidelines which so far have often been missing. In this sense 1997 may be regarded as the starting point of a new approach of the Member States to the common security risks posed by organized crime. Yet the implementation of the ambitious package of measures could well take much more time than foreseen. In December 1997, the Luxembourg President-in-Office had to admit before the European Parliament that, in spite of intense negotiations, the Member States had failed to agree on a common definition of 'organized crime' under national laws, which is of central importance to a successful implementation of the Action Plan.

On some issues of the fight against crime, however, concrete progress was achieved. With the Belgian Dutroux case having highlighted the need for more effective action against sexual abuse of children, the Council adopted on 24 February a Joint Action to combat traffic in human beings and the sexual exploitation of children. It provides for a common broad interpretation of the term 'sexual exploitation', a revision of national laws with the aim of classifying all types of sexual exploitation as criminal offences and new mechanisms of information and co-operation in investigations. On 9 June, the Council adopted a resolution on the exchange of DNA analysis results which invites the Member States to establish national DNA databases based on common standards and envisages the creation of a European DNA database as a second step. The Member States tried to reduce possible concerns over the protection of data on individuals by providing that the exchange of data should be limited to the non-coding part of DNA which contains no information about hereditary qualities. On 5 December, the Council adopted another Joint Action providing for an annual evaluation of the application and implementation at national level of Union and other international instruments of the fight against crime. This Joint Action responded to the concerns of the High Level Group and several Member States about persisting major differences between the Member States in the practice and effectiveness of national implementing measures.

The Member States also took a further step towards the entry into force of the long-delayed Europol Convention through the adoption, on 19 June, of a protocol on the privileges and immunities of Europol and its personnel. This protocol, however, caused considerable controversy in some national parliaments and led to protests by civil rights organizations because of its wide-ranging exemption of Europol personnel from the requirement to appear when summoned before courts and tribunals or parliamentary committees.

In the fight against drugs, particular emphasis was placed on action against synthetic drugs whose production in some of the major trading partners of the Union and in the Member States themselves poses particular problems. In a communication on the control of new synthetic drugs adopted on 22 May, the Commission proposed action at three levels, namely, through legislation, practical co-operation between the Member States against production and trafficking, and international co-operation. On 16 June the Council, partly motivated by an initiative of the Netherlands, adopted a Joint Action on the information exchange, risk assessment and control of new synthetic drugs. This Joint Action provides, *inter alia*, for the Member States to provide each other via the Europol Drugs Unit and the European Monitoring Centre for Drugs and Drug Addiction with a maximum of information on new synthetic drugs, to proceed to a common risk assessment of these drugs and to adopt the necessary national legal measures to submit these new synthetic drugs to control measures and criminal penalties. With national drugs legislation still differing widely between the Member States, there was again no attempt made at harmonization of relevant national law.

Judicial Co-operation

In the area of judicial co-operation, a major breakthrough was achieved by the adoption, on 26 May, of the convention on the fight against corruption, an area which had so far seen hardly any Union action. This convention provides for measures against both passive and active corruption of Community officials or officials of the Member States. It contains detailed provisions on the definition of acts of corruption, the adoption of national legislation on these acts providing for criminal penalties, extradition and prosecution procedures and co-operation between the Member States in areas such as legal assistance, transfer of proceedings and enforcement of sentences passed in another Member State. Article 4 also provides for the principle of assimilation of criminal laws on corruption in relation to government ministers, judges and parliamentarians. The convention has to be regarded as an important step forward not only because it is likely to improve substantially judicial co-operation in criminal matters involving corruption, but also because it is aimed at ensuring that both passive and active corruption are treated as criminal offences across the European Union. There are still a number of loopholes in some national laws, especially as regards acts of corruption involving Community officials or officials of other Member States, which the convention should help to close. Fully in line with the new emphasis placed on the internal fight against corruption, the Council also defined two common positions (on 6 October and 13 November) on the Union's support for a broad definition of corruption of public officials and a comprehensive criminalization of such corruption in the framework of the ongoing negotiations in the Council of Europe and the OECD on new international legal instruments on the fight against corruption.

The Member States also prepared for the implementation of the 1996 convention relating to extradition between the Member States, which is still in the process of ratification. They adopted on 26 May a comprehensive explanatory report on the convention which clarifies the Member States' position on central issues such as extraditable offences, extradition of nationals and the concept of 'presumption of consent' of the requested Member State.

On 26 November the Commission proposed a convention on jurisdiction and the recognition and enforcement of judgments in civil and commercial matters which provides for simplified recognition and enforcement procedures by way of a revision of the 1968 Brussels and 1988 Lugano conventions. The proposed convention provides, *inter alia,* for the limitation of checks on enforcement orders to formal checks only, for a limitation of the grounds for not recognizing a judgment and for easier provisional measures. In a communication submitted together with this proposal, the Commission underlined the problem that, in spite of the presumed equality of citizens and business partners within the integrated area of the internal market, litigants in the European Union do not so far have equal access to weapons of the law of equal performance levels. The Commission suggested a number of 'new avenues' aimed at reducing the heterogeneity of national procedural systems which is at the origin of this problem. These include, for instance, the introduction of a rapid procedure for the payment of money debts, improved measures on seizures of bank accounts and new rules on transparency of assets. While several of the Commission's suggestions met serious objections, the Council agreed on 5 December on a working programme for the revision of the Brussels and Lugano conventions.

III. The Reforms Introduced by the Treaty of Amsterdam

Communitarization and the New Provisions on Decision-making

The reform of 'Co-operation in the Fields of Justice and Home affairs' under Title VI TEU was one of the most controversial issues of the Intergovernmental Conference. While a majority of the Member States regarded communitarization as the best way to strengthen the Union's capacity to act in these areas, a minority – in particular Denmark and the United Kingdom – wanted to retain the existing intergovernmental basis. Yet these were far from forming two homogeneous camps: most of the Member States generally favouring communitarization were reluctant to bring police and judicial co-operation in criminal matters under Community competence, and those generally opposing communitarization were willing to envisage the transfer to the EC framework of some matters already closely related to Community competence, such as combating fraud against the EC budget. In addition, a whole range of staunchly defended national positions needed to be accommodated. Among these were the British and Irish non-participation in the Schengen system, the special position of Denmark as a Schengen member opposing further communitarization, French concerns about jurisdiction of the Court of Justice on national internal security measures, a Dutch interest in limiting applications to the Court in asylum matters, German concerns about the asymmetrical effects of international migratory pressure on Germany and Belgium's reluctance to accept the safe country of origin principle in respect to asylum applications emanating from other Union countries. All these different positions and interests were, in some way or another, incorporated in the Treaty of Amsterdam, creating a large set of new and, in part, extremely complex provisions spreading over different parts of the EC and EU Treaties and several protocols.

A major move towards communitarization was made by the transfer of matters of asylum, immigration, external border controls and judicial co-operation in civil matters into a new Title IV (ex IIIa) of the EC Treaty. This, however, was only possible at the price of a comprehensive opt-out granted to the United Kingdom, Ireland and Denmark (see below under 'Flexibility'). In two areas – customs co-operation and the protection of the financial interests of the Community – communitarization was accepted by all Member States. These were therefore incorporated in other parts of the EC Treaty. Only judicial co-operation in criminal matters and police co-operation were kept within the intergovernmental domain of Title VI TEU.

It had been widely expected that a move towards communitarization would bring a major improvement in decision-making in justice and home affairs which had been affected by the usual drawbacks of intergovernmental decision-making, especially the unanimity requirement. Yet in Amsterdam, Chancellor Kohl blocked the introduction of qualified majority voting in the areas of asylum and immigration because of German anxieties about the particular immigration and refugee pressure on Germany and the involvement of Länder competences in this area. As a result, it was decided that unanimity should be retained under new Title IV TEC for a transitional period of five years. After this period the Council shall take unanimously a decision with a view to making all or parts of the Title on free movement governed by the co-decision procedure which provides for qualified majority voting. On all of the newly communitarized matters of Title IV, majority voting will therefore become possible only after five years if – and this is a big if – this move finds unanimous backing in the Council.

As regards the areas remaining under Title VI TEU, all acts must be adopted by unanimity. An exception is made only for measures implementing a decision which will be taken by a special qualified majority requiring the double qualification of at least 62 votes cast by at least 10 Council members. This mandatory majority voting represents a small step forward because, under the old provisions, it needed an unanimous decision by the Council to proceed to qualified majority voting on implementing measures.

The Commission's right of initiative has been strengthened: the new Treaty will give it an exclusive right of initiative in respect to the measures countering fraud affecting the financial interests of the Community and to customs co-operation, and it will extend its right of initiative to the areas of police and judicial co-operation in criminal matters. Yet the Commission still has to share its right of initiative with the Member States in all the newly communitarized areas under Title IV EC during the transitional period of five years. This restriction on the Commission's role will be made worse by the maintenance of unanimity in the same areas. In this respect 'communitarization' hardly merits the term, and Amsterdam has clearly set a highly questionable precedent for the import of intergovernmental procedures into the Community framework.

New Objectives and New Instruments

The new Treaty removes one of the main deficits of the old third pillar, the absence of clear objectives in justice and home affairs. A new treaty objective was inserted into Article 2 (ex B) TEU providing for the maintenance and the development of the Union 'as an area of freedom, justice and security'. Linked to this central objective are a host of new and detailed policy objectives which have been included under both the new Title IV TEC and amended Title VI TEU. Some of these cover new ground. The competences of Europol, for example, will be extended to the support of specific investigative actions by Member States. Europol will be allowed to ask Member States' authorities to conduct investigations in specific cases. Yet there are also important gaps left in between the different objectives which make the prospects for comprehensive common policies look rather dim. In the areas of asylum and immigration, for instance, no objectives are established as regards the social integration of asylum seekers and immigrants and interior enforcement measures (against clandestine entries and visa overstays). The central issue of burden-sharing between the Member States, an issue repeatedly brought up by Germany, is also only vaguely referred to. On the positive side, it has to be noted that a number of important areas such as external border controls and illegal immigration will be subject to a deadline of five years within which the Council has to act.

The Member States were aware that the new objectives will need more effective instruments for their implementation. In the newly communitarized areas, the old third pillar instruments that are, in part, inadequate, will be automatically replaced by the well-established EC legal acts. In the areas remaining under Title VI TEU, the Treaty introduces two new instruments:

framework decisions for the purpose of approximation of laws which are to be binding upon the Member States as to the results to be achieved but leave the choice of method and form of implementation to the national authorities; and binding *decisions* for any other purpose. As regards *conventions* the Member States have made an effort to speed their ratification by providing that ratification procedures will have to begin within a time limit set by the Council and that conventions shall enter into force as soon as they are adopted by at least half of the Member States. While the instrument of *joint action*, originally taken over from the CFSP but hardly adequate to justice and home affairs, was eliminated, the Member States decided to retain that of *common positions* which could be used to avoid a binding legal act and the need to consult the European Parliament. Yet on the whole the Treaty brings clear progress in terms of the legal quality and potential effectiveness of instruments in the areas of justice and home affairs. It should be added that the Treaty offers also new possibilities for co-operation with third countries by enabling the Council to negotiate and conclude international agreements on subject matters covered by Title VI TEU. The newly communitarized areas (asylum, immigration, etc.) will automatically come under the external competences of the Community.

Democratic and Judicial Control

The deficits of the old third pillar in terms of democratic and judicial control had been widely criticized. Yet the opportunity to strengthen the European Parliament's rather weak position in justice and home affairs was largely missed. In the newly communitarized areas of Title IV TEC, the Parliament, during the transitional period of five years, will need only to be consulted. After the transitional period there could be a move towards the application of the 'co-decision procedure', but this remains subject to a unanimous decision of the Council. As regards the areas remaining under Title VI TEU, the Council will be obliged to consult the European Parliament before adopting any legally binding instruments. This represents a small element of progress with regard to the arbitrary practice of consultation by the Council under the old provisions. The Luxembourg Presidency of the second half of 1997 adapted its consultation practice already to the new provisions. However, since the improved legal instruments are likely to lead to an increased legislative output in EU justice and home affairs it seems regrettable that the Parliament will only be able to influence legislation through the weak instrument of consultation.

With the entry into force of the new Treaty the newly communitarized areas will automatically come under the jurisdiction of the Court of Justice. Yet the Member States decided to limit the use of the preliminary rulings procedure to national courts of last instance, to exclude measures regarding controls on persons at internal borders from the Court's jurisdiction if these relate to the 'maintenance of law and order and the safeguarding of internal security' and to exclude judgments of national courts which have become *res judicata* from the application of rulings of the Court. All these restrictions are new in the Community legal order. In the intergovernmental areas under Title VI TEU the new Treaty introduces for the first time comprehensive possibilities for judicial review by the Court, a major step forward if one considers the protracted struggles over the Court's role under third pillar conventions during the last few years. Yet here as well major restrictions can be found. The most extraordinary of these gives Member States the possibility to decide by the time of the signing of the Treaty or any time thereafter whether they intend to accept preliminary rulings by the Court or not. On the occasion of the signing of the new Treaty only six Member States (Austria, Belgium, Germany, Greece, Luxembourg, the Netherlands), declared they would accept preliminary rulings by the Court. This '*à la carte*' approach, strongly advocated by the British Government during the IGC, clearly poses a threat to the consistency and coherence of the Union's legal *acquis*.

Schengen and 'Flexibility'

Arising from the frustration of some of the at present 13 Schengen members over British opposition against the communitarization of major parts of the third pillar, 'flexibility' became one of the key issues of the IGC negotiations. The Member States eventually agreed on the introduction of a wide range of forms of 'flexibility' in justice and home affairs.

The most prominent case is the incorporation of Schengen into the Union *acquis*. With the entry into force of the protocol the Schengen Executive Committee will be replaced by the Council, which will take the necessary measures to incorporate the 3,000 pages or so of the Schengen *acquis* under the appropriate provisions of the TEC or TEU. While not being bound by the *acquis*, the UK and Ireland may 'at any time' request to take part in some or all of the *acquis*. Yet this 'opt-in' part of the 'opt-out' will be dependent on a unanimous decision by the Schengen members which could be put at risk, for instance, by the Spanish controversy with Britain over Gibraltar which was again in the headlines during autumn 1997.

The Treaty also introduces the possibility of setting up new frameworks of 'closer co-operation' both under the TEC and Title VI TEU, with different legal provisions being applicable under each of these treaty parts. This means, for instance, that each new framework of 'closer co-operation' will lead to the emergence of a different legal *acquis* under the Treaties valid only for some of the Member States.

In addition, a whole range of other 'opt-ins' and 'opt-outs' were inserted into the new Treaty. To name only the most relevant: the UK and Ireland were guaranteed a complete opt-out (the term is, of course, avoided) from new Title IV EC; this however with the opt-in possibility of the adoption of any measure proposed under this title within a period of three months. Ireland was given the possibility of withdrawing from this opt-out protocol. In addition, the UK was granted the continuation of its right to exercise at its frontiers with other Member States controls on persons, and the UK and Ireland secured the right to maintain the 'Common Travel Area'. Denmark was granted an opt-out similar to that of the United Kingdom and Ireland. Yet since Denmark is a Schengen member it was provided that Denmark should have six months to decide whether it will implement any Council decision building on the Schengen *acquis*. Belgium inserted a national reserve in respect to the protocol providing that – except in a number of special cases – Member States shall be regarded as safe countries of origin in asylum matters.

This massive upsurge in 'flexibility' is clearly the most problematic aspect of the Amsterdam reforms in justice and home affairs. While it seems that this was the price which had to be paid for the compromises reached at Amsterdam, it entails major risks of legal fragmentation and political tensions between the 'ins' and 'outs'. An extensive (ab)use of the various forms of 'flexibility' built into the Treaty could easily more than negate all the real elements of progress achieved by the Treaty of Amsterdam in the areas of justice and home affairs.

References

Commission of the European Communities (1997) *Proposal for a Council Act establishing the Convention on jurisdiction and the recognition and enforcement of judgments in civil and commercial matters in the Member States of the European Union*, COM(97) 609, 26 November.

Commission of the European Communities (1997) *Proposal for a Council Act establishing the Convention on rules for the admission of third-country nationals to the Member States*, COM(97) 387, 30 July.

Commission of the European Communities (1997) *Proposal to the Council for a Joint Action concerning temporary protection of displaced persons*, COM(97) 93, 5 March.

Council of the European Union (1997) *Action Plan to Combat Organized Crime*, OJ C 251/1, 15 August.

Council of the European Union (1997) *Convention determining the State responsible for examining applications for asylum lodged in one of the Member States*, OJ C 254/1, 19.08.97; *OJ* L 242, 4 September.

Council of the European Union (1997) *Convention [...] on the fight against corruption involving officials of the European Communities or officials of the Member States of the European Union*, OJ C 195/2, 25 June.

Council of the European Union (1998) *Convention [...] on mutual assistance and co-operation between customs administrations*, OJ C 24/1, 23 January.

Journal of Common Market Studies

Volume 36, Annual Review
September 1998

Developments in the Member States

BRIGID LAFFAN
University College Dublin

I. Introduction

This section of the *Annual Review* analyses the main political developments in the Member States that have implications for the European Union and the EU issues that reverberated in domestic debates on EU policies and programmes. 1997 was the year of the Amsterdam Treaty, preparations for EMU and the publication of the *Agenda 2000* proposals. At Amsterdam in June 1997, the Member States engaged in the end game which completed the Intergovernmental Conference and in July the Commission published it long-awaited *Agenda 2000* proposals. The latter established the broad parameters of the enlargement process and the internal changes needed in EU policies to accommodate a larger Union.

II. Elections and their Consequences

The general elections in the United Kingdom and France returned centre-left governments to power.

United Kingdom

The UK election in May was watched with considerable interest by the UK's partners in Europe. The internal strife within the Conservative Government on

Europe was a serious problem for the EU in a number of policy areas, notably in relation to the IGC and EMU. The Prime Minister, John Major, was unable to prevent his party and Cabinet moving in an increasingly Eurosceptical direction. It was accepted that the Intergovernmental Conference could not end before the UK election was held. The election was called in March for 1 May. The Labour Party, under Tony Blair, had a decisive lead in the polls going into the election campaign and maintained that lead throughout the campaign. In fact, Labour had led in the polls since September 1992 when sterling was forced out of the Exchange Rate Mechanism. The Conservative Government and John Major's authority never recovered from Black Wednesday. Even during the campaign, the Prime Minister was unable to unite his party on Europe; a large number of Conservative candidates went against the Government's 'wait and see' policy on the single currency which served to highlight the deep divisions in the Government and party. Division was exacerbated by the entry into the election of the newly formed Referendum Party, led by the millionaire business man (and French MEP) Sir James Goldsmith, who was strongly opposed to the EU and EMU. The Referendum Party ran candidates in almost every constituency. The challenge for the opposition Labour Party was to maintain its lead in the polls, which it did by presenting itself as 'New Labour' to distinguish itself from 'Old Labour', which had failed in four successive elections.

'New Labour' won a landslide, gaining 419 seats or 64 per cent of the total, a larger majority than it had won in any previous election. The Conservative Party, on the other hand, won only 165 seats, its lowest since 1906 and many high- ranking Conservative ministers lost their seats. The pro-European Liberal Democrats won 46 seats, its largest number since the Second World War. The Referendum Party did extremely badly despite a well-financed campaign. The extent of the Labour landslide owed much to the British 'first past the post' electoral system which gave it 64 per cent of the seats with just 44 per cent of the votes (see Table 1). The defeated Prime Minister, John Major, resigned as leader of the Conservative Party. His speedy departure meant that the defeated, divided and demoralized Conservatives had to elect a new leader. Six candidates ran in the first round, five of them opposed to the single currency. The second round was a contest between Kenneth Clarke, the pro-European former Chancellor of the Exchequer and William Hague, who won despite his youth and relative inexperience. Notwithstanding Hague's attempts to rebuild the party, conflict on Europe continued to bedevil it. In November, when Hague hardened his position on EMU by insisting that he would fight the next election on saving the pound, the pro-European elements of the party revolted.

In the meantime, Tony Blair was installed as British Prime Minister. The UK's partners in Europe waited with considerable interest to see was how the new Government and Prime Minister would act on Europe. During the election

Table 1: The British Election 1997

	Party Seats	% Seats	% Votes Cast
Labour	419	64	44
Conservative	165	25	31
Liberal Democrat	46	7	17
Other	29	4	7

Source: Harrop (1997).

campaign, Tony Blair argued that Britain had a choice in Europe between disengagement, a sullen presence on the sidelines or engagement and leadership. The tone, if not the substance, of British pronouncements on Europe changed very quickly with the new Government. The Foreign Minister, Robin Cook, in his first foreign policy mission statement, spoke of making the UK a 'leading player in a Europe of independent nation states' (FCO, 12 May 1997). This was echoed by the Prime Minister who argued that the UK needed to 'end the isolation of the last twenty years and be a leading partner in Europe' (Prime Minister's Speech, 1 November 1997). The new Government was immediately confronted with two big policy issues – the IGC and EMU – which tested this aspiration.

In office, the new Labour Government launched a process of major constitutional reform which will in the long term have a significant impact on relations between the UK and Europe. In September, two referendums were held, in Scotland and Wales, which paved the way for the creation of devolved assemblies in Edinburgh and Cardiff. The assembly in Scotland was granted tax-raising powers. Although Westminster retains responsibility for foreign affairs, defence and national security, the evolution of the assemblies will inevitably raise the question of relations with the EU and the treatment of European issues in the assemblies. In all of the Member States with regional or federal governments – Germany, Belgium, Italy, France and Spain – relations between the regional, national and EU tiers of government have been the subject of considerable negotiation between national capitals and the regional level. The White Paper on the Scottish Parliament devoted a chapter to the question of relations with the EU. It established the principle that the UK Government was responsible for relations with Brussels but accepted that the Scottish executive would have to be intimately involved in the elaboration of UK positions, as it will have to implement EU policies and laws within its jurisdiction. Devolution may therefore have a major impact on the management of European business in the UK and on relations between the constituent parts of the UK and Brussels (Robbins, 1998).

France

In April, President Chirac, using his power to dissolve Parliament, took the unprecedented step of setting in train Assembly elections one full year ahead of the necessary date. His purpose was to copperfast the Right's hold on power in the Assembly up to the end of his own electoral mandate in 2002, this being especially necessary as his advisers believed that the outlook for the Right would worsen in 1998.

His declared intention was to ensure that the French Government had a renewed mandate to carry out the major reforms necessary to ensure that France participated in the single currency. The President took a gamble which did not pay off. He and his Prime Minister, Alain Juppé, were deeply unpopular because of the austerity measures that they had sanctioned, and because President Chirac had failed to fulfil many of his election promises. High levels of unemployment and doubts about public sector reform led to a serious disenchantment with the Government. As the campaign progressed and a win for the left appeared possible, the President raised the dangers of *cohabitation* and argued that if the Left won, France would be unable to speak with one voice in the European Union.

Voting on 25 May demonstrated just how unpopular the President and the Prime Minister had become. The combined vote for the two right-wing parties, RPR and UDF, fell from 39.5 per cent in 1993 to 31.5 per cent. The vote for the Socialists rose by 6 per cent and the Communists had their highest vote (9.9 per cent) since 1988. The far-right FN attained a vote of 14.9 per cent. Following the first round, Juppé resigned as he had clearly lost his mandate. His technocratic and distant style had not found favour with the French electorate. The outcome of the first round was largely confirmed by the distribution of seats in the second round. The left-wing alliance with 300 seats, including 38 seats for the Communists, had a clear majority. The parties of the Right were routed; the number of RPR–UDF seats had almost halved which led to considerable acrimony within each party (see Table 2). The Gaullist RPR was particularly divided in the aftermath of the election, between those who continue to profess a neo-Gaullist independent line and those who favour increased European integration. Although the FN ended up with only one seat, its vote of 15 per cent demonstrated that its presence in French politics continues to strengthen.

The unexpected election and its unexpected outcome were to have immediate and long-term consequences for French and European politics. Chirac emerged from the election with his position seriously undermined. His snap election had backfired and he now faced the prospect of a long period of *cohabitation* with a left-wing government. He could no longer direct the policies and programmes of the government from the Elysée. Nor could he rely on total control over those areas, such as foreign policy, that fall within the constitutional prerogatives of the

Table 2: The 1997 French Election

Party	% Votes in Round 1	Seats Gained in Round 2
PS+Radicals	26.5	265
PC	9.9	37
Other Left	5.1	9
Ecologists	6.3	8
RPR	16.8	140
UDF	14.7	109
FN	14.9	1
Other Right	5.8	0

Source: Szarza (1997).

President. Chirac would have to establish a working relationship with the new Government and Prime Minister, Lionel Jospin. Jospin fashioned a Government which included three Communist ministers and one Green, a potential source of friction on reform. The challenge facing the administration was to fulfil its electoral promise to create 700,000 new jobs, reduce the working week from 39 hours to 35 and remain within the Maastricht convergence criteria. The Socialists had to reconcile their promise of a boost for consumption with the need for structural reform of many facets of the French economy. In the immediate aftermath of the election, there were fears that the new French Government was not fully behind the single currency and would not undertake the necessary fiscal policies to ensure that France met the criteria. Jospin set out four conditions for participation in EMU, which are discussed below. There were also doubts about the strength of the Franco-German alliance in the context of the new Government in Paris. Furthermore, the policies of the Jospin Government on labour market issues were in stark contrast, for example, to the policies of the Blair Government in the UK. As employment policy becomes the subject of EU deliberation, this contrast will be at the heart of the debate on how to reduce Europe's high levels of unemployment. In power, the Jospin Government adopted a pragmatic approach to implementing their electoral reforms, although French business felt that it was being asked to pay for the Government's policies with increases in corporate taxes and a reduction in the working week without any reduction in salaries.

Ireland

Ireland had two elections in 1997, a general election in June and a presidential election in November. The election in June pitted the sitting government known as the 'Rainbow Coalition' consisting of Fine Gael, the Labour Party and

Democratic Left against the largest party in Irish politics, Fianna Fáil and the smaller Progressive Democrats. The Labour Party had been the big winners in the 1992 election but faced the electorate in 1997 with its popularity on the wane. Following a tame campaign, the outcome of the election was that no one party was capable of forming a government. The opposition, Fianna Fáil, under Bertie Ahern was best placed, however, to harvest a majority in the Parliament by establishing a coalition with the Progressive Democrats. He also needed the support of three independents which makes this government vulnerable and unlikely to serve a full five years in office. The minority government which took office in June was unlikely to lead to any change in Ireland's European policy as there is a very consistent policy line across the political spectrum favouring adherence to the Maastricht convergence criteria and membership of the single currency at the outset, notwithstanding the policy of the UK. In fact, since 1987, Irish politics has been characterized by considerable consensus on economic management and the development of social partnership. The failure of the Rainbow Government to be re-elected, despite a booming economy with rapid convergence to EU average incomes, was consistent with the fact that, since 1969 no incumbent Irish Government has been returned to office. The replacement of one coalition by another demonstrated the extent to which Ireland now follows Continental European patterns of government formation. The big loser in the election was the Labour Party which lost 16 of its seats and 9 per cent of its vote. Following the election, Dick Spring, the former Foreign Minister, resigned as leader of the party and was replaced by Rurai Quinn, the former Finance Minister. The two larger parties, Fianna Fáil and Fine Gael, increased their votes and seats (see Table 3).

The presidential election in the autumn was a less important election, as the Irish President, although directly elected, has no political power. It was impor-

Table 3: The 1997 Irish Election

Party	% Votes	% Seats
Fianna Fáil	39.33	77
Fine Gael	27.95	54
Labour	10.4	17
Progressive Democrats	4.7	4
Democratic Left	2.5	4
Greens	2.7	2
Sinn Fein	2.5	1
Other	9.8	7

Source: Girvin (1998).

tant, however, as it heralded the departure of Mary Robinson from office. Her tenure since 1990 had transformed the Presidency as she sought to promote a more open and tolerant Ireland. She placed considerable emphasis on Ireland's place in Europe and on the multiple strands of Irish identity. Her replacement in 1997 by Mary MacAleese, the first person from Northern Ireland to hold the office, emphasized the changing relations between the two parts of Ireland. MacAleese adopted a far more nationalist tone in her portrayal of her role as Irish President.

III. Other Political Developments

Germany

As 1997 was a pre-election year in Germany, all political actors had their sights on the Bundestag elections scheduled for 27 September 1998. In April, Chancellor Kohl announced that he would stand for a fifth term of office by leading the CDU as its candidate for Chancellor. However, Kohl's position and authority weakened during the year. He failed to get the agreement of the opposition Social Democrats (SPD) to much needed taxation and pension reform. The SPD had a majority in the Upper House, the Bundesrat, and were thus able to paralyse the government's reform proposals. Germany's consensual style of politics, which had served it well in the post-war period, produced gridlock. Within the Government, there was strain between the CDU and the Liberal FDP on taxation and within the Bavarian-based Christian Social Union, between the Finance Minister, Theo Waigel, and the Bavarian Prime Minister, Edmund Stoiber. The latter continued his campaign against the euro. Within the opposition Social Democrats, Oskar Lafontaine and Gerhard Schröder continued their struggle over who would become the SPD candidate for Chancellor. The election of left-wing parties in the UK and France gave them confidence that they could end 16 years of CDU government in 1998.

Italy

In Italy, the Prodi government continued its policy of securing Italy's membership of the single currency. In the autumn, the vulnerability of the governing coalition was exposed when the Reconstructed Communists under Fausto Bertinotti refused to support the 1998 budget proposals. During what was an old-style Italian Government crisis, the Prime Minister, Romano Prodi, offered his resignation. The threat of elections was sufficient to see the 1998 budget through and highlighted once again Italy's determination to be in the first wave of EMU members.

Spain

In June, the opposition Socialist Party, which had lost the 1996 general election had to find a new leader when Philippe González resigned as party leader. He was replaced by Joaquin Almunia, a close associate of the former Prime Minister.

IV. The Intergovernmental Conference

In the first half of 1997, the Member States began the final phase of negotiations that led to the Treaty of Amsterdam. The Dutch Presidency increased the tempo of the negotiators, publishing an addendum to the Irish Draft Treaty in March. Prior to the end game at Amsterdam, the focus in the negotiations was on defence, flexibility and institutional reform. In March, the German Foreign Minister, Klaus Kinkel, submitted a draft text on the full integration of the Western European Union (WEU) into the Union. His proposals were in a joint paper supported by the Belgian, French, Italian, Luxembourg and Spanish Governments, the maximalist camp with regard to the WEU. There was an immediate and hostile reception from the UK, the neutrals and Greece. On institutional reform, the French Government continued to press for a significant reduction in the size of the Commission with rotation of membership of the Commission among the Member States. The smaller states were strongly opposed to a reduction in the size of the Commission which might lead to the loss of a Commissioner. On the question of qualified majority voting, the Italian Government submitted a paper proposing an arithmetic adjustment in the votes of the larger states rather than a system of double majorities.

The negotiations moved into top gear in May when the Blair Government took power in the UK. The Dutch scheduled an informal meeting of Heads of Government on 23 May to enable Tony Blair and his counterparts to meet before the final negotiations in Amsterdam on 16–17 June. It was his first opportunity to outline his Government's position on the major issues confronting the IGC. On social policy, the UK Government moved quickly to signal its agreement to the Maastricht Social Protocol. However, the UK continued to insist that rules on immigration, asylum, and border control must remain national and must remain outside the scrutiny of the European Court of Justice. In addition, the UK continued to oppose strongly the assimilation of the WEU into the Union.

At Amsterdam, the Heads of Government had to resolve their remaining differences on institutional reform, security/defence, flexibility, foreign policy co-operation and free movement. The arrival of the new UK Labour Government was evident when Britain supported increased powers for the European Parliament and increased majority voting in some areas, thereby facilitating agreement on the Amsterdam Treaty. Paradoxically, Chancellor Kohl, a long-term champion of institutional reform, had to insist on the retention of unanimity on decision-making on third pillar issues at Amsterdam, because the Länder share responsibility for asylum seekers with the Bonn Government and the SPD hold a majority in the Bundesrat. The SPD had threatened to veto the Treaty in the Bundesrat if their concerns were not reflected in the final agreement. On flexibility, the UK, Ireland, Greece, Spain and Portugal favoured both restrictive rules and principles for the new articles on closer co-operation. The incorporation of Schengen into the Treaty raised serious issues for the UK and Irish Governments because of their non-membership of that arrangement and their desire to retain border controls. Both governments were given opt-outs from the Schengen arrangements to enable them to continue with the common travel between the two countries. On defence, the desire of the continental states to incorporate the WEU into the EU was defeated by the UK and the neutrals. The new Member States, for whom this was their first IGC, secured their goals of securing an employment chapter in the Treaty and provisions on transparency and openness. The end of the IGC left much unfinished business for the Member States to return to again. The tension between large and small states was not resolved nor were the institutional conditions established to facilitate enlargement.

V. Policy Developments

Economic and Monetary Union

The single currency was the dominant EU policy at issue in domestic politics during 1997. All of the Member States had to position themselves in relation to the decisions being taken in May 1998 on which states should join in the first wave. As the decision will be based on the fiscal and budgetary figures for 1997, this was the critical year in the race for membership. In France, the election of the left-wing Government raised the question of its commitment to the goal of a single currency and fiscal austerity. The new Government had established four conditions for participating in EMU. First, was its preference for the inclusion of Spain and Italy in a broadly-based EMU. Second, was avoiding an overvalued euro. Third, was the establishment of a euro-zone Council, and fourth was the establishment of a growth and employment pact. Conditions three and four brought France into direct conflict with Germany and gave rise to considerable tensions in Franco–German relations in 1997. On a growth and employment pact, in the lead-up to the Amsterdam European Council, Jospin signalled that France wanted more time to study the Stability Pact which had been agreed in Dublin in December 1996. The French argued that it was necessary to find a new equilibrium between monetary and budgetary discipline, on the one hand, and employment and growth, on the other. At Amsterdam, the French had to be satisfied with the renaming of the Stability Pact to the Growth and Stability Pact, and with a summit on employment in the autumn. Their suggestion that the European Central Bank should have a parallel centre of political control in the form of a stability council was met with implacable German hostility. In November, President Chirac surprised his partners when he nominated the President of the French Central Bank, Jean-Claude Trichet, as President of the European Central Bank. All of the other states had assumed that this post would go to the Dutch Central Banker, Wim Duisenberg, current head of the European Monetary Institute.

In Germany, EMU remained the dominant EU issue on the domestic political agenda. The debate focused on whether or not Germany would meet the convergence criteria, on which states would be eligible to join and on economic governance in the Euro zone. In May, the Bonn Government lost a bruising battle with the Bundesbank over a proposal to revalue the Bundesbank's assets in gold in a effort to massage the budgetary figures. Despite signs in the first part of the year that Germany would not meet the 3 per cent deficit criteria, by September the Government was confident that Germany would meet them. In the debate on which countries should join the euro, Italy emerged as the test case in the political and public debate. Notwithstanding the considerable progress that Italy has made towards fiscal consolidation, there remained serious doubts in German political and banking circles about Italy's ability to adopt the mantle of a stability culture over the long term. Concerning economic governance in the euro–zone, the Germans were determined to ensure that the European Central Bank would be free from political interference. However, in the face of French demands for a stability council, they conceded that there could be an informal 'Euro X' Council which would meet before formal meetings of the Ecofin Council to deal with issues of common concern to members of the euro zone. This proposal in turn led to problems for those states which would remain outside the euro zone – the UK, Sweden, Denmark and Greece.

In Britain, one of the first major policy decisions facing the new Blair Government was its attitude to UK membership of the single currency. In October, the Chancellor, Gordon Brown, made a statement on this issue to the House of Commons setting out the Government's policy. He came out in favour of EMU in principle and, unlike the former Conservative Government, he did not make it an issue of sovereignty. He envisaged that Britain would enter the single currency if the economic circumstances were right. Five economic tests were laid down; convergence, flexibility, and the impact of the single currency on employment, financial services and investment. He signalled that Britain would not join in the life of this Parliament, which runs to 2002, but might well join during the life of the next Parliament, provided the economic criteria were met. The Government launched a campaign to persuade business to prepare and it has set about convincing a sceptical public opinion on the benefits of a single currency. The Government had already promised a referendum on the issue before the UK abolishes sterling. Although the Government's decision on EMU marks a decisive shift in policy, the decision to delay participation prevents the UK playing the leading role identified by Blair in the early days of his Government.

The Mediterranean states, apart from Greece, continued to make progress in ensuring that they meet the Maastricht criteria. The participation of the two Iberian states, Spain and Portugal, received a boost with declining inflation and fiscal consolidation. Italy remained the test case with impressive fiscal consolidation but doubts about its political ability to sustain the rigours of a hard currency and fiscal austerity. Doubts were most trenchantly put by the Dutch and Germans. The Ecofin Council in May warned that too many of the Italian measures to meet the convergence criteria were temporary in nature and should be replaced by structural reform. The Greek Government under Prime Minister Simitis continued its programme to modernize its economy and to bring Greece into the single currency by 2002. This will involve major changes in labour markets and the privatization of state controlled assets. The projected government budget for 1998 was designed so that Greece would meet the deficit target in 1998 and the inflation target in 1999. Among the new Member States, Finland and Austria are determined to join EMU in the first wave, whereas Sweden has adopted a wait-and-see policy.

Agenda 2000

The publication of the Commission's *Agenda 2000* proposals in July set the scene for internal debate in the Union on reform of the CAP and the structural funds in the light of enlargement. The battle lines are already drawn between the Member States on the future financial perspective after 1999. Germany and the Netherlands argued that their contributions were out of proportion and would have to be reduced, even in the light of enlargement. The German Government argued that, although Germany accounts only for 25 per cent of EU GDP, it pays half of the net contributions to the budget, and the Dutch argued that they carry the heaviest per capita burden in relation to the budget. Despite their commitment to enlargement, Germany appears far more determined on the budgetary question than it was in the past. The UK supports the Dutch and Germans on budgetary rigour but does not want to forgo its rebates. Among the net recipients, the Spanish Government was determined that its receipts from EU cohesion policy should not decline in the light of enlargement. They have reserved their position on the 1.27 per cent of GNP as a ceiling for budgetary expenditure up to 2006 and, together with the other cohesion countries, have argued that financial transfers are an essential part of the *acquis*. The budgetary debate is set to be one of the most contentious among the Member States in the next two years.

On reform of the CAP, the Commission has a more difficult task as it received support for its proposals only from the UK. Hence the debate on agriculture will depend on the WTO negotiations and on inter-ministerial battles in the Member States between Agriculture ministries and their Finance counterparts. On the question of enlargement, Sweden, Denmark and Italy failed in a bid to get enlargement negotiations started with more than the six countries suggested by the Commission. The Swedes and the Danes argued strongly that the other two Baltic States should be in the first wave of enlargement, together with Estonia.

Tax Harmonization

The single market programme and the approaching EMU has acted as a spur to renewed debate in the EU about tax harmonization, an area requiring unanimity. In January, the French and German Governments highlighted the need for a code of conduct to prevent unfair tax competition among the Member States. The emergence of taxation on the EU agenda underlined the growing tensions among the Member States on this issue. Two countries in the Union have serious reservations about an EU-wide tax regime; Ireland because of the importance of tax incentives in attracting multinational investment and Luxembourg because of the secrecy of its banking laws and the absence of a withholding tax. Other states have their own problems with EU involvement in taxation, notably the UK because of the special tax status of the Channel Islands and Gibraltar, and Spain because of the Canary Islands.

VI. Presidencies

The Netherlands

The Netherlands took over the Presidency from Ireland on 1 January. They were mindful of the difficulties they faced on 'Black Monday' during their last Presidency in 1991 when their proposed draft treaty did not even receive the support of the Belgians. The Dutch did not want to repeat it. For the Dutch, the major objectives were:

- to conclude the Intergovernmental Conference by June
- to prepare for the single currency, and
- enlargement.

Undoubtedly, the major challenge facing the Dutch Presidency was to try to secure agreement at Amsterdam to a new Treaty as this would open the way for enlargement. The Presidency increased the tempo of the negotiations and began to tackle the sensitive issues that would remain unresolved right up to the end of the negotiations. A major problem for the Dutch was that they had to wait until the British election was over to see what kind of package the British would accept. This meant that negotiations were particularly hectic in the four weeks before the Amsterdam summit; the personal representatives on the IGC working group met for 3–4 days each week, the Foreign Ministers met twice, and the Heads of Government had an informal 'getting to know you' session in Nordwijk in May.

Their carefully laid plans to devote the Amsterdam summit entirely to concluding the IGC came unstuck with the unexpected results of the unexpected French election. As noted above, the new French Government signalled that it needed more time to examine the Stability Pact which had been agreed in Dublin in December 1996. EMU rather than the IGC emerged as the dominant agenda item. The Heads of Government devoted most of their political energies and capacity to ensuring that the new French Government maintained a commitment to EMU. This reduced the time available for Treaty negotiations. However, the Dutch managed to keep both agenda items on track. The French were satisfied with the references in the Amsterdam Conclusions to a Growth and Stability Pact and with a separate Resolution on Employment, Competitiveness and Growth. They had managed to make employment a more salient issue on the EU agenda but not at the expense of derailing the EMU project. At Amsterdam, the Heads of Government also reached a conclusion on the IGC negotiations which opened the way to begin enlargement negotiations. The Dutch were well satisfied with the outcome of their Presidency; they concluded the IGC and without a repetition of 'Black Monday'.

Luxembourg

Luxembourg took over the chair in the latter half of 1997, determined to prove that a micro-state can manage the burden of the Presidency. As a member of the Union from the outset, this has never been a problem in the past. Three priorities dominated the Luxembourg Presidency. First, they had to continue preparations for EMU and manage the Franco–German debate on its economic governance. Second, they had to begin the negotiations on the Commission's *Agenda 2000* proposals which were launched in July at the beginning of their Presidency. Third, they had to host a summit on employment in the autumn, even though they were unconvinced of the usefulness of the event. Such tasks demonstrate the extent to which the agenda for each Presidency is pre-determined.

At the concluding summit in Luxembourg in December, the Presidency managed to get agreement on two major issues. Progress was made on economic governance in the euro zone with agreement to establish an informal 'Euro X' Council of members. There was major conflict between those states that are likely to join the single currency in the first wave and those that will not. In the lead-up to the summit, the British Chancellor made a determined bid to ensure that Britain would have a seat at the table. He failed. The conclusions of the European Council were that the euro ministers would meet among themselves to discuss issues relating to the single currency and that only when 'matters of common interest' are involved will the 'pre-ins' be invited to join the discussions.

The second major issue for the Luxembourg Presidency was enlargement. The European Council agreed that six states would begin enlargement negotiations on 30 March 1998 but that this would be preceded by a European Conference at the level of Heads of State for all of the potential members. The five countries in eastern and central Europe that do not form part of the first wave were reasonably happy with the outcome. However, Turkey reacted very strongly to the outcome and said that it would not attend the Europe Conference in 1998. Substantive negotiations on the internal reform required by *Agenda 2000* did not really begin under the Luxembourg Presidency. The Council merely confirmed that the Commission's proposals were 'an appropriate basis for further negotiations'.

VII. Public Opinion

With the conclusion of the IGC and memories of the June 1992 'No' vote in Denmark on the Treaty on European Union, Europe's leaders were more conscious of public attitudes towards European integration than they have been in the past. In 1997, the Commission continued its policy of conducting two Eurobarometer surveys of public opinion in the Member States, in spring and autumn. Respondents to Eurobarometer 48 were asked if they felt that Europe would play a more important role in their lives in the next millennium. A majority felt that the EU would play a more important role (46 per cent) or at least the same role (34 per cent) with only 7 per cent who felt that the EU would play a more restricted role (Eurobarometer 48, p. 7).

In 1997, support for the European Union dipped to a low of 46 per cent in spring, rising again to 49 per cent in the autumn survey. When asked if membership of the European Union was a good or bad thing for one's country, 49 per cent concluded that it was a good thing, 28 per cent neither good nor bad and 14 per cent of respondents concluded that it was a bad thing for their country. These global figures hide significant cross-national variation. Support was highest in Ireland (83 per cent) and lowest in Sweden (46 per cent) and Austria (31 per cent) (see Table 4).

In a related question on perceived benefits from EU membership, 44 per cent of respondents felt that their country had benefited, an increase of 3 per cent from spring. Levels of perceived benefit increased significantly in Italy (+13 per cent), Spain (+8 per cent), Denmark (+6 per cent) and Sweden (+4 per cent). However,

Table 4: National Attitudes towards EU Membership

	B	DK	D	GR	E	F	IRL	I
A good thing	42 +1	53 +3	38 +2	60 −1	53 +4	48 +1	83 +3	69 +7
A bad thing	18 −1	22 −3	15 −	8 −	9 +1	14 +1	3 −	6 −2
Neither	31 +1	21 −2	37 −1	27 +3	26 −4	33 −4	8 −2	19 −2
Don't know	9 −	4 +1	10 −1	5 −2	12 −	5 +1	6 −1	7 −2
Total	100	100	100	100	100	100	100	100

Table 4 Cont.

	L	NL	A	P	FIN	S	UK	EU 15
A good thing	71 −6	76 +4	31 +1	56 +2	39 +2	31 +4	36 −	49 +3
A bad thing	10 +4	9 +3	24 −3	6 −2	25 +2	46 +5	23 −3	14 −1
Neither	16 +1	12 −4	36 +2	29 −1	31 −2	20 −6	29 +2	28 −2
Don't know	3 +1	3 −3	9 −	9 +1	5 −3	4 −1	13 +1	9 −
Total	100	100	100	100	100	100	100	100

Source: Eurobarometer 48, Autumn 1997, p. B30.

Table 5: Perceived Benefits of EU Membership

	B	DK	G	GR	E	F	IRL	I
Benefited	36 −	67 +6	33 −1	70+ 2	48 +8	44 −	88 −	54 +13
Not benefited	41 +1	22 −4	44 +1	17 −2	28 −5	37 +2	4 +1	22 −13
Don't know	23 −1	11 −2	22 −1	13 −	24 −4	20 −	8 −1	25 +1
Total	100	100	100	100	100	100	100	100

Table 5 Cont

	L	NL	A	P	FIN	S	UK	EU 15
Benefited	65 −5	64 −5	35 +3	67 −	36 −1	21 +4	37 +1	44 +3
Not benefited	19 +3	25 +8	43 −1	18 −2	49 +5	61 +7	43 −1	35 −1
Don't know	16 +2	11 −4	2 −1	16 +3	15 −3	19 −10	20 −2	21 −1
Total	100	100	100	100	100	100	100	100

Source: Eurobarometer 48, Autumn 1997, p.B30.

both Luxembourg and the Netherlands registered a drop of 5 per cent. Again the variations across the Member States can be seen in Table 5.

VIII. Implementation

The growing intensity of EC regulation has led to a renewed focus on the implementation of Community law in the Member States. Since the launch of the single market programme, the Commission has adopted a number of strategies to improve the implementation deficit which characterizes EC law. Among the Commission's strategies is a focus on:

- the publication of an annual report monitoring the application of Community law;
- the publication of 'sinner's lists' on the implementation of single market legislation;
- an increase in the number of Art.169 letters and reasoned opinions sent by the Commission to the Member States;
- the possibility of fines contained in the Treaty on European Union;
- and one-to-one dialogues with the Member States about their implementation record.

The purpose of Commission activity was to increase peer pressure on the Member States to take their obligations seriously and to ensure that in all national administrations there was a group of administrators responsible for the implementation phase of EC law. The longer-term aim is to ensure that implementing and enforcing EC law becomes a norm of national administrations and enforcement agencies. In previous years, the *Annual Review* has used figures relating to the implementation of single market legislation to give an overview of cross-national differences. This is no longer appropriate as most single market legislation has been processed and this method neglected other areas of EC law, notably health and safety, the environment and agriculture. It is proposed in this article to use the 1996 report on the implementation of EC law which was published by the Commission in May 1997.

In 1997, the Commission began to use its powers under Art. 171 to ask the European Court of Justice to impose fines on Member States for non-implementation. In January, the Commission raised the threat of a daily 23,900 ECU fine because the Campania region had failed to implement a six-year old directive on waste management. The Spanish Government was threatened with fines in the health and safety area because its implementation record was very poor. The German Government faced the prospect of fines over the quality of ground water and the protection of wild birds. The national governments moved quickly to transpose and enforce the relevant legislation. Fines have added to the panoply of measures in the Commission's arsenal in its attempts to improve the implementation phase of EC law. The Commission continued to hold bilateral meetings with the Member States on implementation. In 1996, meetings were held with eight Member States – the Netherlands, Austria, Germany, Spain France, Greece, the UK and Portugal.

The 1996 report monitoring the implementation of EC law showed that the Commission's activity in this field has increased with 1142 letters of notice under Art. 169 (+9 per cent), 435 reasoned opinions (+224 per cent) and 93 referrals (72 in 1995) to the European Court of Justice (CEC, 1997). The Commission's *Annual Report* for 1997 revealed an even higher level of monitoring. It commenced infringement proceedings in 1422 cases, issued 331 reasoned opinions and referred 121 cases to the Court of Justice (CEC, 1998, p. 405).

By 31 December 1996, the Member States had notified 92.8 per cent of the Community directives that should have been transposed into national law. Denmark continued to occupy the first position on the league table with 98 per cent of all applicable directives transposed, whereas the UK has fallen somewhat to 94 per cent. Apart from the new Member States, Austria and Finland, Italy continued to find itself at the bottom of the league table (see Table 6).

Table 6: Notification of Transposition of European Community Law

Member State	Directives Applicable 31.12.96	Measures Notified	(%)
Belgium	1311	1215	92.68
Denmark	1310	1285	98.00
Germany	1313	1227	93.45
Greece	1304	1189	91.18
Spain	1314	1245	94.75
France	1310	1203	91.83
Ireland	1310	1218	92.98
Italy	1310	1181	90.15
Luxembourg	1309	1223	93.43
Netherlands	1310	1275	97.32
Austria	1306	1153	88.28
Portugal	1311	1204	91.84
Finland	1306	1057	80.93
Sweden	1308	1227	93.80
UK	1309	1233	94.19

Source: Commission 1997, p.17.

References

Commission of the European Communities (1997) *'Fourteenth Annual Report on Monitoring the Application of Community Law'*. *COM* (97) 299 final, 29 May.

Commission of the European Communities (1998) *Annual Report on the Activities of the European Union* (Luxembourg: OOPEC).

Foreign and Commonwealth Office (1997) Mission Statement, Robin Cook, Foreign Secretary, 12 May.

Girvin, B. (1998) 'Consensus and Political Competition in the Irish Republic: The 1997 General Election'. *Parliamentary Affairs*, Vol. 51, No. 1, pp. 84–100.

Harrop, M. (1997) 'The Pendulum Swings: The British Election of 1997'. *Government and Opposition*, Vol. 32, No. 3, Summer, pp. 305–19.

Robbins, K. (1998) 'Britain and Europe: Devolution and Foreign Policy'. *International Affairs*, Vol. 94, No. 1, pp. 105–18.

Speech (1997) by the Prime Minister, Tony Blair, Lord Mayor's Banquet, London, 1 November.

Szarka, J. (1997) 'Snatching Defeat from the Jaws of Victory: The French Parliamentary Elections of 25 May and 1 June 1997'. *West European Politics,* Vol. 20, No. 4, October, pp. 192–9.

Journal of Common Market Studies

Volume 36, Annual Review
September 1998

A Guide to the Documentation of the European Union

IAN THOMSON
Cardiff University
and
JANET MATHER
Manchester Metropolitan University

Abbreviations

Bull.EU	Bulletin of the European Union
COM	Commission Document
CoR	Committee of the Regions
EC	European Community (when noted as the publisher, 'EC' means the Office for Official Publications of the European Communities (EUROPE), L-2985, Luxembourg. EC publications may be obtained from the sales agents of EUR-OP in the Member States and elsewhere. In the UK the sales agent is HMSO.)
EEA	European Economic Area
EP	European Parliament
IGC	Intergovernmental Conference
OJ	Official Journal of the European Communities –Annex: Debates of the European Parliament – C: Information – L: Legislation
PE DOC	Committee Report of the European Parliament
SEC	Internal Commission General Secretariat Document
TEU	Treaty on European Union

Most publications cited in this Guide are available for reference in European Documentation Centres (EDCs, mainly based in academic libraries) and EC Depository Libraries throughout the world. Access to electronic sources is also available in EDCs and Depository Libraries.

Introduction

This Guide lists a selection of the key EU documents and publications of 1997 that highlight the important institutional and policy activities and initiatives of the European Union. In addition, a selection of other significant new publications and series are noted. Some titles issued in the closing weeks of 1996, or titles published in 1996 but which only became available in 1997, are included. The bibliography is divided into five sections:

General
Governance and institutional developments
Financing the Union
Internal policy developments
External policies and relations

Specific legislative proposals and legislation adopted during the year are not included. These can be traced routinely in each issue of *European Access* throughout 1997 in the 'Recent references' section under the appropriate heading and are also listed at the beginning of the section 'Recent publications of interest'.

The majority of references noted in the Guide are to printed sources. It should be noted, however, that the Internet is now a major source of European Union information and this is reflected throughout the Guide, where Internet addresses (or 'urls') are noted, when appropriate. Sources noted as *Press Release, Document* and *Memo* are available on the RAPID database on the Internet.

Note that 'EC' remains the standard term used in *European Access* for material published by the Office for Official Publications of the European Communities (EUR-OP).

General

For an overview of the activities of the EU in 1997 see the European Commission's *General Report on the Activities of the European Union 1997* (published by EUR-OP in February 1998) and issues of the monthly *Bulletin of the European Union*. The latter is now also available on the Internet at http://europa.eu.int/abc/doc/off/bull/en/welcome.htm . It is possible that the *General Report* for 1997 will also be available on the Internet.

The EU legislative database CELEX became available on the Internet during 1997 (http://europa.eu.int/celex). A Eurobases userword and password is required for access. Considerable progress has been made in the project to provide full text information in those sectors of CELEX in which previously only bibliographical information was provided.

The EU bibliographic database SCAD also became (freely) available on the Internet (http://europa.eu.int/scad). A further development has been the launch of SCADPLUS on the Internet (http://europa.eu.int/comm/sg/scadplus) which, in addition to providing access to SCAD, also provides access to a range of additional services such as a 'Calendar' (dates and agendas of meetings in the Council, European Parliament, Economic and Social Committee and Committee of the Regions), 'European Union policies' (summaries of EU policies in all the major policy areas), 'Programmes, networks and observatories concerned with social affairs and education' and a 'Practical guide to the free movement of persons' in the EU.

Also worthy of note has been the launch of EUDOR, an EU document delivery service (http://www.eudor.com), the launch of the MARKETACCESS database providing detailed information about trading conditions and barriers in non-EU countries (http://mkaccdb.eu.int) and the launch of OEIL (L'Observatoire Législatif) providing up-to-date information on the status of EU legislative proposals (http://www.europarl.eu.int/dors/oeilfr/default.htm). During 1997 only a French language version of OEIL was available but further language versions are expected.

The Internet version of the EU's interinstitutional directory called IDEA has remained freely accessible (http://europa.eu.int/idea/ideaen.html), as has the invaluable EU press release database RAPID (http://europa.eu.int/en/comm/spp/rapid.html).

Many of the documents noted throughout this Guide are available on the Internet. For the texts of Green Papers and White Papers and other officials documents of the European Commission, for example, check http://europa.eu.int/comm/off/index-en.htm

Agenda 2000

The Commission launched its *Agenda 2000* initiative on 16 July 1997, its detailed strategy for strengthening and widening the Union in the coming years. The Commission's 1,300 page Communication gives an assessment of the preparedness for membership of the applicant countries from central and eastern Europe. The Communication also addresses the need for internal policy and institutional reform within the EU, and the challenges for financing these changes.

The key sources of information on *Agenda 2000* are:

Commission: *Agenda 2000. For a stronger and wider union*: COM (97)2000 final (Vol.I)
Related publications: *Document* (Commission), DOC/97/6 (15.7.97); *Bull.EU: Supplement*, No.5, 1997

Commission: *Agenda 2000. Reinforcing the pre-accession strategy*: COM (97)2000 final (Vol.II)
Related publications: *Document* (Commission), DOC/97/7 (15.7.97); *Bull EU: Supplement*, No.5, 1997

Commission, Spokesman's Service:*Agenda 2000. Summary and conclusions of the opinions of the Commission concerning the applications for membership to*

the European Union presented by the candidate countries: *Document*, DOC/97/
8 (15.7.97)
Related publications: *Bull.EU: Supplement*, No.5, 1997

The Commission's opinions on the applications to join the EU by the countries of central
and eastern Europe are published as *COM* (97)2001–2010 final (15.7.97) or *Bull.EU:
Supplement*, No.6–15, 1997 (Full bibliographical references are noted in Section E
'Enlargement' below.)

Internet address: http://europa.eu.int/comm/agenda2000/index.htm .

For further information sources on *Agenda 2000*, see *European Access*, No.5, October
1997, pp. 35–8.

Governance and Institutional Developments

Primary Legislation

The Treaty of Amsterdam was agreed at the European Council, Amsterdam, 16–17 June
1997. The Council of the European Union published a copy of the text as agreed at
Amsterdam in June 1997:

Council: *Intergovernmental Conference. Amsterdam European Council. Draft
Treaty*: EC, 1997; EC No.BX-06-97-383-EN-C

Subsequently, the text of the Treaty was revised before the formal signing of the Treaty
of Amsterdam on 2 October 1997. The text adopted on that day was published in:

Council: *Treaty of Amsterdam amending the Treaty on European Union
establishing the European Communities and certain related acts, signed at
Amsterdam, 2 October 1997*: *OJ* C340, 10.11.97, pp. 1–313

A further version of the text was published as:

European Union: *Treaty of Amsterdam*: EC, 1997; ISBN: 92-828-1652-4 EC
No.FX-08-97-468-EN-C

The EU also published a volume containing consolidated texts of earlier treaties as
amended by the Treaty of Amsterdam:

European Union: *Consolidated versions of the Treaty on European Union and
The Treaty establishing the European Community*: EC, 1997; ISBN: 92-828-
1640-0: EC No.FX-08-97-606-EN-C

The text of the Treaty of Amsterdam and the consolidated versions of earlier treaties are
available on the Internet at http://ue.eu.int/Amsterdam/en/en.htm . See also: http://
europa.eu.int/abc/obj/amst/en/index.htm .
  The Council issued a short report in November 1997 seeking to explain the results

(as contained in the second part of the Amsterdam Treaty) of the exercise carried out by the Intergovernmental Conference to simplify the Community Treaties:

Council: *Explanatory report from the General Secretariat of the Council on the simplification of the Community Treaties*: OJ C353, 20.11.97, pp. 1–19

The Intergovernmental Conference

The culmination of the Intergovernmental Conference took place with the signing of the Treaty of Amsterdam in October 1997. Information sources are noted above.

Other information sources to note include:

Parliament: *Resolution: on the general outline for a draft revision of the Treaties*: OJ C33, 3.2.97, pp. 66–73

Parliament: *Resolution: Progress of the Intergovernmental Conference*: OJ C115, 14.4.97, pp. 165–8

Council, General Secretariat: *Intergovernmental Conference on the revision of the Treaties. Italian Presidency (January–June 1996). Collected texts*: EC, 1997: ISBN: 92-824-1365-9; EC No.BX-95-96-382-EN-C

Council, General Secretariat: *Intergovernmental Conference on the revision of the Treaties. Irish Presidency (July–December 1996). Collected texts*: EC, 1997; ISBN: 92-824-1009-9; EC No.BX-03-97-991-EN-C

Brief reports on the closing stages of the IGC negotiations were issued by the UK Representation of the European Commission as *Background Report*, B2/97 and *Briefing Paper* 'The Member States of the European Union and the Inter-Governmental Conference'. Both are available on the Internet at http://www.cec.org.uk .

Commission: *Papers of the Symposium of Jean Monnet Chairs on the 1996 Intergovernmental Conference, Brussels, 6-7.5.97*: EC, 1997: ISBN: 92-827-9048-7. EC No.CM-98-96-744-2A-C

A major source of information on the Intergovernmental Conference was available on the EUROPA server on the Internet. At the time of writing this database is still available and it is assumed that it will remain so. The address is: http://europa.eu.int/en/agenda/igc-home/ .

The Presidency and the European Council

The programmes of the six-monthly Presidencies of the EU are formally presented to the European Parliament in January and July each year. The text of the verbal presentation by the current President of the Council, and the subsequent debate is published in the *OJ: Annex*. Publication of this title is now very delayed. At the time of compilation of this feature neither the *OJ:Annex*, No.4-492, January 1997 (covering the Netherlands Presidency, January–June 1997) nor the *OJ: Annex*, July 1997 (covering the Luxembourg Presidency, July–December 1997) are available. Summaries of the presentations are available in *The Week*, 13–17.1.97, p. 10 and *The Week*, 14–18.7.97, p. 22 (also available on the European Parliament's server – http://www.europarl.eu.int).

A review and debate of each European Presidency also takes place in the European Parliament usually during the last months of each Presidency and following the European Council summit. The review of the Dutch Presidency and the Amsterdam European Council (June 1997) took place in the June 1997 plenary session (*OJ: Annex* not yet published, see *The Week*, 25–26.6.97, p. 8); the review of the Luxembourg Presidency and the Luxembourg European Council (December 1997) took place in the December 1997 plenary session (*OJ: Annex* not yet published, see *The Week*, 15–19.12.97).

Note that the full text of these statements and debates is available on the EUROPARL server under the section *Verbatim Report of Proceedings (Provisional Edition)* but these are not translated reports.

Also of value are the homepages that each EU Presidency makes available on the Internet. The Dutch Presidency pages are available at: http://Hermes.bz.minbuza.nl/europe97/ and the Luxembourg Presidency pages are available at: http://www.etat.lu/uepres/ .

The UK launched its homepages for its January–June 1998 Presidency in November 1997: http://presid.fco.gov.uk/.

The long-term continued existence of these pages cannot be guaranteed.

The conclusions adopted at the end of European Council meetings are published in the *Bulletin of the European Union*, as a *Document* on the RAPID database, and on the EUROPA server on the Internet.

For details of the European Council, Amsterdam, 16–17 June 1997, see *Bull.EU*, No.6, 1997, pp. 8–25 or *DOC*/97/2 (18.6.97) on RAPID. The Internet version was unavailable at the time of compilation of this Guide.

For details of the Extraordinary European Council on Employment, Luxembourg, 20–21 November 1997, see *Bull.EU*, No.11, 1997 (not published at time of compilation), *DOC*/97/23 (21.11.97) or *Press Release* (Council), PRES/97/300 (21.11.97) on RAPID, and http://europa.eu.int/en/comm/dg05/elm/summit/en/papers/concl.htm on EUROPA. The Internet site also provides the texts of all the papers associated with the Jobs Summit.

For details of the European Council, Luxembourg, 12–13 December 1997 see *Bull.EU*, No.12, 1997 (not published at time of compilation), *DOC*/97/24 (14.11.97) or *Press Release* (Council), PRES/97/400 (15.12.97) on RAPID, and http://europa.eu.int/council/off/conclu/dec97.htm on EUROPA.

No formal Conclusions were issued after the informal European Council, Noordwijk, 23 May 1997 (see *Bull.EU*, No.5, 1997, p. 8).

In addition to the sources for the 1997 European Councils listed above it should be noted that the Commission published a new-style booklet bringing together the texts of the Conclusions of the Presidency for the three 1996 European Councils:

> Commission, DG X: *The European Councils. Conclusions of the Presidency 1996*: EC, 1997; ISBN: 92-828-1507-2; EC No.CC-07-97-054-EN-C

The Council of the European Union

Reports of all regular Council meetings are issued as *Press Releases* on the RAPID database with the prefix *PRES*. Agendas for forthcoming Council meeting have been issued in this form in the past but generally were not in 1997. Although not fully complete at the time of compilation a new source for agendas and reports of Council meetings is the 'Calendar' sector of SCADPLUS on EUROPA (http://europa.eu.int/comm/sg/scadplus/) .

The Council seem to have stopped publishing a summary-style annual report. During 1997 the following full annual report was issued:

> Council, General Secretariat: *43rd review of the Council's work. The Secretary-General's report. 1 January–31 December 1995*: EC, 1997; ISBN: 92-824-1427-2; EC No.BX-98-96-873-EN-C

For the first time the review provides brief information on various transparency aspects of Council policy-making such as the outcome of votes taken and any explanation of vote and statements for the minutes which the Council has decided may be released to the public when acting in its legislative capacity.

The Council of the European Union published a three-volume handbook to help officials, and others, understand the working methods of the Institution. Vol.I sets out in a practical context the arrangements surrounding the preparation and running of a Presidency; Vol.II looks at how the rules of procedure are interpreted in practice; Vol.III contains practical information on the planning and running of meetings, the internal organization of the General Secretariat and the services provided for delegates:

> Council, General Secretariat: *Council Guide I – Presidency handbook*: EC, 1997; ISBN: 92-824-1295-4; EC No.BX-76-96-001-EN-C

> Council, General Secretariat: *Council Guide II – Comments on the Council's rules of procedure*: EC, 1997; ISBN: 92-824-1298-9; EC No.BX-76-96-002-EN-C

> Council, General Secretariat: *Council Guide III – Delegates' handbook* EC, 1997; ISBN: 92-824-1301-2; EC No.BX-76-96-003-EN-C

Further information sources of interest are:

> Council: *96/705/Euratom, ECSC, EC: Council Decision of 6.12.96 amending 93/731/EC on public access to Council documents*: *OJ* L325, 14.12.96, p. 19

> Council, General Secretariat: *Council's rules of procedure*: EC, 1997; ISBN: 92-824-1496-5; EC No.BX-01-96-454-EN-C
> *Related publications*: *OJ* L304, 10.12.93, p1; *OJ* L31, 10.2.95, p. 14

The Council's homepage on the Internet is: http://ue.eu.int/ .

© Blackwell Publishers Ltd 1998

The European Commission

The Commission's Work Programme for 1997 was published in the autumn of 1996 as *COM* (96)507 final (17.10.96). This was re-published, along with the text of the speech by Commission President Jacques Santer to the European Parliament on 22 October 1996, and the Resolution of the European Parliament on the 1997 Programme in *Bull.EU: Supplement*, No.1, 1997. The Programme is also available on the Internet at http://europa.eu.int/en/comm/co97pr/index.htm .

In October 1997 the Commission issued its work programme for 1998:

> Commission: *The Commission's Work Programme for 1998. The political priorities*: *COM* (97)517 final (15.10.97)

The Work Programme is available on the Internet at http://europa.eu.int/en/comm/co98pr/index-en.htm . This contains the political priorities and a list of legislative initiatives to be undertaken during 1998, plus a separate section called 'Report on implementation of the Commission programme for 1997'.

Other information sources of interest include:

> Commission: *Access to Commission documents. A citizen's guide*, 2nd ed.:EC, 1997; ISBN: 92-827-8315-4: EC No.CM-96-96-764-EN-C

> Commission, Spokesman's Service: *MAP 2000: Modernisation of administration and personnel: Commission modernises its services: Press Release*, IP/97/369 (30.4.97)

> Commission, Spokesman's Service: *Commission decides to pay interest to creditors for overdue payments*: *Press Release*, IP/97/506 (10.6.97)

> Commission, Spokesman's Service: *The Commission decides to buy the renovated Berlaymont – a long term solution*: *Press Release*, IP/97/616 (8.7.97)

> Commission, Spokesman's Service: *Commission adopts - as first European Institution - a green housekeeping plan for its administration*: *Press Release*, IP/97/694 (24.7.97)

Most Directorates General of the European Commission have sites on the Europa server on the Internet. In addition, there is much further information relating to European Commission activities. The basic address (url) for Europa is http://europa.eu.int .

See Section A above for details of the Commission's General Report.

The European Parliament

Periodically the European Parliament issues a directory of Members of the Bureau, Parliament, political groups, committees and interparliamentary delegations. The latest edition is:

Parliament: *List of Members* (5.11.97): EC, 1997: ISSN: 0256-243X
EC No.AX-AE-97-003-1F-C

Other information sources of interests include:

Parliament: *Rules of procedure*: OJ L49, 19.2.97, pp. 1–76

Parliament: *97/632/ECSC, EC, Euratom: EP Decision of 10.7.97 on public access to European Parliament documents*: OJ L263, 25.9.97, pp. 27–9

Parliament, Publications and Public Events Service: *The European Parliament* EC, 1997; ISBN: 92-823-0988-6; EC No.AX-98-96-938-EN-C
Notes: Introductory booklet

Commission: *Communication ... Financing new buildings for the European Parliament in Brussels and Strasbourg*; COM (97)518 final (29.10.97)

The European Parliament's homepage on the Internet is: http://www.europarl.eu.int .

The European Court of Justice
The more rapid publication of the judgments of the European Court of Justice in a printed version has been maintained, but the most important development during 1997 was the placing on the ECJ homepage on the Internet of the full text of judgments of the ECJ on the day of the judgement (from June 1997). The full text will remain available in this form for twelve months, by which time the printed version should be available as will the text on the CELEX database.

Other information sources of interest include:

Court of Justice: *Note for guidance on references by national courts for preliminary rulings: Proceedings of the Court of Justice...*, No. 34, 1996 (9.12.96), pp. 1–3

Court of Justice: *Amendments to the rules of procedure of the Court of Justice* OJ L103, 19.4.97, pp. 1–7

Court of Justice, Research, Documentation and Library Directorate: *Index A–Z. Numerical and alphabetical index of cases before the Court of Justice of the European Communities. Situation on 31 August 1996*; EC, 1997; ISBN: 92-829-0333-8EC No.DX-03-97-103-EN-C

Court of Justice, Research, Documentation and Library Directorate: *Notes, Références des notes de doctrine aux arrêts de la Cour de justice et du Tribunal de première instance des Communautés européennes. January 1997*: EC, 1997ISBN: 92-829-0335-4: EC No.DX-03-97-377-FR-C

Court of Justice, Library: *Legal bibliography of European Integration, 1996.* 2 vols.: EC, 1997; ISBN: 92-829-0336-2 (Vol.1); 92-829-0337-0 (Vol.2); EC No.DY-14-97-001/2-1F-C

The homepage of the European Court of Justice is: http://www.curia.eu.int

The Economic and Social Committee

The annual report of the Economic and Social Committee for 1996 was published:

Economic and Social Committee: *Annual report 1996*; EC, 1997; ISBN: 92-830-0274-1; EC No.EX-04-97-008-EN-C

The Economic and Social Committee also published its response to transparency initiatives:

Economic and Social Committee: *Decision on public access to ESC documents*: *OJ* L339, 10.12.97, p. 18

The homepage for the Economic and Social Committee is: http://www.esc.eu.int/en/default.htm .

The Committee of the Regions

A summary of the CoR's consultative work was provided:

Committee of the Regions: *Summary of consultative work 1996*: *CdR* 99/97; EC, 1997

A regular summary of the CoR's impact was published showing a mixed reception to CoR Opinions from other EU institutions:

Committee of the Regions: *Impact and follow-up of opinions 1996*: EC, 1997

The CoR also published an introductory booklet:

Committee of the Regions: *Committee of the Regions*: EC, 1997; ISBN: 92-827-9905-0; EC No.GF-01-96-535-EN-C

Following the European Summit of the Regions and Cities, the CoR summarized the proceedings (six issues of a special *Newsletter* covering the summit were also published):

Committee of the Regions: *European Summit of the Regions and Cities, Amsterdam, 15–16.5.97. The message EC, 1997*

The CoR's response to transparency was issued:

Committee of the Regions: *Decision of the Committee of the Regions of 17.9.97 concerning public access to documents of the Committee of the Regions*: *OJ* L351, 23.12.97, pp. 70–1

The homepage of the Committee of the Regions is: http://www.cor.eu.int/ .

The European Court of Auditors

The 20th annual report (for the financial year 1996) of the European Court of Auditors was issued in November 1997:

Court of Auditors: *Annual report concerning the financial year 1996, together with the institutions' replies.* 2 vols: *OJ* C348, 18.11.97, pp. 1–417 (Vol.I); pp. 1–56 + i–xxxix (Vol. II)

Special reports, opinions and other reports of the Court of Auditors issued during 1996 and 1997 are listed at the back of Vol.I of the above report, with an indication of their availability. See also *OJ* C393, 29.12.97, pp. 1–63, which contains the reports from the Court of Auditors on the financial statements and management for 1996 for most of the EU agencies such as CEDEFOP and the European Environment Agency.

The address (url) of the European Court of Auditors site on the Internet is http://europa.eu.int/ca/caudit.html (although the site has apparently not been updated in 1997).

The European Investment Bank (EIB)

The EIB's role is to contribute long-term loans to assist towards the EU's integration. In 1997, it issued annual reports on the EIB and the European Investment Fund:

European Investment Bank: *Annual report 1996*: EC, 1997; ISBN: 92-827-9943-3; EC No.IX-04-97-113-EN-C

The combined 1995 and 1996 annual reports of the EIB are also available on CD-ROM from the Bank; see also the website: http://www.bei.org .

European Investment Fund: *Annual report 1996*: EC, 1997

EIB activity was expanded in 1996, advancing loans for a total of 23.2 bn ECU. A report detailed its operations on finance contracts signed and disbursements:

European Investment Bank: *The European Union's financing institution*: EC, 1997; ISBN: 92-827-9931-X; EC No.IX-04-97-121-EN-C

The Amsterdam Special Programme (ASAP) towards creating jobs was drawn up in 1997. The EIB estimated in a report to the Luxembourg Council in November 1997 that this will generate up to 10 bn ECU of financing:

European Investment Bank: *EIB's growth and jobs action programme – first results; Press Release*, 21.11.97
Related publications: *EIB Information*, No. 94 (No.4, 1997), p. 1

The EIB revised its rules on transparency. Requests for public access to documentation are to be forwarded to the Secretary General of the bank:

European Investment Bank: *Rules on public access to documents*: OJ C243, 9.8.97, pp. 13–15

The homepage for the European Investment Bank is http://www.eib.org .

Other EU Institutions and Organizations

European Agency for the Evaluation of Medicinal Products: *Work programme 1997–98*: EC, 1997; ISBN: 92-9155-006-X; EC No.AM-05-97-567-EN-C

(Annual reports for 1996 and 1997 are available on the Internet at http://www.eudra.org/emea.html).

The EEA's annual report (also available on the Internet at http://www.eea.dk/frdocu.htm) was published:

European Environment Agency: *EEA annual report 1996*: EC, 1997; ISBN: 92-9167-041-3; EC No.GH-03-97-806-EN-C

The European Environment Agency is to accord 'the widest possible' access to documents except where it could undermine public interest, international relations, monetary stability, court proceedings and investigations or where there is individual privacy or financial interests to be protected:

European Environment Agency: *Decision of 21.3.97 on public access to European Environment Agency documents*: OJ C282, 18.9.97, pp. 5–7

Two reports were published by the European Foundation for the Improvement of Living and Working Conditions:

European Foundation for the Improvement of Living and Working Conditions: *Annual report 1996*: EC, 1997; ISBN: 92-826-9717-7; EC No.SX-06-97-658-EN-C

European Foundation for the Improvement of Living and Working Conditions: *Programme of work for 1997*; EC, 1997; ISBN: 92-827-9697-3; EC No.SX-03-97-531-EN-C

The European Monetary Institute published an introductory booklet:

European Monetary Institute: *The European Monetary Institute*: EMI, 1997, ISBN: 92-9166-017-5

Its more substantial annual report covered preparations for EMU and looked at the performance of the Member States' economies:

European Monetary Institute: *Annual report 1996*; EMI, 1997; ISSN: 1024-560X
Notes: See also Section D 'Economic and monetary issues' below.

Other publications of interest include:

Office for Harmonisation in the Internal Market: *Annual activity report 1996*; EC, 1997; ISBN: 92-9156-004-9; EC No.AH-04-97-937-EN-C

Translation Centre for the bodies of the European Union: *Report on the activities 1996*; EC, 1997; ISBN: 92-828-1179-4; EC No.AT-07-97-256-EN-C

Gabriele Winkler has been appointed of the Community Plant Variety Office. the appointment is for five years:

Council: *Decision by common accord... determining the seat of the Community Plant Variety Office*: OJ C36, 5.2.97, p. 1

The Commission took a 'dynamic approach' to the EU's drug policy, setting down the starting point for plans to meet the EU's medium and long-term needs:

Commission: *Report on the activities of the European Monitoring Centre for Drugs and Drug Addiction* (1994–96): *COM* (97)146 final (11.4.97)

The Commission provided an overview of the European Training Foundation's (ETF) experience to date:

Commission: Report... *on the European Training Foundation*: *COM* (97)379 final (18.7.97)
Related publications: *COM* (97)381 final (18.7.97) (ETF annual reports for 1995 and 1996)

As with other EU institutions, the ETF decided upon 'widest possible' public access to its documentation, unless such access threatened the public interest, individual privacy, commercial and industrial secrecy and the EC's financial interests.

European Training Foundation: *Decision of the Governing Board on public access to European Training* Foundation documents: *OJ* C369, 6.12.97, pp. 10–11

Policy-making

The Commission thought that 1996 was a 'good year' for applying Community Law. The number of complaints fell by 15%. The report's introduction, however, includes measures to improve infringement procedures:

Commission: *Fourteenth annual report on monitoring the application of Community law – 1996: OJ* C332, 3.11.97, pp. 1–206
Related publications: *COM* (97)299 final (29.5.97)

In contrast, the EP was concerned that some Member States were not transposing directives and that some had not complied with ECJ judgments:

> Parliament: *Resolution: Monitoring the application of the Community law* OJ C55, 24.2.97, pp. 47–52
> *Related publications*: *PE DO* A4-1/97

The Commission was pleased to report that Santer's aim to 'do less but do better' was being achieved:

> Commission: *Better lawmaking 1997. Commission report to the European Council:COM* (97)626 final (26.11.97)

The EP's response to the Commission's proposal to extend co-decision to the entire legislative field was one of guarded enthusiasm. The EP felt that the proposal left too many 'grey areas':

> Parliament: *Resolution: Scope of co-decision procedure*; OJ C362, 2.12.96, pp. 267–70
> *Related publications*: *PE DOC* A4-361/96; *SEC* (967)1225 final

The Commission's formula for calculating the level of fines for defaulting Member States was a uniform flat rate of 500 ECU per day multiplied by two coefficients, reflecting the seriousness of the infringement and its duration. The result was to be multiplied by a factor reflecting the ability of the state to pay and the number of votes it carried in the Council of Ministers:

> Commission: *Method of calculating the penalty payments provided for pursuant to Article 171 of the EC Treaty*: OJ C63, 28.2.97, pp. 2–4
> *Related publications*: OJ C242, 21.8.96, p. 6

The EP noted its concern about the lack of progress in the implementation of the subsidiarity principle in 1994–96 particularly in relation to the single market:

> Parliament: *Resolution: Application of subsidiarity principle*: OJ C167, 2.6.97, pp. 34–6

For information sources relating to access to documents, in the context of openness and transparency, see *European Access*, No.6, December 1997, pp. 33–4 and under individual EU institution headings above.

European Ombudsman

The 1996 report was the first to cover a full year of activity by the Ombudsman. His report concentrated upon reporting the work of the Ombudsman's office rather than dealing with specific cases:

European Ombudsman: *Annual report for 1996*: EC, 1997; ISBN: 92-823 1012-4; EC No.ME-05-97-486-EN-C

The EP greeted the Ombudsman's report with satisfaction, but urged the Ombudsman to make full use of his powers:

Parliament: *Resolution: Activities of the European Ombudsman in 1996*: OJ C286, 22.9.97, pp. 41–3
Related publications: PE DOC A4-211/97

The homepage for the Ombudsman is: http://www.euro-ombudsman.eu.int/ .

Miscellaneous

Various informative reports about the Commission's working arrangements were published by the Commission:

Commission: *Directory of interest groups*: EC, 1996; ISBN: 92-827-8987-X EC No. CM-94-96-833-3A-C

Commission, DG X: *Working together – the Institutions of the European Community and Union*: *Document*: EC, 1997; ISBN: 92-828-0294-9; EC No.CC-05-97-244-EN-C

'Who's Who' is also available as the IDEA base (http://europa.eu.int/idea/ideaen.html) on the Internet where it is updated fortnightly. The 'hard copy' is:

Commission: *Who's who in the European Union? Interinstitutional Directory. April 1997*: EC, 1997; ISBN: 92-828-0099-7; EC No.FX-04-97-080-EN-C

The Commission's evaluation of the Interchange of Data between Administrations (IDA) programme included proposals on a series of guidelines and for adopting a series of actions and measure to ensure interoperability and access to trans-European networks:

Commission: *Communication ... concerning the evaluation of the IDA programme and a second phase of the IDA programme (+ legislative proposals)*: *COM* (97)661 final (12.12.97)

Financing the Union

1997 Budget

The full text of the 1997 budget was published in:

Parliament: 97/105/ECSC, EC, Euratom: *Final adoption of the general budget of the EU for the financial year 1997*: OJ L44, 14.2.97, pp. 1–1573

Commission: *General budget of the European Union for the financial year
1997. The figures*: *SEC* (97)15; EC, 1997; ISBN: 92-827-9462-8; EC No.C6-
01-96-567-EN-C

1998 Budget

The full texts of the draft budget as it passes through the various legislative stages are
not published. Summaries are available in various secondary sources, notably Part I
Section 5 'Financing Community activities' in the *Bulletin of the European Union* for
the appropriate months.

The Commission approved the preliminary draft budget for 1998 on 30 April 1997
(*Bull.EU*, No.4, 1997, pp. 98–103). The Council adopted a first reading draft on 24 July
1997 (*Bull.EU*, No.7–8, 1997, pp. 113–19 and *Press Release* (Council), PRES/97/248
(24.7.97). The European Parliament voted on the first reading on 21 October 1997
(*Bull.EU*, No.10, 1997). The Council approved a draft 1997 budget at a second reading
on 27 November 1997 (*Bull.EU*, No.11, 1997 and *Press Release* (Council), PRES/97/
362 (27.11.97)). The European Parliament finally adopted the 1998 budget on 16
December 1997 (*Bull.EU*, No.12, 1997(not published at time of compilation) and *The
Week*, 15–19.12.97, p. 9).

The 1998 budget was published in *OJ* L (not available at the time of compilation).

Financial Management

1996 had produced a good climate for borrowing money, and the sum borrowed was an
increase of 36.4 per cent on previous years. However, lending money, especially to non-
EC countries, had been reduced following the conclusion of co-operation agreements:

> Commission, DG II: *Reports on the borrowing and lending activities of the
> Community in 1996*: *European Economy: Supplement A*, No.6, June 1997, pp.
> 1–15
> *Related publications*: *COM* (97)312 final (19.6.97)

The Guarantee Fund totalled 557,510,343.61 ECU at the end of the 1996 financial year:

> Commission: *Annual status report by the Commission on the Guarantee Fund
> and its management in 1996*: *COM* (97)208 final (13.5.97)

EU loans finance macro (balance of payments loans to Member States or non-EU
countries) or microeconomic objectives (on projects to be repaid via self-generating
funds). The Commission's report deals with both categories:

> Commission: *Commission report to the budgetary authority on guarantees
> covered by the General Budget – Situation at 31.12.96*: *COM* (97)273 final
> (5.6.97)
> *Related publications*: *COM* (97)464 final (25.9.97)

The Commission's report on the fight against fraud covered an overview of activities since its strategy was put into place in 1994. In 1996, fraud equalled 5.8 per cent of total revenue collected (increased from 3.6 per cent in 1995), a sum of 1.3 bn ECU (compared with 1.1 bn ECU in 1995):

> Commission: *Protecting the Community's financial interests. The fight against fraud. Annual report 1996*: EC, 1997; ISBN: 92-828-0484-4
> EC No.CM-04-97-234-EN-C
> *Related publications*: *COM* (97)200 final (6.5.97)

A report on the actions taken against fraud focused on six themes: detection of irregularities; recovery of amounts; fraud prevention; sanctions/deterrence; the judicial area for protection of the EC's interests and the preparation for enlargement:

> Commission: *Protection of the Community's financial interests. Fight against fraud. Work Programme 1997/98*: *COM* (97)199 final (6.5.97)

A case study report examined progress on recovery. It examined two types of sample cases: those which involve entitlements of over 500,000 ECU and those which involve over 1,000,000 ECU:

> Commission: *2nd report on the recovery of traditional own resources in cases of fraud and irregularities (Sample B94)*: *COM* (97)259 final (9.6.97)

A report traces the protection of the EC's financial interest from the 1960s. The Commission's emphasis herein was upon the responsibilities of Member States in the fight against fraud:

> Commission: *Explanatory report on the Convention on the Protection of the European Communities' Financial Interests*: *OJ* C191, 23.6.97, pp. 1–10
> *Related publications*: *OJ* C221, 19.7.97, p. 11

A report under Article 18(5) of Council Regulation (EEC, Euratom) No 1552/89 was issued:

> Commission: *Second report ... on the operation of the inspection arrangements for traditional own resources (for period 1993–96)...*: *COM* (97)673 final (8.12.97)

See also 'Justice and Home Affairs' below.

Miscellaneous

The Commission issued a 1997 edition of its survey of the EU's finances:

> Commission: *The Community budget. The facts in figures. 1997 edition*: *SEC* (97)1200; EC, 1997; ISBN: 92-828-0850-5; EC No.C6-06-97-230-EN-C

Internal Policy Developments

Agriculture

The Commission produced a report in accordance with Article 10, Council Regulation (EEC) No 729/10:

> Commission: *Draft 26th financial report concerning the European Agricultural Guidance and Guarantee Fund (EAGGF Guarantee Section). 1996 financial year*: COM (97)589 final (25.11.97)

A report covered the operation of agri-environment regulation up to 1997, showing how it fitted in with CAP and other EC policy instruments:

> Commission: *Report ... on the application of Council Regulation (EEC) No.2078/92 on agricultural production methods compatible with the requirements of the protection of the environment and the maintenance of the countryside*: COM (97)620 final (4.12.97)

Another report focused upon the implementation of flanking methods adopted in 1992 to accompany CAP reform:

> Commission: *Report ... on the application of Regulation (EEC) No.2080/92 instituting a Community aid scheme for forestry measures in agriculture*; COM (97)630 final (28.11.97)

DG VI provided long-term forecasts for key agricultural products for the period 1997–2000:

> Commission, *DG VI: CAP 2000: Long term prospects. Grains, milk and meat markets: Working Documents*: EC, 1997; ISBN: 92-828-0863-7; EC No.CH-04-97-670-EN-C
> *Related publications: Document* (Commission, Spokesman's Service), DOC/97/1 (April 1997)

A similar summary was concerned with rural developments:

> Commission, *DG VI:CAP 2000: Situation and outlook. Rural developments: Working Documents*: EC, 1997; ISBN: 92-828-2053-X; EC No.CH-06-97-666-EN-C
> *Related publications: Memo* (Commission, Spokesman's Service), No.93, 1997 (6.11.97)

The full set of five CAP 2000 *Working Documents* can be found on the Internet at http://europa.eu.int/en/comm/dg06/new/CAP2000/ . In addition to the two reports listed above there are reports on the beef sector, the dairy sector and cereals.

A report detailed consultations from experts and politicians leading up to the BSE recommendations:

Commission: *Final consolidated report to the Temporary Committee of the European Parliament on the follow-up of recommendations on BSE*: COM (97)509 final (20.10.97)
Related publications: *PE DOC* A4-20/97 (Report of the European Parliament Temporary Committee of Inquiry into BSE)

The Commission issued reports on specific products:

Commission: Communication ... Action programme to promote milk consumption in the Community and expand the markets for milk and milk products: *COM* (97)377 final (18.7.97)

Commission: *Forward estimate for the 1997–98 wine year*: *OJ* C383, 17.12.97, pp. 10–11

Commission: *Report ... Sheepmeat. Second Commission report ... on the functioning of the ewe premium (follow-up of the 1997–98 price package)*: *COM* (97)679 final (15.12.97)

Commission: *Report ... on the common organisation of the market in raw tobacco*: *COM* (96)554 final (18.12.96)

Commission: *Note to the Council ... and European Parliament on the olive and olive oil sector ..., the current common market organisation, the need for a reform and the alternatives envisaged*: *COM* (97)57 final (12.2.97)

The third Commission report on the use of animal experiments in cosmetics proposed a postponement of the ban agreed by the Council in June 1993 because alternative measures had not yet been put in place:

Commission: *1996 Commission report on the development, validation and legal acceptance of alternative methods to animal experiments in the field of cosmetics*: *COM* (97)182 final (5.5.97)

Citizens

The Commission's report assessed the application of specific provisions relating to citizenship in 1994–96:

Commission: *Second report ... on citizenship of the Union*: *COM* (97)230 final (27.5.97)

See also 'Justice and Home Affairs' below.

Competition

The Commission publishes a specialized annual report on competition policy:

> Commission, *DG IV: XXVIth report on competition policy 1996*: EC, 1997
> ISBN: 92-828-0721-5; EC No.CM-04-97-242-EN-C

A less dense and technical survey of the year's activities was also produced:

> Commission, DG IV: *European Community competition policy 1996*: EC,
> 1997: ISBN: 92-828-0298-1; EC No.CM-03-97-967-EN-C

An addendum to the consolidated version of competition legislation was published:

> Commission, *DG IV: Competition law in the European Communities. Volume
> IIB. Explanation of the rules applicable to State aid. Situation in December
> 1996*:EC, 1997; ISBN: 92-827-9664-7; EC No.CM-03-97-296-EN-C

A consolidated version of the rules in the international field was produced:

> Commission, DG IV: *Competition law in the European Communities. Volume
> IIIA. Rules in the international field. Situation at 31 December 1996*: EC, 1997
> ISBN: 92-827-7636-0; EC No.CM-89-95-858-EN-C

Articles 85 and 86 of the EC Treaty prohibit restrictive practices between firms and the abuse of dominant positions. DG IV produced a book describing the way in which these Articles were applied by the courts of the 12 countries which were EU members in December 1994:

> Commission, DG IV: *Dealing with the Commission. Notifications, complaints,
> inspections and fact-finding powers under Articles 85 and 86 of the EEC
> Treaty*:EC, 1997; ISBN: 92-828-1724-5; EC No.CV-95-96-552-EN-C

The fifth survey on state aid to manufacturing updated existing data up to the end of 1994 (i.e. before the accession of the newest Member States).

> Commission, DG IV: *Fifth survey on state aid in the European Union in
> the manufacturing and certain other sectors*: *Document*: EC, 1997; ISBN:
> 92-828-0978-1; EC No.CV-06-97-901-EN-C
> *Related publications*: *COM* (97)170 final (16.4.97)

A further publication was:

> Commission, DG IV: *Reports of Commission Decisions relating to State aid.
> Article 93, paragraph 2 (Negative final Decisions)*. 1973–1995: EC, 1996;
> ISBN: 92-827-7751-0; EC No.CM-96-96-465-EN-C

The Commission intended to administer derogatives to the principle of incompatibility of state aid with Common Market guidelines in the fisheries and aquaculture sector:

Commission: Guidelines for the examination of state aid to fisheries and aquaculture: OJ C100, 27.3.97, pp. 12–20

The Commission published guidelines by which Member States could handle the sale of land and buildings in a way which precluded the existence of state aid:

Commission: *Commission Communication on State aid elements in sales of land and buildings by public authorities: OJ* C209, 10.7.97, pp. 3–5

A Commission report detailed a new policy on state aid to maritime transport, which would be focused upon safeguarding EC employment, preserving maritime expertise and improving safety:

Commission: *Community guidelines on State aid to maritime transport: OJ* C205, 5.7.97, pp. 5–15

The EC's guidelines on rescuing firms in difficulty were maintained in a report issued, although an exception was made in the case of agriculture, where some amendments were to be incorporated:

Commission: *Community guidelines on State aid for rescuing and restructuring firms in difficulty: OJ* C283, 19.9.97, pp. 2–12

A Commission document attempted to adjust the framework for state aid to the motor vehicle industry to bring it into line with the new economic situation, emphasizing intangible investments such as research and development, and training initiatives:

Commission: *Community framework for State aid to the motor vehicle industry: OJ* C279, 15.9.97, pp. 1–44

The Commission provided guidance on the way in which it applied the concept of the relevant product and the geographic market in ongoing enforcement of community competition law:

Commission: *Commission notice on the definition of relevant market for the purposes of Community competition law: OJ* C372, 9.12.97, pp. 5–13

The Commission took further steps towards defining the scope of Article 85 (1) in order to facilitate undertakings:

Commission: *Notice on agreements of minor importance which do not fall within the meaning of Article 85(1) of the Treaty establishing the European Community: OJ* C372, 9.12.97, pp. 13–15

Taking the view that the widest possible consultation should take place on its interpretative work, the Commission invited comments from interested parties:

Commission: *Draft Commission Interpretative Communication. Freedom to provide services and the general good in the insurance sector*: OJ C365, 3.12.97, pp. 7–27

The Green Paper was issued because the Commission thought that a review was needed now that the single market in free movement in products was now largely in place:

Commission: *Green Paper on vertical restraints in EC competition policy*: COM (96)721 final (22.1.97)

A memorandum related to new factors in air transport was issued:

Commission: *Memorandum ... Application of the competition rules to air transport*: COM (97)218 final (16.5.97)

The Commission issued a report completing the 1996 calendar year to supplement the first report on the application of the agreement between EC and USA:

Commission: *Report ... on the application of the Agreement between the EC and ... the USA ... regarding the application of their competition law. 1 July 1996 to 31 December 1996*: COM (97)346 final (4.7.97)

See also 'Single Market' below.

Consumers

The Commission issued a report on the action it had taken to reinforce the way in which it obtained and used scientific advice and how it operated its food, veterinary and phytosanitary control and inspection services:

Commission: *Communication ... Consumer health and food safety*: COM (97)183 final (30.4.97)

The Commission issued a recommendation containing comprehensive requirements for transparency and clarification of parties' obligations and liabilities in relation to electronic commerce:

Commission: *Communication ... Boosting customers' confidence in electronic means of payments in the Single Market*: COM (97)353 final (9.7.97)

A report on the approximation of laws concerning consumer credit concluded that financial services industries would prefer the *status quo*, whilst consumers and money advice groups would welcome the proposals:

Commission: *Report on the operation of Directive 87/102 for the approximation of laws ... concerning consumer credit ... Summary report of reactions and comments COM* (97)465 final (24.9.97)

See also 'Industry' below.

Culture

The second report on 'Television without frontiers' covered the application of a directive issued in 1989 from January 1995 until July 1997 so as to provide continuity. This directive was superseded by Directive 97/36/EC which did not enter into force until July 1997:

> Commission: *2nd report from the Commission ... on the application of Directive 89/552/EEC 'Television without frontiers'COM* (97)523 final (24.10.97)

The Commission followed up its Green Paper on the protection of minors in audiovisual and information services with a report which included a proposal for Council recommendation on the issue:

> Commission: *Communication ... on the follow-up to the Green Paper on the protection of minors and human dignity in audiovisual and information services: COM* (97)570 final (18.11.97)

Economic and Monetary Issues

The Commission's *Annual Economic Report for 1997* looked at the economic situation and at structural and macroeconomic policy issues in each Member State:

> Commission, DG II: *Annual Economic Report for 1997: European Economy,* No.63 (1997)
> *Related publications: COM* (97)27 final (12.2.97)

> *European Economy: Supplement A,* No.5, May 1997 (Spring 1997 Economic Forecasts); *European Economy: Supplement A,* No.10, October 1997 (Autumn 1997 Economic Forecasts)

DG II's publication on stability, growth and employment showed moderate economic activity:

> Commission, DG II: *1997 Broad Economic Policy Guidelines. The outcome of the Amsterdam European Council on stability, growth and employment: European Economy,* No.64 (1997)
> *Related publications: COM* (97)168 final (23.4.97); *COM* (97)169 final (23.4.97)

Sufficiently high levels of sustainable convergence had been achieved by too few Member States for an early start to economic and monetary union in 1996. However, the third stage was on target to begin in January 1999:

Commission, DG II: *Report on convergence in the European Union in 1996*
European Economy: Supplement A, No.1, January 1997, pp. 1–31
Related publications: *COM* (96)560 final (6.11.96)

A Council resolution included commitments by Member States, Council and Commission on the stability pact:

Council: *Resolution of the European Council on the Stability and Growth Pact*
(Amsterdam, 17.6.97): *OJ* C236, 2.8.97, pp. 1–2

Preparations for Economic and Monetary Union continued throughout the year. DG II
of the Commission launched a series called *Euro Papers*, which reproduced the texts of
the key initiatives and reports of the year:

Commission, DG II:
1.   *External aspects of economic and monetary union*
2.   *Accounting for the introduction of the euro*
3.   *The impact of the introduction of the euro on capital markets* (also
      published as *COM* (97)337 final (2.7.97)
4.   *Legal framework for the use of the euro* (also published in *European
      Economy: Supplement A*, No.2, February 1997)
5.   *Round Table on practical aspects of the changeover to the euro – May 15,
      1997 – Summary and conclusions*
6.   *Checklist on the introduction of the euro for enterprises and auditors*
7.   *The introduction of the euro: compilation of Community legislation and
      related documents*

The Commission specified the exact size, number and components of the euro:

Commission: *Communication ... European Monetary Institute... Denomina-
tions and technical specifications of euro coins (+ legislative proposal)*:
COM (97)247 final (29.5.97)

The new euro symbol, which was inspired by the Greek epsilon (symbolizing tradition)
and the initial 'E' for 'Europe', crossed by two lines (symbolizing stability), was
recommended:

Commission: *Communication ... The use of the euro symbol*: *COM* (97)418
final (23.7.97)

Further work was carried out on the introduction of the euro:

Commission: *Communication ... Practical aspects of the introduction of the
euro*: *COM* (97)491 final (1.10.97)

Commission: *Communication ... The impact of the changeover to the euro on Community policies, institutions and legislation*: *COM* (97)560 final (5.11.97)

Commission, DG II: *The ECU markets*: *European Economy: Supplement A*, No.8–9, August-September 1997, pp. 1–11

European Monetary Institute: *The single monetary policy in Stage Three. General documentation on ECSB monetary policy instruments and procedures*: EMI, 1997: ISBN: 92-9166-039-6

A progress report addressed the provision of liquidity, pricing policies, operation time, settlement services and the organizational framework of the Target Project:

European Monetary Union: *Second progress report on the Target Project. September 1997*: EMI, 1997; ISBN: 92-9166-040-X

See also 'Other EU Institutions and Organizations' above.

Education, Training and R&D

The Commission's produced a Communication on information systems:

Commission: *Communication ... Towards a Europe of knowledge*: *COM* (97)563 final (12.11.97)

The Commission reported a 'remarkable response' towards the SOCRATES project:

Commission: *SOCRATES: The Community Action Programme in the Field of Education. Report on the results achieved in 1995 and 1996*: *COM* (97)99 final (14.3.97)

An annual report on the TEMPUS programme was issued:

Commission: *TEMPUS. Annual report 1996 (Phare and Tacis) COM* (97)502 final (19.11.97)

The European Voluntary Service was designed to open a space for young people to become involved in the making of their societies. The second report updated information and statistics, identified trends and highlighted issues for future development:

Commission: *European Voluntary Service for young people. Second report of work in progress*: *COM* (97)512 final (20.12.97)
Related publications: *COM* (96)610 final (23.12.96)

The interim report on the LEONARDO DA VINCI programme presented an analysis of trends and of the impact of the programme:

Commission: *Interim report on the implementation of the LEONARDO DA VINCI Programme* (Vocational Training Programme, 1995–99): *COM* (97)399 final (23.7.97)

CEDEFOP was established by the Council of Ministers in February 1975. It contributes to development of vocational training in the EU through its academic and technical activities. Data on training were provided in a report compiled by DG XXII:

Commission, DG XXII/Eurostat/CEDEFOP: *Key data on vocational training in the European Union*: EC, 1997; ISBN: 92-828-1322-3; EC No.C2-05-97-252-EN-C

The independent experts examining the RTD framework programmes concluded that they were not fulfilling their promise. The Commission endorsed the panel's conclusion that it was time for a major review:

Commission: *Communication ... EU research and technological activities. Five-year assessment of the European Community RTD framework programmes. Report of the Independent Expert Panel + Commission's comments*: *COM* (97)151 final (15.4.97)
Related publications: *COM* (97)149 final (16.4.97)

The 1997 annual report on RTD was the third in the series. It complements five-year assessment reports and the annual monitoring reports by independent experts:

Commission: *Research and technological development activities of the European Union. 1997 annual report*: *COM* (97)373 final (18.7.97)

Further information was available:

Commission: *Fifth Framework Programme for Research and Technological Development (1998–2002). Commission Working Paper on the specific programmes: Starting points for discussion*: *COM* (97)553 final (5.11.97)

The 1996 annual report covers activities in fulfilment of the Council decision on JRC specific programmes (1995–98) for the EC and the EAEC:

Commission: *Joint Research Centre. 1996 annual report*: *COM* (97)137 final (3.4.97)

A document providing individual reports on each of the JRC Institutes was provided:

Commission: *Communication ... Evaluation of the Joint Research Centre, 1992–1996: COM* (97)164 final (22.4.97)

See also:

Commission: *The First Action Plan for Innovation in Europe. Innovation for growth and employment*: COM (96)589 final (20.11.96)

The second working paper was designed to pave the way for a new stage in the framework programmes setting out a more detailed idea for the possible content of the Fifth Framework programme:

Commission: *Commission Working Paper: Towards the Fifth Framework Programme:Scientific and Technological Objectives*: COM (97)47 final (12.2.97)

The final evaluation of the FORCE Programme summarized its overall implementation:

Commission, DG XXII: *Final evaluation of the FORCE Programme* EC, 1997; ISBN: 92-828-1391-6; EC No.C2-07-97-119-EN-C *Related publications*: COM (97)384 final (22.7.97)

The final report on the PETRA Programme aimed to give a global analysis of the period 1988–94:

Commission: *Final report on the implementation of the PETRA Programme (Action Programme for the Vocational Training of Young People and their preparation for Adult and Working Life)*: COM (97)385 final (22.7.97)

The EUROTECNET Programme ended in 1994. The final report summarized its impact:

Commission: *Final report from the Commission on the EUROTECNET Programme ..., January 1990–December 1994*: COM 997)386 final (22.7.97)

A Commission report responded to a Council decision for independent evaluation of the TEDIS Programme on its completion:

Commission: *Communication ... on the evaluation of the Trade Electronic Data Interchange Systems (TEDIS) Programme*: COM (97)335 final (3.9.97)

See also 'Agriculture' above.

Energy

A Commission document followed up its 1995 White Paper: 'An Energy Policy for the European Union' with 'a first step which could open the way to a new and more coherent presentation of energy actions':

Commission: *Communication ... an overall view of energy policy and actions*: COM (97)167 final (23.4.97)

A report aimed to analyse the main elements which needed to be considered in relation to natural gas and electricity interconnections with third countries:

Commission: *Communication ... The external dimension of trans-European energy networks*: COM (97)125 final (26.3.97)

An information document on trans-European networks covered the EC's objectives and priorities, lines of action, projects of common interest, priority projects and rules for granting financial support:

Commission, DG XVII: *Trans-European energy networks. Policy and actions of the European Community. Information document, September 1997*: EC, 1997: ISBN: 92-828-1386-X; EC No.CS-BR-97-001-EN-C

The Commission summarized the situation of EC solid fuel markets in 1996, presenting forecasts for 1997:

Commission: *The market for solid fuels in the Community in 1996 and the outlook for 1997 (revision)*: OJ C376, 11.12.97, pp. 3–6

The Commission thought that it was appropriate to reconsider main issues in relation to nuclear energy:

Commission: *Communication ... on the nuclear industries in the European Union*: COM (97)401 final (25.9.97)

The ALTENER Programme was set up in 1993 to promote renewable energy sources for the EC. The Commission issued a report summarizing the first three years:

Commission: *Report ... on the results of the ALTENER Programme*: COM (97)122 final (12.3.97)

The White Paper on energy also committed the Commission to evolving a strategy to reduce emissions of greenhouse gases by means of developing CHP:

Commission: *Communication ... A Community strategy to promote combined heat and power (CHP) and to dismantle barriers to its development*: COM (97)514 final (15.10.97)

The second stage in the Commission's two-stage approach for increasing use of renewable energy sources was its White Paper:

Commission: *Energy for the future: Renewable sources of energy. White Paper for a Community strategy and action plan*: COM (97)599 final (26.11.97)

The Commission issued a report in preparation for the third conference of the UN Framework Convention on Climatic Change, due to be held in December 1997:

Commission: *Communication ... The energy dimension of climate change*: COM (97)196 final (14.5.97)

See also 'Environment' below.

Environment

A Guide on EU environmental legislation was published to help senior policy-makers and officials in applicant states deepen their understanding of the environmental *acquis*:

Commission: *Guide to the approximation of European Union environmental legislation*: *SEC* (97)1608 final (25.8.97)

(This document can be downloaded from the Internet at http://europa.eu.int/en/comm/ dg11/guide/contents.htm) .

Brochures describing some of the EC's most important policies and activities in implementing *Agenda 21* were published:

Commission, DG XI: *Agenda 21. The first five years. Implementation of Agenda 21 in the European Community*: EC, 1997; ISBN: 92-828-0393-7; EC No.CR-05-97-082-EN-C

Commission, DG XI: *Agenda 21. The first five years. European Community progress on the implementation of Agenda 21 – 1992–97*: EC, 1997; ISBN: 92-828-0361-9; EC No.CR-04-97-630-EN-C

A publication presented major facts and trends concerning the environment, EU activities and the responsibilities of various participants:

Commission, DG XI: *Caring for our future. Action for Europe's environment*: EC, 1997; ISBN: 92-828-1367-3; EC No.CR-04-97-064-EN-C

A Commission report covered the period since LIFE was first implemented and looked at its three aspects: nature; environment and Third Countries:

Commission: *Report pursuant to Article 7(3) of Regulation (EC) No.1404/96 (LIFE)*: *COM* (97)633 final (12.12.97)

A Commission document supported the implementation of fiscal instruments within Member States to make environmental policy more efficient and cost effective:

Commission: *Communication ... environmental taxes and charges in the Single Market*: *COM* (97)9 final (26.3.97)

See also:

Commission: *Communication ... on environment and employment (Building a sustainable Europe)*: *COM* (97)592 final (18.11.97)

A Commission report examined possibilities for improving urban development and increasing the effectiveness of EC intervention in urban areas:

Commission: *Communication ... Towards an urban agenda in the European Union: COM* (97)197 final (6.5.97)

Following a decision by the Environmental Council in December 1995 for a coherent acidification strategy to be presented for early 1997, the Commission reviewed the problem and the methodology to be used by the Commission in developing its strategy:

Commission: *Communication ... on a Community strategy to combat acidification (+ legislative proposals): COM* (97)88 final (12.3.97)

In March 1997, the Environmental Council adopted a negotiation position which included establishing a quantified emission reduction objective. The Commission's Communication put this negotiation position into context and demonstrated its feasibility:

Commission: *Communication ... Climate change – the EU approach for Kyoto: COM* (97)481 final (1.10.97)

Six years after the adoption of the nitrates directive, most Member States had failed to implement it. The Commission reported that 13 states were the subjects of legal proceedings on the issue:

Commission: *Report ... The implementation of Council Directive 91/676/EEC concerning the protection of waters against pollution caused by nitrates from agricultural sources: COM* (97)473 final (1.10.97)

The 1991 Council directive (91/692/EEC) aimed at standardizing and rationalizing reports on certain environmental directives. In waste management national reports were to be issued every three years. The Commission reported on the current position:

Commission: *Communication ... concerning the application of Directives 75/439/EEC, 75/442/EEC, 78/319/EEC and 86/278/EEC on waste management: COM* (97)23 final (27.2.97)

See also 'Agriculture' and 'Energy' above and 'Asia' below.

Fisheries

A Commission report on fisheries policy was the second report of its kind, supplementing the original Report on Monitoring the Common Fisheries Policy (Doc (96) fin 18.03.96) to include Finland and Sweden:

Commission: *Report ... Monitoring the Common Fisheries Policy 1995: COM* (97)226 final (13.6.97)

The annual report on multi-annual guidance programmes for the fishing fleets was the fifth and final one in the series:

Commission: *Annual report ... on the results of the multi-annual guidance programmes for the fishing fleets at the end of 1996*: COM (97)352 final (11.7.97)

See also:

Commission: *Communication ... The future for the market in fisheries products in the European Union: Responsibility, partnership and competitiveness:* COM (97)719 final (16.12.97)

Health

A legal basis for the EC to undertake action in the field of public health was created under Arts 3 (o) and 129, TEC. A 1997 report focused upon the prevention of intentional and unintentional injuries and accidents:

Commission: *Communication ... concerning a Community action programme on injury prevention in the context of the framework for action in the field of public health (+ legislative proposal)*: COM (97)178 final (14.5.97)
Related publications: OJ C202, 2.7.97, p. 20

The Commission's report on rare diseases was issued under the rationale that they have an economic impact:

Commission: *Communication ... concerning a programme of Community action on rare diseases within the framework for action in the field of public health (+ legislative proposal)*: COM (97)225 final (26.5.97)
Related publications: OJ C203, 3.7.97, p. 6

See also:

Commission: *Communication ... concerning a programme of Community action on pollution-related diseases in the context of the framework for action in the field of public health (+ legislative programme)*: COM (97)266 final (4.6.97)

A Commission document contributed to a review of existing and possible future anti-smoking strategies at EC and Member State level and set out options for future action:

Commission: *Communication ... on the present and proposed Community role in combating tobacco consumption*: COM (96)609 final (18.12.96)

European Cancer Week 1995 'had a major impact on EU citizens' improving their knowledge of cancer prevention and reinforcing EC action in the public health field:

Commission: *Report ... on the evaluation of European Cancer Week 1995:* COM (97)19 final (10.2.97) 2 vols

The second health status report focused on women's health. It was based on work carried out by the University of Limerick:

Commission, DG V: *The state of women's health in the European Community Employment and Social Affairs: Public Health*: EC, 1997; ISBN: 92-828-1062-3: EC No.CE-06-97-521-EN-C
Related publications: *COM* (97)224 final (22.5.97); *OJ* C394, 30.12.97, p. 1

A report was issued in accordance with Article 3 (2) of the EP and Council Decision No. 1729/95/EC on action against AIDS:

Commission: *Report ... on the implementation of the 'Europe against Aids' Action Plan 1994–1995*: *COM* (96)720 final (15.1.97)

A second annual report on the drugs problem was published alongside a 'Summary and highlights' booklet of the annual report which is available on the Internet at http://www.emcdda.org :

European Monitoring Centre for Drugs and Drug Addiction: *Annual report on the state of the drugs problem in the European Union 1997*: EC, 1997
ISBN: 92-9168-013-3; EC No.AO-06-97-262-EN-C

Following a rise in concern about the use of 'designer drugs' by young people, the Commission responded to the Dublin European Council's instruction to work towards reducing domestic production and trafficking:

Commission: *Communication ... on the control of new synthetic drugs (designer drugs)*: *COM* (97)249 final (23.5.97)

DG X's report on action against drugs showed initiatives taken by the EU:

Commission, DG X: *The European Union in action against drugs*: EC, 1997ISBN: 92-828-0426-7

As part of its new series *Employment and Social Affairs* DG V of the Commission launched a sub-series called *Public Health*. Amongst the titles published within this sub-series in 1996, in addition to the newsletter *Prevention*, are:

Commission, DG V: *Public health in Europe*; *Employment and Social Affairs*: *Public Health*; EC, 1997; ISBN: 92-828-0390-2; EC No.CE-05-97-608-EN-C

Commission: *Homeopathic medicinal products. Commission report ... on the application of Directives 92/73 and 92/74*:*COM* (97)362 final (14.7.97)

Commission: *Classification for the supply of medicinal products for human use. Commission report to the Council on the application of Directive 92/26/ EEC*: *COM* (97)581 final (14.11.97)

Commission, DG V: *Europe for the prevention of AIDS. Community Programme 1996–2000: Employment and Social Affairs: Public Health*; EC, 1997 ISBN: 92-827-6907-0; EC No. CE-95-96-035-EN-C

See also 'Miscellaneous' above. Also see 'Social Policy and the Labour Market' below for further titles published in the Employment and Social Affairs *series.*

Industry

DG III's 'panorama' study of EU industry provided a macroeconomic survey of EU industry and services:

Commission, DG III/ Eurostat: *Panorama of EU Industry 1997. An extensive review of the situation and outlook of the manufacturing and service industries in the European Union. 2 vols*: EC, 1997; ISBN: 92-827-9304-4 (Vol.1)/ 92-827-9307-9 (Vol.2): EC No.C0-57-96-001/2-EN-C

(DG III and Eurostat also launched a new journal called *Monthly Panorama of European Industry* replacing *Panorama of EU Industry: Short-term Supplement* and *Industrial Trends*)

A fourth report on European enterprises follows the Commission's White Paper: 'Growth, competitiveness and employment':

Commission, Eurostat/DG XXIII: *Enterprises in Europe. 4th report*: EC, 1996 ISBN: 92-827-7296-9; EC No.CA-94-96-162-EN-C

The Commission published a current analytical foundation for examination of the key issues relating to competitiveness of the request from the Council in November 1994:

Commission: *The competitiveness of European industry*: EC, 1997 ISBN: 92-827-8079-1; EC No.CO-95-96-245-EN-C

DG II noted that profits were higher in 1995, but less strongly than in 1994. The share of goods and purchases was up; financial costs were stable and staff costs had reduced:

Commission, DG II: *Financial situation of European enterprises European Economy: Supplement A*, No.7, July 1997, pp. 1–31

A Commission report defined potential obstacles to the efficient operation of new capital markets in Europe:

Commission: *Communication ... European capital markets for SMEs: prospects and potential obstacles to progress: COM* (97)187 final (5.5.97)

A Commission report was drawn up following a Council decision in December 1996 in relation to the third multinational programme on SMEs:

Commission: *Report ... on the coordination of activities to assist small and medium-sized enterprises (SMEs) and the craft sector 1997*: COM (97)610 final (25.11.97)

An update on the third report (COM (96)552) on EC interest subsidies was published. A fifth report is to follow in 1998:

Commission: *Fourth report of the Commission relative to the implementation of the decision regarding the provision of Community interest subsidies on loans for small and medium-sized enterprises extended by the European Investment Bank under its temporary lending facility (the SME Facility)*: COM (97)645 final (2.12.97)

A Commission document provided a 'coherent policy framework for future EC action' with the object of 'establishing a common European position to achieve global consensus through international negotiations in electronic commerce':

Commission: *Communication ... A European Initiative in electronic commerce*: COM (97)157 final (16.4.97)

A Commission document followed up on *COM* (96)463, 9.10.96 and the Round Table report: 'Benchmarking for policy makers – the way to competitiveness, growth and job creation' issued in October 1996:

Commission: *Communication ... Benchmarking. Implementation of an instrument available to economic actors and public authorities*: COM (97)153 final (16.4.97)

The Commission set out the results of its consultative paper on financial services:

Commission: *Communication ... Financial services: Enhancing consumer confidence. Follow-up to the Green Paper on 'Financial Services: Meeting consumers' expectations'*: COM (97)309 final (26.6.97)

There were signs of increasing demands for steel, but the Commission concluded that the priority remained a lasting period of stability for the EC steel market:

Commission: *Forward programme for steel for the first half of 1997 and for 1997 as a whole*: OJ C50, 20.2.97, pp. 3–16

The ESCS is due to be phased into the EC Treaty in 23 July 2002. The Commission noted that there was a need for the revenue from outstanding reserves to be used for a research fund for related sectors:

Commission: *Communication ... Expiry of the ECSC Treaty – financial activities*: COM (97)506 final (8.10.97)

The Commission presented a report in accordance with Article 1 (7) of the Council Regulation (EEC) No 3030/93 on the textile and clothing sector:

Commission: *Report ... on the respect of market access commitments by WTO Members in the textiles and clothing sectors*: COM (97)219 final (15.5.97)

The Commission's plan of action in this sector took note of conclusions reached at Industry Council meetings held 28 March and 14 November 1996:

Commission: *Communication ... Plan of action to increase the competitiveness of the European textile and clothing industry*: COM (97)454 final (29.10.97)

A working document 'Ship building policy – options for the future' was issued in April 1997 in preparation for the expiry of the existing regime on state aids to shipbuilding at the end of the year. The Commission presented a follow-up to that document:

Commission: *Communication ... Towards a new shipbuilding policy:* COM (97)470 final (1.10.97)

The Commission concluded that the EU needed to take a more proactive and coherent approach in the satellite communications area:

Commission: *Communication ... EU Action Plan: Satellite communications in the Information Society*: COM (97)91 final (5.3.97)

The Commission issued its first contribution on ICT industries, citing them as a critical component of the European economy:

Commission: *Communication ... The competitiveness of the European information and communication technologies (ICT) industries*: COM (97)152 final (16.4.97)

The Commission issued a follow-up to its consultative paper on numbering policy. The consultation had showed wide support for the Green Paper proposals:

Commission: *Communication ... regarding the consultation on the Green Paper on a numbering policy for telecommunications services in Europe*: COM (97)203 final (21.5.97)

The Commission presented an overview of developments responding to a Council Green Paper on mobile and wireless communication:

Commission: *Communication ... on the further development of mobile and wireless communications. Challenges and choices for the EU*: COM (97)217 final (29.5.97)

The regulatory framework for telecommunications was nearing completion. The Commission reviewed the current status of the legislation involved and progress in implementing it:

Commission: *Communication ... on the implementation of the telecommunications regulatory package COM* (97)236 final (29.5.97)
Related publications: *COM* (97)504 final (8.10.97)

The Commission aimed to develop a European policy for a common framework to ensure the functions of the European market for cryptographic services and products:

Commission: *Communication ... ensuring security and trust in electronic communication. Towards a European framework for digital signatures and encryption*:*COM* (97)503 final (8.10.97)

The Commission responded to a call from Council and EP for proposals for further action to ensure continuing support towards the third generation in UMTS, following its mobile Green Paper:

Commission: *Communication ... Strategy and policy orientations with regard to further development of mobile and wireless communications (UMTS). Outcome of the public consultation and proposals for creating a favourable environment*: *COM* (97)513 final (15.10.97)

The Commission's Communication on the safe use of the Internet included a proposal for a Council Decision adopting a Multiannual Community Action Plan:

Commission: *Communication ... Action plan on promoting safe use of the Internet (+ legislative proposal)*: *COM* (97)582 final (26.11.97)

Other publications include:

Commission: *Green Paper on the convergence of the telecommunications, media and information technology sectors, and the implications for regulation. Towards an Information Society approach*: *COM* (97)623 final (3.12.97)

Commission: *Communication ... The European aerospace industry. Meeting the global challenge*: *COM* (97)466 final (24.9.97)

The Commission analysed the principle factors which influenced the competitiveness of the construction industry:

Commission: *Communication ... The competitiveness of the construction industry*:*COM* (97)539 final (4.11.97)

A report on defence-related industries was issued:

Commission: *Communication ... Implementing European Union strategy on defence-related industries*: *COM* (97)583 final (4.12.97)

See also 'Competition' above and and 'Social Policy and the Labour Market' and Developing Countries' below.

Justice and Home Affairs

The Commission document incorporated the findings of the Stockholm Congress (August 1996) on child sex tourism and proposed specific measures towards combating it:

> Commission: *Communication ... on combating child sex tourism*: *COM* (96)547 final (27.11.96)

The EC needed to take co-ordinated action to fight corruption. The Commission set out the main elements of a comprehensive strategy:

> Commission: *Communication ... on a Union policy against corruption*: *COM* (97)192 final (21.5.97)

The Council had to examine periodically the functioning of the extradition convention and the general operation of extradition procedures among the Member States:

> Council: *Convention relating to extradition between the Member States of the European Union. Explanatory report:OJ* C191, 23.6.97, pp. 13–26
> *Related publications*: *OJ* C78, 30.3.95, p1; *OJ* C313, 23.10.96, p. 11

The Council Conclusions on the Dublin Convention added a 'time limit for replying to a request that an applicant be taken in charge' and made provisions for urgent procedures:

> Council: *Council Conclusions of 27.5.97 concerning the practical implementation of the Dublin Convention*: *OJ* C191, 23.6.97, pp. 27–8
> *Related publications*: *OJ* L281, 14.10.97, p. 1

The Council issued a description of Cirea activities for 1994–96:

> Council: *Activity reports on the Centre for Information, Discussion and Exchange on Asylum (Cirea) (1994–96)*: *OJ* C191, 23.6.97, pp. 29–35

A High Level Group had been created to draw up a comprehensive plan to combat rising rates in organized crime. Its 15 political guidelines and 30 specific recommendations along with an implementation timetable were issued by the Council:

> Council: *Action plan to combat organised crime:OJ* C251, 15.8.97, pp. 1–18

DG V looked at immigration policy:

> Commission, DG V: *The Member States of the EU and immigration in 1994: Less tolerance and tighter control policies (RIMET): Employment and Social Affairs: Social Dialogue and Social Rights*: EC, 1997 ISBN: 92-827-9731-7 EC No. CE-02-96-577-EN-C

DG V provided its first comprehensive publication of key texts on racism:

Commission, DG V: *The European Institutions in the fight against racism: Selected texts: Employment and Social Affairs: Social Dialogue and Social Rights*: EC, 1997; ISBN: 92-827-9841-0; EC No.CE-01-96-438-EN-C

Four issues of a Newsletter, providing information about initiatives and including a 'Diary of Events' were published for the Year Against Racism:

Commission, DG V: *Newsletter for the European Year Against Racism*, January 1997–

Information on the European Year Against Racism also available on the Internet at http://www.europeanyear1997.org .

For further titles in the Employment and Social Affairs *series, see 'Social Policy and the Labour Market' below. See also 'Citizens' above.*

Single Market

The Commission issued a summary report on the single market, concluding that there had been positive results but that Member States had not been sufficiently diligent in putting in place single market measures and enforcing its rules:

Commission: *The 1996 single market review. Background information for the report for the report to the Council and European Parliament*: EC, 1997; ISBN: 92-827-9627-2; EC No.C1-03-96-022-EN-C
Related publications: SEC (96)2378 (16.12.96); *COM* (96)520 final (30.10.96)

A single market action plan with four targets (making rules more effective; dealing with key market distortions; removing sectoral obstacles to market integration; delivering a single market for the benefit of citizens) with an implementation date of January 1999 was set:

Commission: *Action Plan for the Single Market. Communication of the Commission to the European Council: CSE* (97)1 final (4.6.97); EC, 1997; EC No.C1-06-97-189-EN-C
Related publications: COM (97)184 final (6.5.97)

One of a series of publications examining the competitiveness of the single market assessed its economic impact:

Commission, DG II: *Economic evaluation of the Internal Market: European Economy: Reports and Studies*, No.4, 1996 (published 1997)

The Commission launched its strategy for simple legislation for the single market (SLIM) in May 1996. A report summarized its results and put in place two new phases to begin in January and May 1998:

Commission: *Report ... on the results of the second phase of SLIM and the follow-up of the implementation of the first phase recommendations*: COM (97)618 final (24.11.97)

A report was issued containing a range of proposals to combat the problem of transit fraud and move towards the reform of customs transit systems:

Commission: *Communication ... Action Plan for transit in Europe. A new customs policy*: OJ C176, 10.6.97, pp. 3–34
Related publications: COM (97)188 final (30.4.97); *PE DOC* A4-53/97 (European Parliament Report of the Committee of Inquiry into the Community Transit System)

A Commission Green Paper reported that European public authorities spend 720 bn ECU (11 per cent of the EU's GDP) on goods and services and looked at a potential framework for open and competitive public procurement:

Commission: *Green Paper. Public procurement in the European Union: exploring the way forward*: COM (96)583 final (27.11.96)

The Commission thought that it was necessary to set out its position in relation to the application of the ECJ's principles to the specific problems raised by the Second Banking Directive:

Commission: *Commission Interpretative Communication. Freedom to provide services and the interest of the general good in the Second Banking Directive*: OJ C209, 10.7.97, pp. 6–22

There is still no single system of patent protection. The Green Paper proposed measures for removing the practical and political obstacles to devising a system:

Commission: *Promoting innovation through patents. Green Paper on the Community patent and the patent system in Europe*: COM (97)314 final (24.6.97)

Following an informal meeting of Ecofin in September 1997, the Presidency decided to hold an orientation debate on taxation in October. The Commission submitted a paper as a basis for discussion at this meeting:

Commission: *Communication ... Towards tax co-ordination in the European Union. A package to tackle harmful tax competition*: COM (97)495 final (1.10.97)
Related publications: COM (97)564 final (5.11.97)

The Commission issued a report based on the criterion set down in Art. 99 (EC) which specifies that VAT harmonization is needed to ensure the effectiveness of the single market:

Commission: *Report ... in accordance with Article 12(4) of the Sixth Council Directive of 17.5.77 on the harmonisation of the laws of the Member States relating to turn-over taxes – Common system of value added tax: uniform basis of assessment*: COM (97)559 final (13.11.97)

A High Level Panel was constituted to report on measures to enable people to take advantage of their rights to free movement within the EU. A total of 80 recommendations were put forward, but the conclusion was that Member States needed to improve co-operation among themselves:

High Level Panel on the Free Movement of Persons: *Report presented to the Commission on 18 March 1997 (chaired by Mme Simone Veil)*: EC, 1997

This report was not formally published, but is available on the Internet at http://europa.eu.int/comm/dg15/en/people/index.htm .

A Commission paper built on the final report of the High Level Panel on the Free Movement of Persons. It addressed the Panel's conclusions that some flaws and lacunae still remained in the legal framework and in a range of practical problems and obstacles:

Commission: *Communication ... An action plan for free movement of workers*: COM (97)586 final (12.11.97)

A report which should have been presented in 1990 regarding a directive on the minimum training qualifications for architects was submitted. It had been postponed because of the accession of the new Member States; German unification and delay by the Member States in transposing the directive into national law:

Commission: *Report ... Review, on the basis of experience, of Council Directive 85/384/EEC of 10.6.85 pursuant to Article 30 thereof*: COM (97)350 final (8.7.97)

See also 'Consumers' above and 'Social Policy and the Labour Market' below.

Social Policy and the Labour Market

DG V of the Commission reorganized its publications programme during 1997. The journals *Social Europe* (plus its Supplements) and *Social Europe Magazine* ceased. Instead, a new programme under the generic series heading *Employment and Social Affairs* was created with a number of distinctive sub-series 'themes': Employment and Labour Market; Public Health; Social Dialogue and Social Rights; Social Protection and Social Action; Equal Opportunities; European Social Fund; Health and Safety at Work. Under each theme a number of one-off reports will be published each year plus, in a number of instances, new periodical titles. Specific new titles of importance published during 1997 are listed throughout the Guide mainly in the section below but also under the section headings 'Health' and 'Justice and Home Affairs'. A new journal called *Forum* (replacing *Social Europe Magazine*) has been launched (Issue No.1, October

1997) and the first issue lists all new publications of DG V of 1997. A special issue of *Forum* was also published to mark the Extraordinary European Council, Luxembourg, 20–21 November 1997 ('the Jobs Summit').

The achievements of the social action programme in its first period were reported:

Commission, DG V: *Progress report on the implementation of the medium-term social action programme 1995–97: Social Europe: Supplement*, No.4, 1996: *Employment and Social Affairs*: EC, 1997; ISBN: 92-827-6315-3: EC No.CE-NC-96-004-EN-C

The Copenhagen summit (June1993) had adopted a declaration on social development and had proposed a three-pronged action plan aimed at eradicating poverty, increasing employment and fostering social integration. The Commission highlighted remaining areas upon which the EU could focus:

Commission: *Communication ... The European Union's follow-up to the World Summit for Social Development*: COM (96)724 final (14.2.97)

The previous demographic report (1995) had shown an increase in persons aged over 60 and a fall in numbers of young people. The latest report confirmed these trends, but also noted changes in age distribution among the EU's regions:

Commission: *Demographic report 1997*: COM (97)361 final (9.7.97)

A Commission communication illustrated the rising importance of the voluntary sector, and the prospects for increasing its contribution towards European integration:

Commission: *Communication ... on promoting the role of voluntary organisations and foundations in Europe*: COM (97)241 final (6.6.97)

The Commission noted a 'defining moment' in the history of combating unemployment provided by the Treaty of Amsterdam which will make unemployment a matter for common concern. A report presented the latest trends in the labour market:

Commission, DG V: *Employment in Europe 1997*: *Employment and Social Affairs: Employment and Labour Affairs*; EC, 1997; ISBN: 92-828-1575-7; EC No.CE-05-97-729-EN-C
Related publications: COM (97)479 final (1.10.97)

An overview of principle labour measures undertaken by the EU were presented. The document was intended as an instrument by which to assess structural reform of labour markets:

Commission, DG V: *Employment Observatory. Tableau de Bord 1996. Follow-up to the conclusions of the Essen European Council on employment policies*

Employment and Social Affairs: Employment and Labour Market: EC, 1997
ISBN: 92-827-9023-1; EC No.CE-98-96-574-EN-C

The Commission prepared for the extraordinary European Council meeting to be held 20–21 November 1997:

Commission: *Communication ... Proposal for guidelines for Member States employment policies 1998*: *COM* (97)497 final (1.10.97)

Unless policies change, the Commission found that the unemployment rate will remain at its present 9.7 per cent EU-wide until 1999. The Communication reported a need for an overall strategy to fight this trend:

Commission: *Communication ... Community policies in support of employment*: *COM* (97)611 final (12.11.97)

In September 1993, the Commission had published an Opinion on Equitable Wages. Following this a questionnaire had been sent to Member States' governments asking for information on progress. A report summarized the findings:

Commission: *Equitable wages – a progress report*: *COM* (96)698 final (8.1.97)

The Commission noted that Council Directive 77/197/EEC, 14.02.77 had proved to be an 'invaluable instrument for the protection of workers'. It published a memorandum with the aim of increasing public information and guidance on its application by the ECJ:

Commission: *Memorandum ... on acquired rights of workers in cases of transfers of undertakings*: *COM* (97)85 final (4.3.97)

The Commission issued a Green Paper with the aim of stimulating debate on work organization:

Commission: *Green Paper. Partnership for a new organisation of work*: *COM* (97)128 final (16.4.97)

The Commission's White Paper on exclusions from the Working Time Directive analysed the current situation, put forward options and set out its views on the way forward:

Commission: *White Paper on sectors and activities excluded from the Working Time Directive*: *COM* (97)334 final (15.7.97)

The European Industrial Relations Observatory (EIRO) is a major new database on industrial relations. It publishes a regular newsletter on related subjects.

European Foundation for the Improvement of Living and Working Conditions: *EIRO Observer*, No.1, 1997– ; ISSN: 1028-0588; EC No.SX-AB-97-00-EN-C

A report commissioned by DG V analysed and assessed the system of employee participation in company bodies, also looking at potential avoidance tactics and considering what kind of rules for worker involvement should be applied:

Commission, DG V: *Group of Experts European systems of worker involvement (with regard to the European Company Statute and the other pending proposals). Final report (Chairman: Etienne Davignon): Employment and Social Affairs: Social Dialogue and Social Rights*: EC, 1997; ISBN: 92-828-1113-1; EC No.CE-06-97-739-EN-C

The Commission followed a request by the Florence European Council, June 1996 to report on apprentice training. Its report recommended a sharing of 'best practice' throughout the Member States:

Commission: *Communication ... Promoting apprenticeship training in Europe: COM* (97)300 final (18.6.97)

The Commission summarized progress towards integrating the social dimension, based upon its 1996 Green Paper: 'Living and Working in the Information Society: People First':

Commission: *Communication ... on the social and labour market dimension of the Information Society. People first – the next steps: COM* 997)390 final (23.7.97)

The Commission argued that there was a need to adapt systems of social protection (which account for 28 per cent of total EU GDP) because of the changing nature of work and demographic factors:

Commission: *Communication ... Modernising and improving social protection in the European Union: COM* (97)102 final (12.3.97)

Building on a Commission paper on social protection, a 1997 Green Paper developed a number of ideas about certain aspects of supplementary pensions, noting that the present ratio of people of working age to pensioners is 4:1. By 2040 it will be 2:1:

Commission: *Supplementary pensions in the Single Market. A Green Paper COM* (97)283 final (10.6.97)

DG V issued a guide on social security rights:

Commission, DG V: *Your social security rights when moving within the European Union. A practical guide*: EC, 1997 *Employment and Social Affairs: Social Dialogue and Social Rights* EC, 1997; ISBN: 92-827-5607-6; EC No.CE-92-95-174-EN-C

DG V issued its first in a series of annual reports on equal opportunities:

Commission, DG V: *Equal opportunities for women and men in the European Union – 1996: Employment and Social Affairs: Equal Opportunities*: EC, 1997 ISBN: 92-827-8237-9; EC No.CE-98-96-566-EN-C
Related publications: *COM* (96)650 final (12.2.97)

(As part of the reorganization of its publishing programme DG V have launched a new quarterly journal called *Equal Opportunities Magazine*.)

See also 'Environment', 'Health' and 'Justice and Home Affairs' above for further titles published within the Employment and Social Affairs *series.*

Structural Policy

The eighth annual report on Structural Funds was compiled in accordance with Article 16 of Regulation (EEC) No 2052/88:

Commission, DG XVI: *The Structural Funds in 1996. Eighth annual report*: EC, 1997; ISBN: 92-828-1786-5; EC No.CX-08-96-751-EN-C
Related publications: *COM* (97)526 final (30.10.97)

DG XVI published a factsheet looking at the way in which rules for qualification for expenditure under the Structural Funds were being applied and giving new recommendations clarifying the eligibility criteria:

Commission, DG XVI: *Eligible expenditure under the Structural Funds. Factsheets*: EC, 1997; ISBN: 92-828-0888-2; EC No.CX-06-97-698-EN-C

A communication encompassing principal elements of EC assistance for the 2nd programming period under Objective 2 was published. It reported that 65 new single programming documents had been approved:

Commission: *Communication ... The new regional programmes 1997–1999 under Objective 2 of the Community's Structural Policies – focusing on job creation*: *COM* (97)524 final (14.11.97)

The annual report on the Cohesion Fund fulfilled legal requirements and was intended to be a reference for parties interested in the promotion of economic and social cohesion of the EU:

Commission, DG XVI: *Annual report on the Cohesion Fund 1996*: EC, 1997 ISBN: 92-828-1107-7; EC No.CX-06-97-844-EN-C
Related publications: *COM* (97)302 final (23.6.97)

See also:

Commission, DG XVI: *European Cohesion Forum. Speeches and summaries, 28–30 April 1997*: EC, 1997; ISBN: 92-828-1099-2; EC No.CX-06-97-917-EN-C

DG XVI's study provided input for the preparation of a Report on Economic and Social Cohesion:

Commission, DG XVI: *The impact of structural policies on economic and social cohesion in the Union 1989–99; Regional Development Studies, No.26*: EC, 1997; ISBN: 92-827-9167-X; EC No.GA-01-96-672-EN-C

The Financial Mechanism was established 01.01.94, under Art. 115–116, EEA Agreement and Protocol 38. A report noted activities from mid-1996 to mid-1997:

Commission: *Third annual report ... The European Economic Area Financial Mechanism: COM* (97)567 final (27.11.97)

Two publications on spatial planning systems were provided:

Commission, DG XVI: *The EU compendium of spatial planning systems and policies. Regional Development Studies*, No.28; EC, 1997; ISBN: 92-827-9752-X: EC No.CX-03-97-870-EN-C

Commission, DG XVI: *European spatial development perspective. First official draft. Presented at the informal meeting of Ministers responsible for spatial planning of the Member States of the European Union, Noordwijk, 9–10 June 1997*: EC, 1997; ISBN: 92-828-1499-8: EC No.CX-08-97-218-EN-C

See also:

Commission, DG XVI: *Community involvment in urban regeneration: added value and changing values: Regional Development Studies*, No.27: EC, 1997; ISBN: 92-827-9787-2; EC No.CX-03-97-862-EN-C

A report complemented the 1996 Green Paper 'Living and Working in the Information Society: People First' with regard to economic and social cohesion:

Commission: *Communication ... Cohesion and the Information Society: COM* (97)7 final (22.1.97)

An interim report in fulfilment of the Brussels European Council mandate to submit an annual report on TENs was published. A detailed annual report is to follow in 1998 when outturn figures are available:

Commission: *Trans-European Networks. 1997 report: COM* (97)654 final (4.12.97)

See also 'Energy' and 'Environment' above.

Transport

Based upon Eurostat data, two issues of a statistical pocket book on transport, covering the period 1970–date, were published:

Commission, DG VII/ Eurostat: *EU transport in figures. Statistical pocket-book. 1st issue 1997*: EC, 1997; ISBN: 92-827-9693-0; EC No.C3-03-97-604-EN-C

Commission, DG VII/ Eurostat: *EU transport in figures. Statistical pocket-book. 2nd issue 1997*: EC, 1997; ISBN: 92-828-0959-5; EC No.C3-05-97-543-EN-C

The Commission thought that there was a need for a joint approach towards sustainable network planning:

Commission: *Communication ... connecting the Union's transport infrastructure to its neighbours. Towards a co-operative pan-European transport network policy*: COM (97)172 final (23.4.97)

The Commission addressed the question of freight transport:

Commission: *Communication ... Intermodality and intermodal freight transport in the European Union. A systems approach to freight transport. Strategies and actions to enhance efficiency, services and sustainability*: COM (97)243 final (29.5.97)

A report was drawn up based upon the findings from a questionnaire sent to Member States and professional bodies:

Commission: *Report ... on the application during the years 1993 to 1995 of Council Directive 92/106/EEC of 7.12.92 on the establishment of common rules for certain types of combined transport of goods between Member States*: COM (97)372 final (18.7.97)

A High Level Group set up by Commissioner Kinnock in 1996 had concluded that public–private partnerships could accelerate trans-European network projects. The Commission proposed measures to implement the Group's recommendations:

Commission: *Communication ... on public-private partnerships in Trans-European Transport Networks projects*: COM (97)453 final (10.9.97)

A decline between 1970 and 1995 of almost 25 per cent in freight carried by rail had prompted the issue of a report by a group set up by Kinnock, 'The Future of Rail in Europe', which recommended the setting-up of trans-European rail freight freeways. The Commission's communication advised methods of implementation:

Commission: *Communication ... Trans-European rail freight freeways*: COM (97)242 final (29.5.97)

Unless policies are changed, an estimated one in 80 European citizens will die as a result of road accidents. The Commission communication gave details of the effects of the first action plan set up by *COM* (93) 246, and proposed a new strategy towards road safety:

Commission: *Communication ... Promoting road safety in the EU. The programme for 1997–2001*: *COM* (97)131 final (9.4.97)

See also:

Commission: *Report ... on the implementation in 1993–94 of Regulation (EEC) No.3820/85 on the harmonisation of certain social legislation relating to road transport (18th report ...)*: *COM* (97)698 final (12.12.97)

A second report on maritime and island cabotage analysed the social and economic effects of implementation of Council Regulation 3577/92:

Commission: *Report ... on the implementation of Council Regulation 3577/92 applying the principle of freedom to provide services to maritime cabotage (1995–96) and on the economic and social impact of the liberalisation of island cabotage*: *COM* (97)296 final (17.6.97)

See also:

Commission: *Communication ... External relations in the field of maritime transport*: *COM* (96)707 final/2 (17.4.97)

Commission: *Green Paper on sea ports and maritime infrastructure*: *COM* (97)678 final (10.12.97)

The first EU code of conduct for CRSs was adopted by Council in July 1992 and amended in October 1993. A report proposed a revision of that code:

Commission: *Report on the application of Council Regulation (EEC) No.2299/ 89 on a code of conduct for computerised reservation systems (CRSs)(+ legislative proposal)*: *COM* (97)246 final (9.7.97)

A report, presented in accordance with Art. 5 of Council decision 92/41/EEC, gave an overview of EC measures affecting tourism:

Commission: *Report ... Community measures affecting tourism (1995–96)*:*COM* (97)332 final (2.7.97)

See also 'Competition' above.

Miscellaneous

In 1995, the EU had supported the Northern Ireland peace process through its Special Support Programme. This was a five-year plan, resourced initially for three years. The Commission recommended further funding in 1998 of 100m ECU, with a similar allocation for 1999:

Commission: *Communication ... on the Special Support Programme for Peace and Reconciliation in Northern Ireland and the Border Counties of Ireland (1995–1999)*: *COM* (97)642 final (26.11.97)

Enforcement procedures were addressed:

Commission: *Communication ... 'Towards greater efficiency in obtaining and enforcing judgments in the European Union*: *COM* (97)609 final (26.11.97)

External Policies and Relations

General

In a third report of its kind, the Commission described the main activities followed in 1995 under 'the European initiative for democracy and the protection of human rights':

Commission: *Report ... on the implementation of measures intended to promote observance of human rights and democratic principles (for 1995)*: *COM* (96)672 final (17.1.97)

Macro-financial assistance is now extended to third countries. The intention is to extend efforts towards political and economic reform:

Commission: *Report ... on the implementation of macro-financial assistance to Third Countries in 1995*: *COM* (96)695 final (8.1.97)
Related publications: *European Economy: Supplement A*, No.10–11, October–November 1996, p. 1

The Commission provided a report on regional co-operation referring to countries outside the EU in fulfilment of an undertaking given to the Dublin European Council:

Commission: *Report ... on regional co-operation in Europe*: *COM* (97)659 final (1.12.97)

Common Foreign and Security Policy (CFSP)

Statements and declarations made within the CFSP framework in 1997 are issued in the form of *Press Releases* from the Council of the European Union. They can be traced on the RAPID database using the *PESC* prefix. Statements can also be located on the EU Presidency homepages.

A regular account of CFSP activities is published in the monthly *Bull.EU* throughout the year as a part of Section 3: 'Role of the Union in the world'. Legislative acts adopted are noted in that source and reproduced in the *Official Journal* 'L' series and on CELEX.

European University Institute: *European Foreign Policy Bulletin*, Vol.10, 1994: EC, 1997; ISBN: 92-827-9571-3; EC No.OY-03-97-111-2A-C

Enlargement

The issue of EU enlargement was a key one in 1997. The Commission investigated the progress made by ten prospective Member States. For Hungary, Poland, Estonia, the Czech Republic and Slovenia, immediate negotiations for entry were recommended, with a further report to be issued no later than December 1998. For Romania, Slovakia, Latvia, Lithuania and Bulgaria, the Commission recommended opening negotiations as soon as each state had made sufficient progress to satisfy conditions for membership as defined by the Copenhagen Council (June 1993):

Commission: *Commission opinion on Hungary's application for membership of the European Union*: *Bull.EU: Supplement*, No.6, 1997; ISBN: 92-828-1259-6: EC No.CM-NF-97-006-EN-C
Related publications: *COM* (97)2001 final (15.7.97)

Commission: *Commission opinion on Poland's application for membership of the European Union*: *Bull.EU: Supplement*, No.7, 1997; ISBN: 92-828-1270-7; EC No.CM-NF-97-007-EN-C
Related publications: *COM* (97)2002 final (15.7.97)

Commission: *Commission opinion on Romania's application for membership of the European Union*: *Bull.EU: Supplement*, No.8, 1997; ISBN: 92-828-1303-7: EC No.CM-NF-97-008-EN-C
Related publications: *COM* (97)2003 final (15.7.97)

Commission: *Commission opinion on Slovakia's application for membership of the European Union*: *Bull.EU: Supplement*, No.9, 1997; ISBN: 92-828-1248-0; EC No.CM-NF-97-009-EN-C
Related publications: *COM* (97)2004 final (15.7.97)

Commission: *Commission opinion on Latvia's application for membership of the European Union*: *Bull.EU: Supplement*, No.10, 1997: ISBN: 92-828-1292-8: EC No.CM-NF-97-010-EN-C
Related publications: *COM* (97)2005 final (15.7.97)

Commission: *Commission opinion on Estonia's application for membership of the European Union*: *Bull.EU: Supplement*, No.11, 1997; ISBN: 92-828-1281-2: EC No.CM-NF-97-011-EN-C
Related publications: *COM* (97)2006 final (15.7.97)

Commission: *Commission opinion on Lithuania's application for membership of the   European Union*: *Bull.EU: Supplement*, No.12, 1997: ISBN: 92-828-1204-9: EC No.CM-NF-97-012-EN-C
Related publications: *COM* (97)2007 final (15.7.97)

Commission: *Commission opinion on Bulgaria's application for membership of the European Union*: *Bull.EU: Supplement*, No.13, 1997; ISBN: 92-828-1215-4: EC No.CM-NF-97-013-EN-C
Related publications: *COM* (97)2008 final (15.7.97)

© Blackwell Publishers Ltd 1998

Commission: *Commission opinion on the Czech Republic's application for membership of the European Union: Bull.EU: Supplement*, No.14, 1997; ISBN: 92-828-1226-X: EC No.CM-NF-97-014-EN-C
Related publications: COM (97)2009 final (15.7.97)

Commission: *Commission opinion on Slovenia's application for membership of the European Union: Bull.EU: Supplement*, No.15, 1997; ISBN: 92-828-1237-5; EC No.CM-NF-97-015-EN-C
Related publications: COM (97)2010 final (15.7.97)

External Trade

Developments in world trade were assessed:

Commission, DG I: *The European Union and world trade. European Union trade developments for the year 1995, comparison with the United States and Japan:* EC, 1996; ISBN: 92-827-7188-1; EC No.CN-97-96-984-EN-C

The Commission published an introduction to TARIC in accordance with Article 6, Regulation (EEC) No. 2658/87:

Commission: *Integrated tariff of the European Communities (TARIC). Introduction: OJ* C102, 1.4.97, pp. 1–29
Related publications: OJ C102A, 1.4.97. 4 vols

The fifteenth annual report concentrated upon EC activities for 1996, commenting on each case opened, measures taken and cases terminated without action:

Commission: *Fifteenth annual report ... on the Community's anti-dumping and anti-subsidy activities (1996): COM* (97)428 final (16.9.97)

Asia

During the year in which sovereignty of Hong Kong was handed back to China, the Commission published its ideas on the impact of this on the EU:

Commission: *Communication ... The European Union and Hong Kong: beyond 1997: COM* (97)171 final (23.4.97)

The Commission issued a Communication analysing the impact of overall co-operation between Europe and Asia in the field of the environment:

Commission: *Communication ... on a Europe–Asia Cooperation Strategy in the field of the environment: COM* (97)490 final (13.10.97)

Developing Countries (ACP)

Commission, DG VIII: *Development cooperation policy in the run-up to 2000. Collection of Communications from the Commission ... and of relevant resolutions, declarations and conclusions of the Council of Ministers, May 1992–May 1995: Europe Information: Development*: EC, 1996; ISBN: 92-827-6487-7; EC No.CF-94-96-607-EN-C

Major political and economic changes have taken place at international level and within the ACP states and the EU itself since the Lomé IV convention was signed. A report from DG VIII put forward proposals for the future:

Commission, DG VIII: *Lomé IV revised. Changes and challenges*: *Europe Information: Development*, DE 89 (December 1996)

An account of progress in financial co-operation was provided:

Commission, DG VIII: *Financial cooperation under the Lomé Conventions. Aid situation at the end of 1996*: *Europe Information; Development*, DE 92, (November 1997)

See also:

Commission: *Communication ... Guidelines for the negotiations of new cooperation agreements with the African, Caribbean and Pacific (ACP) countries*: *COM* (97)537 final (29.10.97)

A Communication proposed further measures to alleviate debt problems in ACP states:

Commission: *Communication ... Support for structural adjustment and debt relief in heavily indebted ACP States. A Community response to the HIPC Debt Initiative*: *COM* (97)129 final (25.3.97)

The Commission suggested a long-term strategy to improve market access for least developed countries on the basis of the WTO Action plan adopted in Singapore:

Commission: *Communication ... Improving market access for least developed countries*: *COM* (97)156 final (16.4.97)

A Communication responding to requests from both the Council and the Member States made in June 1995 looked at scientific and technological research:

Commission: *Communication ... scientific and technological research – a strategic part of the European Union's development co-operation with developing countries*: *COM* (97)174 final (25.4.97)

The Copenhagen summit (June 1993) argued that more attention should be drawn to the social effects of globalization. The Commission report addressed this question:

Commission: *Commission report ... on the Scheme of Generalised Preferences. Summary of work conducted within the OECD, ILO and WTO on the link between international trade and social standards / ... on the relationship between international trade and the environment*: COM (97)260 final (2.6.97)

A Communication presented guidelines and mechanisms to encourage the role of developing countries in the Information Society:

Commission: *Communication ... The Information Society and development: the role of the European Union*: COM (97)351 final (15.7.97)

Following Article 31 (3) of the financing and administration of Community Aid States, a Commission report paid special attention to the allocation of transfers for 1995:

Commission: *Commission report on the operation in 1996 of the export earnings stabilisation system under the fourth ACP–EC Convention as revised by the Agreement signed in Mauritius*: COM (97)374 final (18.7.97)

In compliance with Article 152 EC, the Council requested the Commission to carry out a diagnostic study of tariff arrangements, which was completed in 1997:

Commission: *Communication ... on the management of preferential tariff arrangements*: COM (97)402 final (23.7.97)

Assistance in 1996 amounted to 656 m ECU (a reduction from the 1995 figure of 692 m ECU). Sixty countries had benefited:

Commission: *Annual report 1996 on humanitarian aid*: COM (97)437 final (3.9.97)

The Commission reported on the International Grains Agreement:

Commission: *Communication ... The extension of the International Grains Agreement, 1995 and the negotiation of a successor agreement*: COM (97)717 final (16.12.97)

See also Industry' above.

Eastern and Central Europe

Previously unpublished data on price developments were published in the form of case studies undertaken by external experts:

Commission, DG II: *The CAP and enlargement. Agrifood price developments in five associated countries*: European Economy: Reports and Studies, No.2, 1997

The issue of cross-border co-operation under the TACIS programme has become one of increasing importance in recent years. A Commission Communication gave details of the implementation of a new budget created in 1996:

Commission: *Communication ... on cross-border cooperation within the framework of the TACIS Programme*: COM (97)239 final (27.5.97)

See also 'Enlargement' and Section D 'Education, training and R & D' and 'Transport' above.

Mediterranean and Middle East

A Communication reviewed the first 15 months of partnership between the EU and the Mediterranean region:

Commission: *Communication ... Progress report on the Euro-Mediterranean partnership and preparations for the Second Conference of Foreign Affairs Ministers*: COM (97)68 final (19.2.97)

The Cannes European Council (June 1995) agreed a figure of 4685m ECU for the EU's financial co-operation with Mediterranean partners 1995–99. A Commission report was issued on the first part of this programme

Commission: *Commission report ... on cooperation with the Mediterranean Partners*: COM (97)371 final (18.7.97)

The Commission fulfilled its undertaking to the February Agricultural Council, by issuing a report focused on 'sensitive' import products in relation to third countries of the Mediterranean region:

Commission: *Report ... Mediterranean concessions impact study*: COM (97)477 final (1.10.97)

North America

DG I reported on US/EU trade:

Commission, DG I: *Report on United States barriers to trade and investment 1997: EC, 1997* (not formally published)

See also 'Competition' above.

Turkey

A Communication on development of relations with Turkey was issued. It reconfirmed that Turkey was eligible for EU membership but it included the condition of 'the achievement of a just and lasting settlement in Cyprus'.

Commission: *Communication ... on the further development of relations with Turkey*: COM (97)394 final (15.7.97)

Journal of Common Market Studies

Volume 36, Annual Review
September 1998

Chronology of Key Events 1997

ADRIAN RANDALL
and
GEORG WIESSALA
De Montfort University Bedford

January	1	Dutch Presidency took over from Ireland with IGC conclusion, preparation for the single currency and enlargement as priorities.
	8	System for calculating financial penalties for Member States that do not comply with ECJ judgments set out by Commission. Penalties to start at 500 ECU per day.
	13	Spanish MEP José Maria Gil-Robles Gil-Delgado is elected new President of the EP to succeed Klaus Hänsch.
	30–31	'European Year Against Racism' launched in the Hague.
February		European Ombudsman Jacob Söderman recommended the European institutions adopt rules on public access to documents to avoid accusations of maladministration.
	6	Leonardo training programme launched for 1997.
	13–14	12th Ministerial meeting EU/ASEAN in Singapore.
March		First Annual Report on equal opportunities for women and men adopted by the Commission.
	25	Ceremony in Rome to commemorate 40th anniversary of the signature of the Treaty of Rome.
	27	Shift in emphasis for the PHARE programme from a demand-driven to an accession-driven initiative approved by Commission.

April	15–16	Second Euro-Mediterranean Conference of Foreign Ministers in Malta.
	23	Commission adopted Communication: The EU and Hong Kong: Beyond 1997.
	24	ACP–EC Council of Ministers adopted the protocol on South Africa's accession to the amended Lomé IV Convention.
	29	First Co-operation Agreements with Cambodia and Laos.
	30	Commission adopted proposal for the Fifth Framework Programme for Research and Technical Development (1998–2002)
May	1	General Elections in the UK. Labour gained 419 seats or 44% of votes case. Conservatives: 165 seats (31%); Liberal Democrats: 46 seats (17%).
	9	Europe day. Solidarity and citizenship were the priorities for the commemorative celebrations in 1997.
	12–13	Paris Declaration on co-operation between the EU and the WEU and the WEU and NATO.
	25	First round of voting in the French General Election. The combined vote for right-wing RPR and UDF fell to 31.5%, vote for Socialists rose by 6% and Communists had their highest vote since 1988. Far-right FN attracts a vote of 14.9%.
June	6	General Election in Ireland. Fianna Fáil gained 77 seats, or 39.33% of votes, Fine Gael: 54 seats (27.95%). Labour: 17 seats (10.4%).
	12	EU reaffirms its commitment to EU–ASEAN dialogue as ASEAN enlarges to accept Burma (Myanmar), Cambodia and Laos.
	16–17	EU Council meeting in Amsterdam reaches agreement on draft Treaty.
	23	Commission adopts amendment to Directive 90/220: genetically modified organisms (GMO) will have to be labelled as such.
	26	Commission President Santer attended G 8 summit in Denver. Russia took part for the first time. EU–Australia Joint Declaration signed.
	30	Television Without Frontiers Directive enters into force.
July	1	Luxembourg takes over the helm of the Presidency from the Netherlands. Priorities are EMU, *Agenda 2000* and unemployment.
	8	Commission agrees to buy the renovated Berlaymont building.
	8–9	NATO summit in Madrid; invitations to the Czech Republic, Hungary and Poland to start accession negotiations.

16 Jacques Santer announces the Commission's *Agenda 2000* programme. This is designed to meet the twin challenges of enlargement and internal reform.

Commission also delivers favourable opinions with regard to accession negotiations with the Czech Republic, Estonia, Hungary, Poland and Slovenia. Negotiations with the remaining five, Bulgaria, Latvia, Lithuania, Romania and Slovakia to start when they satisfy conditions for membership laid down by the Copenhagen Council in June 1993. The Council had decided that negotiations with Cyprus would start six months after the end of the IGC, following the positive 1993 opinion by the Commission.

22 Brussels Declaration on the WEU's relationship with the EU and NATO in the light of the Amsterdam Treaty.

30 Commission cleared Boeing/McDonnell-Douglas merger, subject to conditions to be fulfilled by Boeing.

September 1 Dublin Asylum Convention enters into force.
Devolution referendums in Scotland and Wales

October 2 EU Foreign Ministers formally sign the Amsterdam Treaty. It amends and updates the 1992 Maastricht Treaty.

6 'Ariane' Programme to encourage reading adopted by Council and EP.

13 'Raphael' Programme concerning cultural heritage adopted by Council and EP.

22 Commission President Jacques Santer presents the Commission's 1998 Work Programme to the EP. It concentrates on the priority areas of employment, the single currency, *Agenda 2000*, external relations and serving the public.

28 Youth Council endorses an EU-wide voluntary service initiative for young people.

29 Commission adopts guidelines for EU–ACP relations.

30 Presidential Election in Ireland: Mary MacAleese becomes successor to Mary Robinson.

November Commission starts second phase of 'Citizens First' campaign concentrating on 'buying goods and services', 'travelling' and 'equal opportunities'.

20–21 EU Employment summit in Luxembourg discussed the implementation of the new Employment Chapter in the Amsterdam Treaty. It also concentrated on employment policy guidelines, employability, entre-

entrepreneurship, equal opportunities and adaptability. It supported an EIB initiative to lend up to 10bn ECU extra to encourage SMEs, new technology and TENs.

December 1–10 International conference on climate change in Kyoto.

1 Partnership and Co-operation Agreement between the EU and Russia enters into force.

3 International Convention on Anti-Personnel Landmines signed in Ottawa.

4 Council agrees to ban tobacco advertising.

12–13 The Luxembourg European Council launched the accession process for ten applicant countries of central and eastern Europe and Cyprus. This will start on 30 March 1998 and will be all-embracing, inclusive and responsive to events. There will be a European Conference.

Final practical arrangements for the implementation of the third stage of EMU are to be accelerated.

The Council adopted a declaration on the 50th anniversary of the European Convention of Human Rights (ECHR).

18 1998 Budget adopted after two EP readings.

The Commission's 'Europa' Internet server is being accessed more than 15 million times per month.

Journal of Common Market Studies

Volume 36, Annual Review
September 1998

Books on European Integration

BRIAN ARDY AND JACKIE GOWER

Thames Valley University

The following list includes all books submitted to the *Journal of Common Market Studies* during 1997, whether these were reviewed or not. Each book is entered only once even though, inevitably, some titles are of relevance to more than one section.

General Studies

Bideleux, R and Jeffries, I: *A History of Eastern Europe: Crisis and Change* (London, Routledge, 1998, ISBN hb 0415161118, pb 0415161126) xii + 685 pp., hb £60.00, pb £19.99.

De Giustino, D: *A Reader in European Integration* (Harlow, Longman, 1996, ISBN 058229200X) xvi + 296 pp., pb £16.99.

Dehousse R (ed): *Europe: The Impossible Status Quo* (Basingstoke, Macmillan, 1997, ISBN hb 033368205X, pb 0333699408) xix + 132 pp., hb £42.50, pb £15.99.

Della Porta, D: *Democracy and Corruption in Europe* (London, Pinter, 1997, ISBN hb 1855673665, pb 1855673673) viii + 208 pp., hb £45.00, pb £13.99.

East, R and Pontin, J: *Revolution and Change in Central and Eastern Europe* (London, Pinter, 1997, ISBN hb 1855673606, pb 1855673614) xii + 340 pp., hb £45.00, pb £16.99.

Gowan, P and Anderson, P (eds): *The Question of Europe* (London, Verso, 1997, ISBN hb 1859848362, pb 1859841422) xv + 399 pp., hb £40.00, pb £15.00.

Harryvan, A G and van der Harst, J (eds): *Documents on European Union* (Basingstoke, Macmillan, 1997, ISBN hb 0333658671, pb 033365868X) xvii + 313 pp., hb £45.00, pb £14.99.

McAllister, R: *From EC to EU: An Historical and Political Survey* (London, Routledge, 1997, ISBN hb 0415142652, pb 0415142660) xxvii + 254 pp., hb £45.00, pb £14.99.

Rhodes, M, Heywood, P and Wright, V (eds): *Developments in West European Politics* (Basingstoke, Macmillan, 1997, ISBN hb 0333651278, pb 0333651286) xi + 363 pp., hb £42.50, pb £13.99.

Salmon, T and Nicoll, W (eds): *Building European Union: A Documentary History and Analysis* (Manchester, Manchester University Press, 1997, ISBN hb 0719044456, pb 0719044464) xiv + 297 pp., hb £45.00, pb £14.99.

Stirk, P M R: *A History of European Integration since 1914* (London, Pinter, 1996, ISBN hb 1855674114, pb 1855674122) xi + 308 pp., hb £42.50, pb £16.99.

Urwin, D: *A Political History of Western Europe since 1945* (Harlow, Addison Wesley/ Longman, 1997, 5th edn, ISBN hb 0582316189, pb 0582253748) xii + 359 pp., hb £44.00, pb £16.99.

Weidenfeld, W and Wessels, W: *Jahrbuch der Europäischen Integration 1996/97* (Bonn, Europa Union Verlag GmbH, 1997, ISBN 3771305500) 552 pp., DM 89.

Government and Institutions

Bennett, R J (ed): *Trade Associations in Britain and Germany: Responding to Internationalisation and the EU* (London, Anglo-German Foundation, 1997, ISBN 1900834057) ii + 118 pp., pb £12.00.

Budge, I, Newton, K et al.: *The Politics of the New Europe; Atlantic to Urals* (Harlow, Addison Wesley/Longman, 1997, ISBN 0582234344) xvi + 412 pp., pb £19.99.

Cram, L: *Policy-making in the EU* (London, Routledge, 1997, ISBN hb 0415146259, pb 0415146267) xix + 210 pp., hb £50.00, pb £15.99.

Duff, A: *The Treaty of Amsterdam* (London, Federal Trust, 1997, ISBN hb 0901573671, pb 0901573655) xl + 322 pp., hb £45.00, pb £12.95.

Edwards, G and Pijpers, A (eds): *The Politics of European Treaty Reform: The 1996 Intergovernmental Conference and Beyond* (London, Pinter, 1997, ISBN hb 1855673584, pb 1855673592) viii + 353 pp., hb £59.95, pb £16.99.

Federal Trust, TEPSA: *Britain's Agenda in Europe: The United Kingdom Presidency of the European Union January to June 1998* (London, Federal Trust, 1997, ISBN 090157368X) 32 pp., pb £5.00.

Greenwood, J: *Representing Interests in the European Union* (Basingstoke, Macmillan, 1997, ISBN hb 333611772, pb 0333611780) xx + 292 pp., hb £45.00, pb £14.99.

Hix, S and Lord, C: *Political Parties in the European Union* (Basingstoke, Macmillan, 1997, ISBN hb 0333609204, pb 0333609212) xv + 240 pp., hb £42.50, pb £13.99.

Jeffery, C: *The Regional Dimension of the European Union: Towards a Third Level in Europe?* (London, Frank Cass, 1997, ISBN hb 0714647489, pb 0714643068) 223 pp., hb £27.50, pb £14.50.

Johansson, K M: *Transnational Party Alliances: Analysing the Hardwon Alliance between Conservatives and Christian Democrats in the EP* (Lund, Lund University Press, 1997, ISBN 9179664172) 272 pp., pb SEK 230.00.

Jorgensen, K E (ed): *Reflective Approaches to European Governance* (Basingstoke, Macmillan, 1997, ISBN 0333656792) xi + 262 pp., hb £35.00.

Lothian Foundation: *Annals of the Lothian Foundation, Volume IV* (London, Lothian Foundation Press, 1996, ISBN 187221009X) 397 pp., pb np.

Mair, P: *Party System Change: Approaches and Interpretations* (Oxford, Oxford University Press, 1997, ISBN 019829235X) xiv + 244 pp., hb £35.00.

Mouritzen, H: *External Danger and Democracy: Old Nordic Lessons and New European Challenges* (Aldershot, Dartmouth, 1997, ISBN 1855218852) x + 173 pp., hb £39.50.

Mouritzen, H, Waever, O and Wiberg, H: *European Integration and National Adaptations: A Theoretical Enquiry* (New York, Nova Science, 1996, ISBN 1560722916) 338 pp., hb £50.99.

Nugent, N (ed): *At the Heart of the Union: Studies of the European Commission* (Basingstoke, Macmillan, 1997, ISBN 0312174136) xii + 328., hb £50.00.

Page, E C: *People Who Run Europe* (Oxford, Oxford University Press, 1997, ISBN 0198280793) x + 178 pp., hb £30.00.

Plant, R and Steed, M: *PR for Europe* (London, Federal Trust, 1997, ISBN 0901573663) 21 pp., pb £10.00.

Richardson, J (ed): *European Union: Power and Policy-Making* (London, Routledge, 1996, ISBN hb 0415129168, pb 0415129176) x + 300 pp., hb £45.00, pb £13.99.

Van Deth, J W: *Private Groups and Public Life: Social Participation, Voluntary Associations and Political Involvement in Representative Democracy* (London, Routledge, 1997, ISBN 0415169550) xvi + 244 pp., hb £50.00.

Wallace, H and Young, A R (eds): *Participation and Policy-Making in the European Union* (Oxford, Oxford University Press, 1997, ISBN 0198280602) xxiv + 280 pp., hb £35.00.

Zirakzadeh, C E: *Social Movements in Politics: A Comparative Study* (Harlow, Longman, 1997, ISBN hb 0582209471, pb 0582209463) xiv + 629 pp., hb £40.00, pb £15.99.

Internal Policies and the Law

Armstrong, K and Bulmer, S J: *The Governance of the Single European Market* (Manchester, Manchester University Press, 1998, ISBN hb 0719044561, pb 071904457X) xii + 340 pp., hb £45.00, pb £15.99.

Bachtler, J and Turok, I (eds): *The Coherence of EU Regional Policy* (London, Jessica Kingsley, 1997, ISBN 1853023965) 416 pp., pb £25.00.

Bovis, C: *EC Public Procurement Law* (Harlow, Longman, 1997, ISBN 0582294398) x + 133 pp., pb £15.99.

Collier, U, Golub, J and Kreher, A (eds): *Subsidiarity and Shared Responsibility: New Challenges for EU Environmental Policy* (Baden-Baden, Nomos, 1997, ISBN 3789046477) viii + 196 pp., pb DM 54.50.

Deflorian, L A: *La Struttura Istituzionale Del Nouvo Diritto Comune Euoropeo: Competizione E Circolazione Dei Modelli Giuridici* (Trento, Italy, Universita degli Studi dialogue Trento, 1996, ISBN 8886135580) xx + 412 pp., pb L. 50.000.

Ehlermann, C D and Laudati, L L (eds): *Proceedings of the European Competition Forum* (Chichester, Wiley, 1997, ISBN 0471966681) xxviii + 248 pp., hb £50.00.

Fennell, R: *The Common Agricultural Policy: Continuity and Change* (Oxford, Oxford University Press, 1997, ISBN 0198288573) xiv + 439 pp., hb £48.00.

Field, J: *European Dimensions: Education, Training and the European Union* (London, Jessica Kingsley, 1997, ISBN 1853024325) vii + 215 pp., pb £19.95.

Grant, W: *The Common Agricultural Policy* (Basingstoke, Macmillan, 1997, ISBN hb 0333604652, pb 0333604660) xii + 244 pp., hb £42.50, pb £13.99.

Haaland Matláry, J: *Energy Policy in the European Union* (Basingstoke, Macmillan, 1997, ISBN hb 0333643488, pb 0333643496) xiii + 174 pp., hb £40.00, pb £12.99.

Hoekman, B M and Mavroidis, P C (eds): *Law and Policy in Public Purchasing: The WTO Agreement on Government Procurement* (Michigan, University of Michigan Press, 1997, ISBN 0472108298) xiv + 343 pp., hb £50.00 / $65.00.

Ingersent, K A, Rayner, A J and Hine, R C (eds): *The Reform of the Common Agricultural Policy* (Basingstoke, Macmillan, 1998, ISBN 033368771X) xiv + 223 pp., hb £45.00.

Johnson, D and Turner, C: *Trans-European Networks: The Political Economy of Integrating Europe's Infrastructure* (Basingstoke, Macmillan, 1997, ISBN 0333649842) xvii + 228 pp., hb £45.00.

Laffan, B: *The Finances of the European Union* (Basingstoke, Macmillan, 1997, ISBN hb 0333609859, pb 0333609867) xvi + 294 pp., hb £45.00, pb £14.99.

Lehning, P B and Weale, A: *Citizenship, Democracy and Justice in the New Europe* (London, Routledge, 1997, ISBN hb 0415158192, pb 0415158206) xi + 212 pp., hb £45.00, pb £14.99.

Liefferink, D and Andersen M S (eds): *The Innovation of EU Environmental Policy* (Copenhagen, Scandinavian University Press, 1997, ISBN 8200376877) 198 pp., pb DKK 220.

Meijers, H: *Democracy, Migrants and Police in the European Union: the 1996 IGC and Beyond* (Utrecht, FORUM, Institute for Multi-Cultural Development, 1997, ISBN 905714011X) 196 pp., pb Hfl 49.50.

Plender, R (ed): *European Courts Practice and Precedents* (London, Sweet & Maxwell Ltd, 1996, ISBN 0421523204) cxxxi +1208 pp., hb £210.00.

Stefanou, C and Xanthaki, H: *A Legal and Political Interpretation of Articles 224 and 225 of the Treaty of Rome: The Former Yugoslav Republic of Macedonia Cases* (Aldershot, Dartmouth, 1997, ISBN 1855218941) vii + 146 pp., hb £42.50.

Tufano, M L: *La C.D. Eccezione di Invalidita Delgi Atti Communitari* (Naples, Editoriale Scientifica, 1996, ISBN 8885370705) 129 pp., pb L. 20.000.

Turner, C: *Trans-European Telecommunication Networks: The Challenges for Industrial Policy* (London, Routledge, 1997, ISBN 041516186X) xii + 177 pp., hb £40.00.

Uçarer, E and Puchala, D: *Immigration into Western Societies: Problems and Policies* (London, Pinter, 1997, ISBN 1855674513) xv + 350 pp., hb £59.95.

External Relations and Developments

Friedman, G and Starr, H: *Agency, Structure, and International Politics: From Ontology to Empirical Inquiry* (London, Routledge, 1997, ISBN 0415152593) viii + 170 pp., hb £40.00.

Galal A and Hoekman, B (eds): *Regional Partners in Global Markets: Limits and Possibilities of the Euro–Med Agreements* (London, CEPR/ECES, 1997, ISBN 1898128286) xviii + 317 pp., pb £16.95.

Hirsch, S and Almor, T (eds): *Outsiders' Response to European Integration* (Copenhagen, Handleshojskolens Forlag, 1996, ISBN 8716132335) 196 pp., hb £22.00.

Hocking, B and Smith, M: *Beyond Foreign Economic Policy: The United States, the Single European Market and the Changing World Economy* (London, Pinter, 1997, ISBN hb 1855672685, pb 1855672693) 216 pp., hb £45.00, pb £14.99.

Holmes, J W: *The United States and Europe After the Cold War: A New Alliance?* (Columbia, University of South Carolina Press, 1997, ISBN 157003107X) ix + 225 pp., hb $ 34.95.

Larsen, H: *Foreign Policy and Discourse Analysis: France, Britain and Europe* (London, Routledge, 1997, ISBN 0415159768) vi + 243 pp., hb £50.00.

Laursen, F and Riishoj, S (eds): *The EU and Central Europe: Status and Prospects* (Esbjerg, Vestkystens Bogtrykkeri, 1996, ISBN 8777801024) ix + 282 pp., pb Dkr 260.00.

Maresceau, M (ed): *Enlarging the European Union; Relations Between the EU and Central and Eastern Europe* (Harlow, Addison Wesley/Longman, 1997, ISBN 0582318483) xxv + 403 pp., hb £58.00.

Milner, H V: *Interests, Institutions, and Information; Domestic Politics and International Relations* (Princeton, Princeton University Press, 1997, ISBN hb 069101177X, pb 0691011761) xii + 309 pp., hb £35.00, pb £14.95.

Regelsberger, E; de Schoutheete de Tervarent, P and Wessels, W (eds): *Foreign Policy of the European Union: From EPC to CFSP and Beyond* (London, Lynne Rienner, 1997, ISBN 1555877052) ix + 406 pp., hb np.

Sachwald, F: *L'Europe et la Mondialisation* (France, Flammarion, 1997, ISBN 2080354949) 128 pp., pb 41.00 Ff.

Sperling, J and Kirchner, E: *Recasting the European Order: Security Architectures and Economic Cooperation* (Manchester, Manchester University Press, 1997, ISBN hb 071903986X, pb 0719039878) x + 287 pp., hb £45.00, pb £14.99.

Wyatt-Walter, H: *The European Community and the Security Dilemma, 1979–92* (Basingstoke, Macmillan, 1997, ISBN 0333673530) xiv + 339 pp., hb £45.00.

Economic Developments in Europe and Beyond

Ahn, S-J: *From State to Community: Rethinking South Korean Modernization* (Colorado, Aigis Publications, 1994, ISBN 1883930022) xiv +108 pp., pb $ 9.50.

Allen, L: *Capital Markets and Institutions: A Global View* (Chichester, Wiley, 1997, ISBN 0471130494) xx + 734pp., hb £23.00.

Ambrus-Lakatos, L and Schaffer, M E (eds): *Fiscal Policy in Transition: Forum Report of the Economic Policy Initiative* (London, Centre for Economic Policy Research, 1997, ISBN 18981128308) xv + 83pp., pb £14.95.

Asante, S K B: *Regionalism and Africa's Development; Expectations, Reality and Challenges* (Basingstoke, Macmillan, 1997, ISBN 0333711289) xvii + 206 pp., hb £45.00.

Batchelor, RE and Chebli-Saadi, M: *French for Marketing: Using French in Media and Communications* (Cambridge, Cambridge University Press, 1997, ISBN hb 0521585007, pb 052158535X) xvii + 350 pp., hb £45.00, pb £16.95.

Begg, D, Giavazzi, F, von Hagen, J, Wypolosz, C: *EMU: Getting the End-Game Right* (London, Centre for Economic Policy Research, 1997, ISBN 189812826X) xiv + 75 pp., pb £10.00.

Bishop, G, Perez, J, van Tuyll van Serooskerken, S (eds): *User Guide to the Euro* (London, Federal Trust, 1996, ISBN 0901573620) xxii + 184 pp., pb £9.95.

Black, S W: *Europe's Economy Looks East: Implications for Germany and the European Union* (Cambridge, Cambridge University Press, 1997, ISBN 0521572428) xvi + 363 pp., hb £45.00.

Brusse, W A: *Tariffs, Trade and European Integration, 1947–1957* (Basingstoke, Macmillan, 1997, ISBN 0333717694) xiii + 318 pp., hb £35.00.

Buckley, P, Campos, J, Mirza, H and White, E (eds): *International Technology Transfer by Small and Medium-Sized Enterprises* (Basingstoke, Macmillan, 1997, ISBN 0333564871) xxv + 504 pp., hb £65.00.

Burda, M and Wyplosz, C: *Macroeconomics: A European Text* (Oxford, Oxford University Press, 1997, 2nd edn, ISBN hb 0198774699, pb 0198774680) xxv + 613 pp., hb £50.00, pb £22.99.

Cencini, A: *Monetary Theory: National and International* (London, Routledge, 1997, ISBN 0415110556) x + 384 pp., pb £17.99.

Curwen, P: *Restructuring Telecommunications: A Study of Europe in a Global Context* (Basingstoke, Macmillan, 1997, ISBN 0333722299) xii + 220 pp., hb £40.00.

Dent, C M: *The European Economy: The Global Context* (London, Routledge, 1997, ISBN hb 0415134870, pb 0415134889) xxii + 455 pp., hb £ 60.00, pb £ 16.99.

Eichengreen, B: *Globalizing Capital: A History of the International Monetary System* (Princeton, Princeton University Press, 1996, ISBN 069102880X) viii + 224 pp., hb $24.00.

El-Agraa, A M (ed): *Economic Integration Worldwide* (Basingstoke, Macmillan, 1997, ISBN hb 033365482X, pb 0333654838) xix + 434 pp., hb £50.00, pb £18.50.

Estrin, S, Hughes, K and Todd, S: *Foreign Direct Investment in Central and Eastern Europe; Multinationals in Transition* (London, Cassell, 1997, ISBN 1855674815) vii + 276 pp., hb £45.00.

Ethier, D: *Economic Adjustment In New Democracies: Lessons from Southern Europe* (Basingstoke, Macmillan, 1997, ISBN 0333695569) xii + 180., hb £42.50.

Grahl, A: *After Maastricht: A Guide to European Monetary Union* (London, Lawrence & Wishart, 1998, ISBN 0853158223) viii + 264 pp., pb £12.99.

Hesse, D: *Deregulation and Employment in Britain and Germany* (London, Anglo-German Foundation, 1997, 1900834022) 58pp., pb £12.00.

Josselin, D: *Money Politics in the New Europe: Britain, France and the Single Financial Market* (Basingstoke, Macmillan, 1997, ISBN 0333681096) xviii + 235 pp., hb £50.00.

Jovanovic, M N: *European Economic Integration: Limits and Prospects* (London, Routledge, 1997, ISBN hb 0415095484, pb 0415095492) xx + 389 pp., hb £65.00, pb £19.99.

Karadeloglou, P (ed): *Exchange Rate Policy in Europe* (Basingstoke, Macmillan, 1997, ISBN 0333698193) xxv + 231 pp., hb £50.00.

Kostecki, M & Fehérváry, A (eds): *Services in the Transition Economies: Business Options for Trade and Investment* (Oxford, Pergamon, 1996, ISBN 0080425828) xxv + 278 pp., hb $66.00.

Lecher, W and Platzer, H W (eds): *European Union – European Industrial Relations* (London, Routledge, 1998, ISBN 0415158729) xiii + 312 pp., hb £50.00.

McGuire, S: *Airbus Industrie: Conflict and Cooperation in US–EC Trade Relations* (Basingstoke, Macmillan, 1997, ISBN 0312175329) viii + 224., hb £42.50.

Minkkinen, P and Patomäki, H (eds): *The Politics of Economic and Monetary Union* (Helsinki, Finnish Institute of International Affairs, 1997, ISBN 9517690606) 229 pp., pb np.

Mironesco, C: *Un Enjeu Démocratique: Le Technology Assessment. Maîtrise de la Technologie aux Etats-Unis et en Europe* (Geneva, Georg Editeur, 1997, ISBN 2825705748) 189 pp., pb 129.00 Ff.

O'Brien, R: *Subsidy Regulation and State Transformation in North America, the GATT and the EU* (Basingstoke, Macmillan, 1997, ISBN 0333692462) xiv + 210 pp., hb £45.00.

Overturf, S F: *Money and European Union* (Basingstoke, Macmillan, 1997, ISBN 0333726561) xi + 303 pp., £35.00.

Pelkmans, J: *European Integration: Methods and Economic Analysis* (Harlow, Addison Wesley/ Longman, 1997, ISBN 0582277590) xviii + 346 pp., pb £18.99.

Pennant-Rea, R (ed): *The Ostrich and The EMU: Policy Choices Facing the UK* (London, Centre for Economic Policy Research, 1997, ISBN 1898128316) xiv + 51 pp., pb £7.50 / $12 US.

Pomfret, R: *The Economics of Regional Trading Arrangements* (Oxford, Oxford University Press, 1997, ISBN 0198233353) xiv + 440 pp., hb £48.00.

Rabellotti, R: *External Economies and Cooperation in Industrial Districts; A Comparison of Italy and Mexico* (Basingstoke, Macmillan, 1997, ISBN 0333693876) xiii + 213 pp., hb £45.00.

Radaelli, C M: *The Politics of Corporate Taxation in the European Union: Knowledge and International Policy Agendas* (London, Routledge, 1997, ISBN 0415149991) xi + 254 pp., hb £47.50.

Scobie, H M (ed): *European Monetary Union: Progress and Prospects* (London, Routledge, 1998, ISBN 0415174082) x + 133 pp., hb £45.00.

United Nations: *International Investment Instruments: A Compendium; Multilateral Instruments; Regional Instruments; Regional Integration* (Geneva, United Nations Publications, 1996, ISBN 9211044634) xlii +371; xv + 577; xv + 389 pp., pb np.

United Nations Commission on Trade and Development: *World Investment Report 1997: Transnational Corporations, Market Structure and Competition Policy* (New York, United Nations, 1997, ISBN 9211124131) xxxv + 381 pp., pb £34.00.

van der Zee, F A: *Political Economy Models and Agricultural Policy Formation: Empirical Applicability and Relevance for the CAP* (Leiden, Backhuys, 1997, ISBN 9067544841) xi + 272 pp., pb NLG 80.00.

Watson, A M S: *Aspects of European Monetary Integration: The Politics of Convergence* (Basingstoke, Macmillan, 1997, ISBN 0333645227) xiii + 226 pp., hb £45.00.

Ziegler, J: *Governing Ideas: Strategies for Innovation in France and Germany* (New York, Cornell University, 1997, ISBN hb 0801433118, pb 0801483719) xi + 258 pp., hb £27.50, pb np.

Member States

Geyer, R: *The Uncertain Union: British and Norwegian Social Democrats in an Integrating Europe* (Aldershot, Avebury, 1997, ISBN 185972504X) vii + 229 pp., hb £37.50.

Hanf, K and Soetendorp, B (eds): *Adapting to European Integration: Small States and the European Union* (Harlow, Longman, 1997, ISBN 0582286999) xv + 202 pp., pb £14.99.

Howorth, J and Menon, A (eds): *The European Union and National Defence Policy* (London, Routledge, 1997, ISBN hb 0415164842, pb 0415164850) xiii+ 185 pp., hb £47.50, pb £15.99.

Lavdas, K A: *The Europeanization of Greece: Interest Politics and the Crises of Integration* (Basingstoke, Macmillan, 1997, ISBN 0312174632) xiv + 337 pp., hb £50.00.

Ludlow, N P: *Dealing With Britain: The Six and the First UK Application to the EEC* (Cambridge, Cambridge University Press, 1997, ISBN hb 0521592429, pb 0521595363) xiii + 282 pp., hb £50.00, pb £16.95.

Lynch, F M B: *France and the International Economy: From Vichy to the Treaty of Rome* (London, Routledge, 1997, ISBN 0415142199) xv + 277 pp., hb £45.00.

Newton, M, T and Donaghy, P, J: *Institutions of Modern Spain: A Political and Economic Guide* (Cambridge, Cambridge University Press, 1997, ISBN hb 0521573483, pb 0521575087) xxviii + 379 pp., hb £45.00, pb £15.95.

Roberts, G K: *Party Politics in the New Germany* (London, Cassell, 1997, ISBN hb 1855670291, pb 1855673118) xxvi + 227 pp., hb £45.00, pb £16.99.

Wiberg, M (ed): *Trying to Make a Democracy Work; the Nordic Parliaments and the European Union* (Södertälje, The Bank of Sweden Tercentenary Foundation, 1997, ISBN 9178442664) 125 pp., pb np.

Index

© Blackwell Publishers Ltd 1998, 108 Cowley Road, Oxford OX4 1JF, UK and 350 Main Street, Malden, MA 02148, USA

© Blackwell Publishers Ltd 1998

INDEX